W9-CIF-172

The Global Water Crisis

Books in the **Contemporary World Issues** series address vital issues in today's society such as genetic engineering, pollution, and biodiversity. Written by professional writers, scholars, and nonacademic experts, these books are authoritative, clearly written, up-to-date, and objective. They provide a good starting point for research by high school and college students, scholars, and general readers as well as by legislators, businesspeople, activists, and others.

Each book, carefully organized and easy to use, contains an overview of the subject, a detailed chronology, biographical sketches, facts and data and/or documents and other primary source material, a forum of authoritative perspective essays, annotated lists of print and nonprint resources, and an index.

Readers of books in the Contemporary World Issues series will find the information they need in order to have a better understanding of the social, political, environmental, and economic issues facing the world today.

The Global Water Crisis

A REFERENCE HANDBOOK

David E. Newton

An Imprint of ABC-CLIO, LLC
Santa Barbara, California • Denver, Colorado

Hot Topic
333.91
N562
2016

Copyright © 2016 by ABC-CLIO, LLC

All rights reserved. No part of this publication may be reproduced, stored in a retrieval system, or transmitted, in any form or by any means, electronic, mechanical, photocopying, recording, or otherwise, except for the inclusion of brief quotations in a review, without prior permission in writing from the publisher.

Library of Congress Cataloging-in-Publication Data

Names: Newton, David E., author.
Title: The global water crisis : a reference handbook / David E. Newton.
Description: Santa Barbara, California : ABC-CLIO, 2016. | Series: Contemporary world issues | Includes bibliographical references and index.
Identifiers: LCCN 2015051083 | ISBN 9781440839801 (alk. paper) | ISBN 9781440839818 (ebook)
Subjects: LCSH: Water-supply—Encyclopedias. | Water resources development—Encyclopedias. | Droughts—Encyclopedias.
Classification: LCC TD348 .N49 2016 | DDC 333.91—dc23
LC record available at http://lccn.loc.gov/2015051083

ISBN: 978-1-4408-3980-1
EISBN: 978-1-4408-3981-8

20 19 18 17 16   1 2 3 4 5

This book is also available as an eBook.

ABC-CLIO
An Imprint of ABC-CLIO, LLC

ABC-CLIO, LLC
130 Cremona Drive, P.O. Box 1911
Santa Barbara, California 93116–1911
www.abc-clio.com

This book is printed on acid-free paper ∞

Manufactured in the United States of America

Documents

Preface

A close observer of the world's condition today might be excused for being overwhelmed by a host of seemingly insoluble—or at least enormously challenging—problems and issues ranging from endless conflict in the Middle East and other parts of the world to global poverty and hunger to debates over the amounts and types of energy that humans need to survive and improve their lives to a variety of devastating diseases and medical conditions to the growing threat of global climate change to the mass movement of migrants and refugees in a variety of regions. Under such circumstances, it might be understandable that the observer would ignore a crisis affecting one of the simplest and most fundamental of all substances on the planet: water.

Yet, evidence begins to accumulate that humans are already facing a number of daunting challenges related to water scarcity and water stress, the lack to one degree or another of adequate supplies of clean water to meet even the simplest everyday domestic, agricultural, industrial, and other needs we face every day. Hardly a day goes by without new stories of water shortages in California or other parts of the American West, in the Middle East, in sub-Saharan Africa, and in southern Asia or reports of communities and nations facing the growing challenge of obtaining and delivering adequate quantities of *safe* water to their inhabitants.

Those individuals who live in developed nations may be somewhat surprised by growing concerns about a global water "crisis." Yet, such a crisis is hardly a new phenomenon in human history. Droughts are, perhaps, the most dramatic example of conditions in which the very survival of individual humans and human communities is threatened, and droughts have been around as long as human history has existed. Disputes over water are also as old as the human race, with written stories ranging back more than 5,000 years to fights between nations over the use of water resources. Even today, many people who live in developed nations might be shocked to learn how many of their peers in developing nations may face a daily struggle to find enough clean water with which to wash, cook their meals, and clean themselves. Global water issues may seem like a new and strange problem to some of the world's more prosperous communities, but it is a fact of life in billions of homes around the world today.

A number of factors are responsible for this problem, including a growing global population, increasing urbanization of most parts of the globe, competition among growing agricultural and industrial operations along with domestic needs, and, perhaps most important of all, increasingly obvious global climate changes. In addition to problems of quantity—obtaining adequate amounts of water—there are growing problems of quality—lack of access for hundreds of millions, if not billions, of people to adequate amounts of water to follow safe and sanitary handwashing and other disease-preventative practices.

Many national, regional, and international organizations, along with a host of general and special-interest nongovernmental organizations, are now launching vigorous campaigns to educate people about problems of water scarcity and WASH (water, sanitation, and hygiene) in almost every part of the world. These organizations are also creating and putting into practice a variety of active programs designed to solve problems of water shortages and lack of adequate WASH facilities and practice. Some progress has been made over the past two decades as a result of these programs, but far more needs to be done to ensure that the world's population will have access to safe water for all human needs.

The Global Water Crisis is offered as a resource for young adults who would like to learn more about the topic and/or as a reference base for use in future research projects. The first two chapters of the book provide a comprehensive introduction to the topic of water supplies: a review of the amount and kind of water available on the planet's physical environment; a summary of the history of some fundamental types of water technology, such as irrigation and dam-building, water treatment systems, and power production; a description of the growth of water law in its various forms; a detailed analysis of the current factors that contribute to the development of the world's water crisis, such as population growth, urbanization, drought, and climate change; an explanation of the types of disputes that have and can continue to develop over water resources; and a description of the major factors involved in the concern over adequate access to water, sanitation, and adequate hygiene worldwide.

Each of the first two chapters is accompanied by reference sections which are included not only to identify the sources of information presented in a chapter, but also to help guide interested readers in finding and following up on useful resources on the topics discussed in each chapter. These references should be considered as research adjuncts to the extensive annotated bibliography provided in Chapter 6.

Chapter 3 is a popular feature of books in the Contemporary World Issues series in that it provides interested experts in the field with an opportunity to write brief essays about topics of special interest to them and, hopefully, to the reader. Chapter 4 offers biographical and descriptive essays about important individuals and organizations in the field of water, sanitation, hygiene, and related topics. Chapter 5 contains portions of important laws and legal cases dealing with water issues, as well as a number of data tables on water topics. The bibliography of Chapter 6 brings together useful books, articles, reports, and Internet sources dealing with a variety of water-related topics. Chapter 7 offers a chronological timeline of important events in the history of water, while the glossary consists of important terms used in a study of the subject.

The Global Water Crisis

1 Background and History

It's 6 a.m. and Alieyah has just left to get water for the day. Although she is only eight years old, Alieyah plays an essential role in her family's daily life. She walks two miles every morning to the Ugulwara River to get freshwater, and then two miles back to her home in the village of Mbuma. She can't carry much water, but her family depends on the water she is able to provide for the day. Freshwater is a rare and treasured resource in Togo, and thousands of children living in that poor country are a main source for that resource in villages around the country.

The Yakima River Valley of Washington State has long been called *Apple Valley* because of all the lush apple orchards there. Today, its residents are more likely to think of it as "grape valley," because farmers are tearing out apple orchards and replacing them with grape vines. Why? Simple. Grapes take far less water to grow than do apples. And water is becoming a scarce resource in the Pacific Northwest.

Newspapers, magazines, television, and the Internet today carry endless numbers of stories about the world's water crisis. Mbumba and Apple Valley are thousands of miles apart, but they are very similar in one important way: both areas are suffering from a shortage of clean water needed for the simplest activities of daily life as well as for the operation of agricultural, industrial, commercial, and other operations.

Reduced water supplies often mean that jobs in agriculture, dairying, and other occupations will no longer be available. (©2015 Trudy E. Bell t.e.bell@ieee.org)

So what do people mean when they talk about "global water crisis"? This phrase refers to a number of different phenomena, such as:

- Individuals, families, and communities not having enough freshwater to drink, cook with, and use for cleaning purposes.
- Farmers lacking adequate water to grow their crops.
- Rivers and streams running so low that fish are not able to survive.
- Natural landmasses becoming so dry that they can no longer support wildlife that lives there.
- Developed regions lacking the water needed to maintain the lifestyle to which a community has become accustomed, which may involve golf courses, lush lawns, ornamental fountains, and other nonessential uses of water.

Earth's Water Resources

One of the most famous literary commentaries on Earth's water resources is found in a 1798 poem by English poet Samuel Taylor Coleridge, "The Rime of the Ancient Mariner." In the poem, a sailing ship is becalmed near the Antarctic Sea, and its crew begins to fear for its survival. One member of the crew, the "ancient mariner," reflects on their situation. From the deck of the ship, all that can be seen is the wide ocean; Earth might contain no land at all, for all their senses can tell. "Water, water, everywhere," the ancient mariner observes.

And the mariner's observation certainly makes sense, for Earth truly is "the blue planet" or "the water planet." Had the mariner access to the modern technology used by the U.S. National Aeronautics and Space Administration and other research organizations, he might well have come to the same conclusion about the endless availability of water on the planet (see, e.g., Advancing the Science: Google Earth 2015). Alone among the planets that make up our solar system—and, in fact, all other known planets—Earth contains the water resources that appear to be necessary for the survival of most forms of life. Those resources occupy a total of about 332,500,000 cubic miles (1,386,000,000 cubic kilometers), or nearly three-quarters (70.9%) of the planet's surface (Water Basics 2015). Water, water, everywhere. Indeed!

But the ancient mariner also made another keen observation immediately thereafter. He went on,

And all the boards did shrink;
Water, water, everywhere,
Nor any drop to drink.

In other words, the vast extent of water visible to the mariner and his crew was of little value to them since it was not *fresh* water; they could not use the water to relieve their thirst.

And this fact is confirmed by modern estimates of the amount of *fresh* water available on Earth. Of the 332,500,000 cubic miles of water on Earth's surface, about 96.5 percent is found in the oceans, with another 2.5 percent in the form of lakes, rivers, streams, and other freshwater (also called *freshwater*) resources, and less than 1 percent in the form of saline water. The term *saline* refers to water that contains dissolved salts, such as sodium chloride, potassium chloride, and magnesium chloride. Saline water can be further classified as *slightly saline* (1,000–3,000 parts per million [ppm]), *moderately saline* (3,000–10,000 ppm), and *highly saline* (10,000–35,000 ppm). By comparison, freshwater is usually defined as having less than 1,000 ppm of dissolved salts, and seawater as having more than 35,000 ppm (Saline Water 2015).

For many purposes, the statistic with which humans (e.g., the ancient mariner) are most interested is the amount of freshwater available on the planet. Of the approximately 8,312,000 cubic miles of freshwater on Earth, by far the greatest amount (68.7%) is stored in glaciers and ice caps, vast fields of frozen water that, for all practical purposes, are unavailable for human use. Another 30.1 percent occurs underground in the form of so-called groundwater. (Groundwater is generally defined as any water that occurs beneath the surface of the ground.) This leaves only 1.2 percent of all freshwater available in lakes, rivers, swamps, water stored in living organisms, soil moisture, and other sources (The World's Water 2015). These data make it clear that, in spite of the vast amounts of water available on the planet, only a relatively small quantity is actually readily available for human use. The rest occurs in a form that is less convenient for use (saline water) or that is stored in inaccessible locations, such as underground or in glaciers and ice caps.

This summary reflects a fairly traditional method of calculating Earth's water resources, so-called blue water resources. The term *blue water* is used to describe groundwater and surface water, as discussed in the preceding paragraph. Blue water can be thought of as rainwater that falls on Earth's surface and then soaks downward to become groundwater or that runs across the ground and empties into rivers and lakes. Another form of water that has traditionally been ignored to some extent is so-called *green water*. Green water is rainwater that falls on the land and soaks into the ground, where it is available for growing plants. Current estimates suggest that twice as much rainwater ends up in the form of green water as in blue water. That is, for every 100 cubic feet of rainwater that falls on Earth's surface, about 35 cubic feet eventually ends up in rivers and lakes, and the remaining 65 cubic feet ends up as green water that is then taken up by forests (about 41 cubic feet), grasslands (16 cubic feet), wetlands (1 cubic foot), and crops (7 cubic feet) (Ringersma, Batjes, and Dent 2003, Figure 1, page 2; estimates differ somewhat from study to study; see also, e.g., Hoekstra and Mekonnen 2011).

A third form of water resource is also sometimes identified, *gray water*. Gray water is defined as the water required to carry away the waste products of some industrial, municipal, agricultural, or other human activities, that is, polluted water. According to one recent survey of the total freshwater resources on Earth available between 1996 and 2005, about 74 percent of those resources could be classified as green water, 11 percent as blue water, and 15 percent as gray water (Hoekstra and Mekonnen 2011, 3232).

The Distribution of Water on Earth

It probably goes without saying that the availability of freshwater is not even nearly distributed equally in various countries on Earth. For example, citizens of the Middle Eastern nation of Bahrain have available to them an estimated 3 m³ (cubic meters) of freshwater. By comparison, the residents of Iceland have an estimated 525,074 m³ of freshwater *per person*. Table 1.1 lists the amount of freshwater per capita in various nations around the world.

Table 1.1 Availability of Freshwater per Capita in Various Countries, 2010–2014

Country	Freshwater per Capita (m³)
Australia	21,275
The Bahamas	53
Bahrain	3
Bangladesh	671
Bhutan	103,456
Canada	81,062
Chad	1,170
China	2,072
Egypt	22
Germany	1,327
Guyana	301,396
Iceland	524,074
Israel	93
Kuwait	0
Maldives	87
Nigeria	1,273

(continued)

Table 1.1   (*continued*)

Country	Freshwater per Capita (m³)
Norway	75,202
Pakistan	302
Russian Federation	30,054
Saudi Arabia	83
Spain	2,385
Sudan	81
United Kingdom	2,262
United States	8,904
West Bank and Gaza	195

Source: Renewable Internal Freshwater Resources per Capita (cubic meters). World Bank. http://data.worldbank.org/indicator/ER.H2O.INTR.PC. Downloaded on July 12, 2015.

The interesting point about these data is that they do not necessarily reflect the likelihood that a particular nation is or is not experiencing (or likely to experience) water issues. The United States, for example, would appear to have a relatively large amount of water per capita available for a variety of uses. Yet, some people would argue that the United States faces water issues as severe in some respects as many other nations in the world, a point to be discussed in greater detail later in this book.

Note also that the location of a country on or near the oceans does not necessarily guarantee a ready supply of *fresh* water. The Bahamas, situated in the middle of the Caribbean Sea, ranks low in the amount of freshwater available to its residents, a striking contrast, for example, with landlocked Chad, in the middle of the continent of Africa, with more than 20 times as much as freshwater per capita as the Bahama Islands.

The Origin of Earth's Water

One of the questions that has long fascinated researchers is where and when Earth collected its current supply of water. The most common theory is that water did not appear on the planet until very long—perhaps hundreds of millions of years—after it was originally formed. Formation theories suggest that the young Earth was very hot, perhaps molten in some places, conditions that would not have allowed liquid water to remain on the planet. Water must have come, according to the most popular theories, from asteroids, comets, and other bodies that carried water within their structures and then released that water when they collided with the primordial Earth (Ball 2000).

In recent years, researchers have come closer to understanding the how and why of water formation on Earth. It now appears that water may have been present on the planet from almost the first moments of its formation and that the most likely source of the water was asteroids striking Earth, and not comets, as had previously been suspected (Beatty 2015; Sarafian, et al. 2014).

Whatever the origin of Earth's water, one essential fact remains: that water is almost certainly a nonrenewable resource. That is, the amount of water that was present on the primordial Earth is probably almost the same as the amount available on the planet today and that is the amount humans have to live with for the foreseeable future.

The Water Cycle

Most people probably take it as a given that water is a nonrenewable resource. Yet, the testimony of one's senses might easily raise questions about that fact. After all, rain falls from the sky, apparently adding water to the planet's water resources, and lakes and rivers run dry, apparently depleting those resources. In fact, precipitation and evaporation are only two phases of an interconnected series of events through which all water passes at one time or another in its history.

The water cycle really has no beginning or no ending, but for purposes of description might be imagined as originating with water stored in the atmosphere. Water in the atmosphere makes up a vanishingly small amount of the total water on Earth (about 0.001%), as well as a very small amount of total

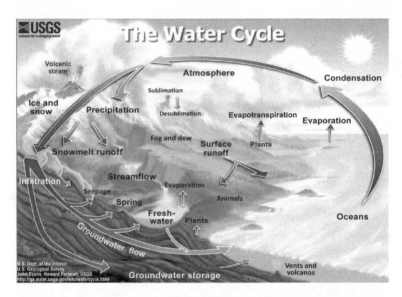

Figure 1.1   The Water Cycle. (United States Geological Survey. Available online at http://water.usgs.gov/edu/watercycle.html)

freshwater on the planet (0.04%) (How Much Water Is There on, in, and above the Earth 2015). Water in the atmosphere can exist in any one of three states: solid (ice), liquid, or gas (water vapor), depending on ambient conditions (the conditions, such as temperature and pressure, at which the water exists). When water first reaches the atmosphere from Earth's surface, it usually does so in the form of water vapor. As it rises to higher altitudes, it tends first to liquefy, forming liquid droplets of water, and then to freeze, forming tiny ice crystals.

At times, water in the atmosphere is visible in the forms of clouds made up of liquid droplets or ice crystals. At other times, the water is so widely dispersed that it is invisible from the ground. Whatever the form in which it occurs, water remains in the atmosphere for periods of less than about two weeks, depending on whether it is situated over water (an average residence time of about 9 days) or over land (an average residence time of about 15 days) (Bice 2015). (Residence time is the average length of time water will remain in a specific part of the water cycle, such as the atmosphere.)

Water remains in the atmosphere for only a relatively short period of time because individual water molecules, water droplets, and ice crystals tend to collide with each other, forming increasingly larger structures. Eventually these structures (larger water droplets and ice crystals) become heavy enough to start falling to Earth's surface in the form or precipitation such as rain, snow, hail, sleet, or fog. An estimated 398×10^{15} kilograms of water per year falls on the oceans by this process, compared with an estimated 108×10^{15} kilograms of water falling on land (of which 99% is rain and less than 1%, snow) (Bice 2015).

The vast majority of the water that falls on the oceans (435×10^{15} kilograms of water per year) and on land (71×10^{15} kilograms per year) is returned to the atmosphere by the process of evaporation, in which liquid (and very rarely, solid) water changes back to the gaseous state and rises into the atmosphere. This return process tends to be very slow for ice, with a residence time of about 27,500 years in its Earth reservoirs, 3,110 years for ocean water, and about 2.57 years for surface water on land (such as rivers and lakes) (Bice 2015).

A relatively small amount of precipitation (34×10^{15} kilograms per year) runs off land by way of lakes, rivers, and steams into the oceans, after which it also evaporates to the atmosphere. The smallest fraction of precipitation (about 2×10^{15} kilograms per year) soaks into the ground (a process known as *infiltration*) and becomes a component of groundwater. Except for ice reservoirs, groundwater has the longest residence time of any water resource on Earth, a period of about 4,100 years. This number means that once water gets relatively deep into the earth beneath ground level, it tends to stay there for very long periods of time.

The Nature of Groundwater

Groundwater is an extraordinarily important feature of Earth's water resources and a key element in many of the problems associated with current global water shortages. Groundwater is supplied when precipitation falls on the surface of the ground and sinks into the ground. This water continues to sink further until it reaches a point at which the ground is permanently saturated. The upper boundary of that region is called the *water table*, and the region itself is referred to as an *aquifer*. The land above the water table remains unsaturated because water is able to flow out of it, across the water table, and into the aquifer. The openings between rocks, stones, gravel, sand, and other particles in the upper unsaturated zone are lined with, but not filled with, water. Within the aquifer, however, the spaces between particles, cracks in the rocks, and all other openings in the ground are filled with water. The aquifer is, therefore, like a huge sponge that soaks up large quantities of precipitation that fall on the land's surface.

Water in an aquifer flows from higher to lower elevations, just as does surface water, but at a far more leisurely pace. The water in most rivers and streams flows at the rate of a few miles per hour; in comparison, groundwater may flow at the rate of a foot or so a day, a foot per year, or even a foot per decade (General Facts and Concepts about Ground Water 2015). The water stored in an aquifer is, therefore, relatively stable, accounting for typically high residence times of a few thousand years.

The water in an aquifer is relatively easy to access in many cases. If one sinks a well into an aquifer, the pressure exerted by water around the well will push it up the well pipe to a height above the water table and, in some cases, directly out of the well onto the land. If the water does not rise to that height on its own, one can then install a pump to raise the water the rest of the way to the surface of the ground, providing a simple and long-used method of extracting water from an aquifer. Vast agricultural projects around the world depend on such wells for the water they need to supply their crops.

Aquifers can truly be of enormous size and of unparalleled importance to the world's water needs. Table 1.2 lists a dozen of the world's largest aquifer systems, the most extensive of which is the West Siberian Basin aquifer system that underlies central Russia and covers an area estimated at about 3.1 million square kilometers with a maximum thickness of 6,000

Table 1.2 Some of the World's Largest Aquifers

Aquifer	Location	Area* (10^3 km²)	Thickness* (m)
West Siberian Basin	Russia	3,200	6,000
Russian Platform Basins	Russia	3,100	20,000
Nubian Aquifer System	Chad, Egypt, Libya, Sudan	2,199	3,500
Taoudeni-Tanezrouft Basin	Algeria, Mali, Mauritania	2,000	4,000
Northern Great Plains Aquifer	Canada, United States	2,000	n/a
Lake Chad Basin	Chad, Cameroon, Central African Republic, Niger, Nigeria,	1,917	7,000
Great Artesian Basin	Australia	1,700	3,000
Amazon Basin	Bolivia, Brazil, Colombia, Peru	1,500	2,000
Arabian Aquifer System	Bahrain, Jordan, Kuwait, Qatar, Saudi Arabia	1,485	6,500
Guaraní Aquifer System	Argentina, Brazil, Paraguay, Uruguay	1,195	800
Atlantic and Gulf Coastal Plains Aquifer	Mexico, United States	1,150	12,000
North Western Sahara Aquifer System	Algeria, Libya, Tunisia	1,019	1,600

*Estimated and approximate

Source: Margat, Jean, and Jac van der Gun. *Groundwater around the World: A Geographic Synopsis*. Boca Raton, FL: CRC Press, 2013, Table 3.2, page 45.

meters. By comparison, the largest aquifer in the United States is the Northern Great Plains aquifer that lies beneath North Central United States and South Central Canada with an area of about 2.0 million square kilometers. The most famous American aquifer, and one of the best known and most thoroughly studied, is the Ogallala (or High Plains) aquifer that underlies parts of the states of Colorado, Kansas, Nebraska, New Mexico, Oklahoma, South Dakota, Texas, and Wyoming. The Ogallala is among the most frequently mentioned of all world aquifers because of its critical role in the agricultural system of the western United States. (For a map of the world's largest aquifers, see http://www.whymap.org/whymap/ EN/Downloads/Global_maps/whymap_largeaquifers_pdf .pdf?__blob=publicationFile&v=3. For a comprehensive list of aquifers in the United States, see https://water.usgs.gov/ogw/ aquiferbasics/alphabetical.html.)

Water and the Rise of Human Civilization

It probably goes without saying that water is one of the most essential substances on Earth. Plants and animals—including humans—depend absolutely on a constant supply of freshwater for their very survival. Humans use water on a largely daily basis for drinking, washing, cleaning, growing of crops, and other essential activities. Over the centuries, its role in transportation, power production, and other activities has also grown substantially.

So it is hardly surprising that early human civilizations almost inevitably had their beginnings on the shores of dependable sources of freshwater, usually streams and rivers (Tvedt and Coopey 2010). Possibly the oldest human settlements of which we have any records are those that developed along the shores of the Nile River, in modern-day Egypt. Those settlements date to at least 5500 BCE, although they did not yet qualify as organized communities characteristic of later societies at that early date (Midant-Reynes 2000).

Credit for being the earliest true human civilizations usually goes to a series of settlements that evolved in the region that constitutes modern-day Iraq, at the confluence of the Tigris and Euphrates Rivers, the eastern portion of what is now known as the *Fertile Crescent*. In fact, that early civilization took its name from that location, *Mesopotamia* meaning "between the rivers."

Beginning almost simultaneously with the first Egyptian settlements on the Nile, the Mesopotamian cultures include those of Samarra, Akkadia, Ur, Babylonia, Minoa, Assyria, and the Hittites, all names familiar to any student of ancient history (Roaf 2008).

Civilizations of eastern Asia followed a similar pattern of development. By about 2600 BCE, the first human settlements were being organized in the region of modern-day India along the banks of the Indus River. Archaeologists now know of more than 1,500 such settlements constructed between about 2600 BCE and 1900 BCE, providing a detailed picture of the type of lives lived by residents of the area (Kenoyer 2011, 17). And in adjacent China, a similar process had begun by about 1700 BCE along the banks of the Yellow River (Nilsson 2015). Of course, even settlements that were located in coastal areas still had to be sited near rivers or streams, since the vast quantities of saltwater available to them from the seas were of no help in meeting the communities' daily need for a dependable supply of freshwater.

In a few locations on Earth, early humans had to be especially resourceful in order to begin building settlements where freshwater was either entirely absent or in short supply. The modern-day nation of Saudi Arabia, for example, has no permanent rivers or lakes, and an annual rainfall of about 5.9 cm (2.3 in), environmental conditions that have existed in the Arabian Desert at least since the end of the Holocene epoch, about 12,000 years ago. The region would be completely uninhabitable were it not for the vast aquifers underlying the area. Early humans discovered that they could recover the freshwater they needed to survive either by seeking out natural seeps from such aquifers (*oases*) or by digging wells into an aquifer. One of the earliest settlements built on such a site, if not the earliest, is called Qaryat al-Faw, located on the western edge of the desert (Al Ansary 1981).

Desert settlements depend, therefore, entirely on the water stored in these aquifers, sometimes known as *fossil water* because it was deposited on Earth's surface hundreds or thousands of years earlier. This fossil water is nonrenewable because once it is gone, it is gone forever; annual rainfall is not nearly sufficient to recharge the aquifer (Foster and Loucks 2006).

The History of Water Wells

Water wells are among the earliest structures found to have been associated with ancient civilizations. As humans abandoned their nomadic lifestyle and settled into permanent communities, they may have found it necessary to find ways of accessing the water they needed for their daily activities. Apparently, one such method was simply digging into the ground until the water table was reached, after which groundwater would begin to flow into the well under artesian pressure.

Such wells were relatively simple to build in concept, but often required a somewhat specific set of skills to produce permanent and dependable structures. The crucial component of such structures was a lining to hold the well's shape and allow water to collect in its lower levels. Archaeologists have found a number of systems for achieving this result, involving the use of wood, fiber, stone, metal, and other materials for the linings of water wells. The oldest well yet discovered, for example, was found in eastern Germany and dates to 5469–5098 BCE. Its inner lining is made of oak timbers that have survived sufficiently well to permit carbon dating of their age. The sophistication of the workmanship involved prompted the wells' discoverers to suggest that the first farmers were also "the first carpenters" (Tegel, et al. 2012).

Accessing the water collected in a well was the second technical challenge facing early inventors. One of the simplest methods was to make the well large enough to allow the installation of steps leading down into the well, making it possible for a person to simply go down into the well and collect the water. Another straightforward method involved hanging a bucket on a windlass at the top of the well. Lowering the bucket into the well was a simple method of collecting the water, one that has been used until recent times on some agricultural facilities. With the development of pumps in the 15th century, a newer and easier method of drawing water from a well was made available, a system that now dominates the construction of nearly all modern water well systems in the world (Segrest 2015).

Today, water wells are often classified as one of three primary types: dug, driven, and drilled. These names come from the method by which they are made, by (often) hand-digging into the ground, by driving a pipe into the ground, or by drilling ("boring") into the ground and then inserting a pipe. In each case, the fundamental problem is a simple one: extending the shove, pipe, or drill into the ground to a point at which it penetrates the water table, and then shoring up the hole produced to prevent it from caving in during use (Groundwater: Wells 2015). The deepest and most sophisticated water wells in use today are almost always produced by drilling.

The deepest hand-dug water well on record as of early 2016 is the Woodingdean Well, near Brighton, England, constructed from 1858 to 1862. It is 1,285 feet deep (Grant 2015). Woodingdean is not necessarily the largest water well, however, as it is exceeded in width by the Big Well of Greensburg, Kansas, which, only 109 feet deep, is 32 feet in diameter (World's Largest Hand Dug Well 2015). Finally, the hand-dug water wells with the greatest total capacity appear to be to very old wells, the Well of Joseph in the Cairo Citadel and St. Patrick's Well in Orvieto, Italy (Fisk 1822, 290; McGowan 2015).

Driven and drilled water wells are generally much deeper than hand-dug wells. The world's current record for the deepest water well is apparently the Stensvad Well 11-W1 located in Rosebud County, Montana, with a depth of 7,320 feet. The well was originally drilled by the Great Northern Drilling Company (Sagmit and Soriano 1998, 194).

A discussion of water wells may seem like a somewhat mundane topic to the general observer. After all, a person or community wants access to freshwater not available from a nearby river, stream, or lake, so he or she or it decides to sink a well into a convenient aquifer and withdraws the water he or she or it needs for his or her or its everyday operations. But the fresh-water obtained from aquifers is a very large component—often a majority—of all the freshwater collected and used by a community, a region, or a nation. Studies of groundwater withdrawal, which occurs almost entirely through systems of water wells, provide an excellent overview of the way communities and nations are collecting freshwater, the purposes for which that freshwater is used, and the ultimate consequences of removing the water from aquifers.

Probably the most comprehensive study of groundwater withdrawal, although now somewhat dated, is a study conducted for the International Hydrological Programme of the United Nations Educational, Scientific and Cultural Organization (now UNESCO) that has been in operation since 1975. The study, "Groundwater Resources of the World and Their Use," provides a plethora of information about the location, extent, withdrawal, and use of groundwater resources in every region of the world (Zekster and Everett 2004; also see Foster and Loucks 2006). Perhaps the most important generalization that can be made about groundwater withdrawal resulting from the study is that it represents the largest single extraction process in the world, resulting in the release of somewhere between 600 and 700 billion m³ of freshwater every year. This water is used primarily for three purposes: drinking water (about 65% of all water removed), irrigation and livestock (about 20%), and industry and mining (about 15%) (Foster and Loucks 2006, 24).

No firm data are available for the number of water wells needed for this extraction process. But one source cites the data provided in Table 1.3 as estimates for these numbers.

These numbers are somewhat misleading, however, as the collection and use of groundwater vary widely from country to country around the world. According to the National Groundwater Association (NGWA), the country that removes the

Table 1.3   Estimated Number of Water Wells in Selected Countries, as of 2010

Country	Estimated Number of Water Wells
United States	15.9 million
India	12.3 million
China	3.4 million
Germany	500,000
South Africa	500,000
Taiwan	37,100
Mongolia	27,000
Botswana	7,500
Costa Rica	5,000

Source: California Groundwater Awareness Month. California Regional Water Quality Control Board. http://www.grac.org/gwawareness.pdf. Accessed on July 14, 2015. (Data attributed to National Groundwater Association, but unverified.)

largest volume of freshwater for domestic use is India, which extracted about 251 cubic kilometers of groundwater in 2010. Of that amount, the vast majority of freshwater (89%) went for irrigation, 9 percent for domestic use, and 2 percent for industrial uses. Other nations that relied heavily on groundwater extraction are listed in Table 1.4.

NGWA also announced that the country worldwide that depended most heavily on groundwater resources was Bahrain, which obtained all (100%) of its domestic and industrial water from groundwater sources and almost all (90%) of its agricultural water from that source. Other nations heavily dependent on groundwater resources are listed in Table 1.5. (An invaluable resource for detailed information on the location and nature of groundwater resources around the world is a pair of maps produced by the United Nations Educational, Scientific and Cultural Organization and the [German] Federal Institute for Geosciences and Natural Resources (BGR), "Groundwater Resources of the World," released in 1999, and its latest update, "The Global Map of Groundwater Vulnerability to Floods and Droughts," published in 2015. The maps can be found on a

Table 1.4   Nations with Largest Estimated Groundwater Extraction Rates, as of 2010

Country	Quantity of Groundwater Extracted			
	Total (km³/yr)	Irrigation (%)	Domestic (%)	Industrial (%)
China	111.95	54	20	26
United States	111.70	71	23	6
Pakistan	64.82	94	6	0
Iran	63.40	87	11	2
Bangladesh	30.21	86	13	1
Mexico	29.45	72	22	6
Saudi Arabia	24.24	92	5	3
Indonesia	14.93	2	93	5
Turkey	13.22	60	32	8
Russia	11.62	3	79	18
Syria	11.29	90	5	5
Japan	10.94	23	29	48
Thailand	10.74	14	60	26
Italy	10.40	67	23	10

Source: "The 15 Nations with the Largest Estimated Annual Groundwater Extractions (2010)." Facts about Global Groundwater Usage. National Groundwater Association. http://www.ngwa.org/Fundamentals/use/Documents/global-groundwater-use-fact-sheet.pdf. Accessed on July 15, 2015. Data for all 234 nations worldwide are available on request from NGWA, as per footnote for this table.

Table 1.5   Nations with Greatest Dependence on Groundwater Resources

Country	Groundwater Share of All Freshwater Use			
	All Water Use	Irrigation	Domestic	Industrial
Bahrain	100	90	100	100
Barbados	100	n/a	n/a	n/a
Malta	100	100	100	100
Montenegro	100	n/a	100	n/a
Palestinian Territory	100	61	69	n/a
Oman	100	97	100	100
Qatar	100	84	100	0

| | Groundwater Share of All Freshwater Use | | | |
Country	All Water Use	Irrigation	Domestic	Industrial
United Arab Emirates	100	84	0	0
Denmark	98	n/a	n/a	n/a
Libya	98	97	100	100
Croatia	97	n/a	100	100
Iceland	97	n/a	n/a	n/a
Djibouti	95	95	67	100
Saudi Arabia	95	94	100	100
Mongolia	91	83	100	100

n/a: Data not available.

Source: "The 15 Nations with Groundwater Having the Largest Share in Total Annual Freshwater Withdrawals, Ranked by All Water Use Sectors." Facts about Global Groundwater Usage. National Groundwater Association. http://www.ngwa.org/Fundamentals/use/Documents/global-groundwater-use-fact-sheet.pdf. Accessed on July 15, 2015. Data for all 234 nations worldwide are available on request from NGWA, as per footnote for this table.

number of sites, including http://www.whymap.org/whymap/EN/Downloads/Global_maps/whymap_largeaquifers_pdf.pdf?__blob=publicationFile&v=3, for the former, and http://unesdoc.unesco.org/images/0023/002324/232431e.pdf, for the latter.)

The History of Irrigation Systems

Removing freshwater from underground aquifers is often only the first step in making use of this valuable resource. This water must then be distributed to those individuals, communities, companies, and other entities who will make use of it, such as purification plants, where it can be prepared for domestic use, or industrial plants, where it is employed for a vast variety of purposes. Perhaps the greatest challenge, however, has long been to move water from its source (e.g., a deep well) to the wide-flung agricultural fields where it is used for the growing of crops and watering of domestic animals. When did humans first develop methods for such systems of distribution, for *irrigation* systems?

Historical records suggest that the first irrigation systems were constructed in at least the sixth millennium BCE in Egypt. These systems took advantage of the country's primary source of freshwater—the Nile River—as its major (and sometimes only) source of providing water for its crops. During flood stage, the Nile's waters were diverted from the river itself into surrounding areas, where they flowed through sometimes complex systems of dams and canals to fields where the crops were grown. At the conclusion of the flood season, the excess water in the fields was then returned to the river (Irrigation Museum 2015).

Similar irrigation systems were developed throughout the Fertile Crescent (the region ranging from Egypt through the Middle East, which is considered to be the birthplace of human civilizations). The first laws dealing with the construction and use of irrigation systems are thought to date to about 1790 BCE as expressed in the legal code of King Hammurabi. The code described how irrigated water was to be distributed, what a landowner's responsibility for maintaining the system was, and how the operation of the canal was to be administered (Law Code of Hammurabi (1780 B.C.), 53–56).

For at least four millennia, farmers relied entirely on surface waters (e.g., the Nile River) for their irrigation water. (According to the best estimates now available, about 61.3% of all irrigation systems still use surface water, rather than underground water [Siebert, et al. 2010, Table 2, 1868]). Then, in about 1700 BCE, someone invented the first device for extracting water from below ground and using it for irrigation, the *shaduf* (or *shadoof*). The shaduf is almost the simplest possible water-transferring machine that one can imagine, consisting of a long horizontal pole that pivots on a vertical post. A bucket hangs from one end of the horizontal pole, and a weight (e.g., a rock) at the opposite end. The bucket is lowered into a water well, filled with water, and then raised by pushing down on the opposite end. The horizontal pole can then be pivoted to move the bucket over an irrigation ditch, where it is emptied. The shaduf is still in use in parts of the world that do not have access to more sophisticated systems of groundwater transfer.

The greatest disadvantage of the shaduf, of course, was that it was able to transfer only a relatively small volume of water at a time, with considerable effort by the shaduf operator. An important breakthrough in the capture and transfer of groundwater occurred in about 550 BCE with the invention of the *qanat*. The qanat is a system that consists of a long tunnel dug underground into the water table, sloping downward with an outlet on the side of the hill. (For a video description of a qanat, see https://www.youtube.com/watch?v=ieBVMOPRYJ0.) The development of the qanat made possible for the first time the use of underground water as the primary source of the substance in regions where surface water was limited or nonexistent (Irrigation Museum 2015). As with the shaduf, qanats are still widely used and are essential to the existence of human settlements and agricultural projects in the driest parts of the world (Information Center of Qanat 2015).

Figure 1.2 A woman in Egypt collects water with a *shaduf*. (Library of Congress)

Nearly coincidental with the invention of the qanat was the invention of the *sakia*, or Persian waterwheel. The sakia was the first of many similar devices designed to move underground water to the surface by mechanical means, using animal, water, electrical, fossil fuel, solar, wind, or some other form of power. In that respect, the sakia is the grandfather of all systems for the use of groundwater for irrigation systems today. The type of pump for any given system is determined by a number of factors, including the volume of water to be transferred, access to power to operate the pump, and the ability of a user to pay for the pump system (Irrigation Handbook 2015, 47–49).

Irrigation Today

According to the most recent data available (2010), just more than 300 million hectares (740 million acres) of land are now equipped for irrigation of crops worldwide, of which about a third (113 million hectares; 279 million acres) is equipped for irrigation with groundwater. The amount of land *actually being irrigated*, however, is somewhat less, about 98 million hectares (242 acres), or about 87 percent of all land equipped for groundwater irrigation. These groundwater systems account for a total consumption of 543,359 Mm³/yr (cubic megameters per year). Table 1.6 provides a summary of these data for various regions of the world. (More complete, detailed, and recent data may be available on groundwater irrigation systems at Aquastat, http://www.fao.org/nr/water/aquastat/data/query/index.html?lang=en.)

Table 1.6   Groundwater Use for Irrigation

Region	AEI_GW (ha)	AEI_GW (%)	AAI_GW (HA)	ICWU_GW (Mm³/yr)
Northern Africa	2,092,196	32.8	1,817,844	15,685
Sub-Saharan Africa	413,758	5.7	340,134	2,178
Mexico	2,489,785	38.8	191,011,27	11,386

Region	AEI_GW (ha)	AEI_GW (%)	AAI_GW (HA)	ICWU_GW (Mm³/yr)
United States and Canada	16,657,638	57.4	13,547,200	88,498
South America	1,717,288	14.9	1,558,158	6,221
Central Asia	1,149,245	7.8	780,969	4,719
Iran	5,151,186	62.1	3,987,912	30,153
Middle East	10,838,415	46.0	9,059,714	71,261
Arabian Peninsula	2,467,433	88.4	1,938,015	20,759
Near East	3,072,219	29.7	3,026,457	19,848
Southeast Asia	68,594,798	39.5	62,690,325	322,651
Europe	7,349,929	32.4	4,816,935	18,206
Russian Federation	475,020	20.0	338,112	856
Australia and New Zealand	949,172	24.0	812,693	3,301
World	112,936,434	37.5	97,821,180	545,359

Key:
AEI_GW: Area equipped for irrigation with groundwater.
AEI_GW (%): Percentage of irrigated land equipped for groundwater.
AAI_GW: Area actually being irrigated with groundwater.
ICWU_GW: Consumptive use of groundwater for irrigation annually.

Source: Siebert, S., et al. 2010. "Groundwater Use of Irrigation—A Global Inventory." Hydrology and Earth System Sciences. 14: 1863–1880, Table 2, 1868. http://www.fao.org/docrep/013/al816e/al816e00.pdf. Accessed on July 15, 2015.

The History of Dams

In many ways, surface irrigation systems are much easier to build and maintain than are groundwater irrigation systems. Collecting water from a river or lake and diverting it to an agricultural field can, at least in concept, be a relatively simple process. One can imagine that humans at a very early stage of agriculture simply dug a canal from the river or lake to the area where they wanted to plant their crops, and their water problem was solved. Of course, as agricultural systems grew larger and more complex, the surface irrigation systems they required also grew in complexity and size. One of the key elements that such advanced systems often required was a dam to force water into an artificial reservoir from which it was easier to collect.

The history of dams is well studied, one that includes constant technological developments leading to larger, more efficient dams that have been increasingly effective at delivering water for (primarily) irrigation and power systems. The earliest known structure that qualifies as a dam is probably an earthen structure built at the ancient site of Jawa in Mesopotamia, now in modern-day Lebanon, dating to about 3000 BCE. The dam was about 30 feet high and about 3 feet wide, a part of a system of structures along the Rajil River. The system of dams around Jawa was supposedly designed to collect water in the dry season, as well as collecting surface runoff water (Helms 1977; Tanksley 2015; Violet 2010).

The Jawa dam was a *gravity dam*, one that remains in position because of the weight of the materials of which it is composed. This weight is greater than the force of the water behind the time (An Introduction to Gravity Dams 2015). Essentially, all dams built prior to Roman era were either gravity dams or *embankment dams*. An embankment dam is similar to a gravity dam in that it relies on the weight of the material of which it is made to resist the force of water stored behind the dam. The two dam types differ primarily in the type of material of which they are made: heavy materials, such as rock and stone for gravity dams, and lighter materials, such as sand and dirt for embankment dams. Today, gravity dams are usually defined as those structures that consist of concrete and other masonry materials, while embankment dams are defined as those made of earthy materials and rocks.

The first embankment dam of which scientists know is one built at the ancient Egyptian site of Sadd Al-Kafara in about 2700 BCE. It was about 45 feet in height and more than 370 feet in length. The dam was apparently designed to harness the severe, but infrequent, floods that struck the Sadd Al-Kafara valley. It was under construction for more than 10 years before being destroyed by the type of flood against which it was supposed to protect. It was then apparently never completed (Sadd

Al-Kafara 2015; for a comparison of gravity and embankment dams, see Technology of Dams 2015).

The next technological development in dam building did not occur for nearly three millennia. In about the first century BCE, those master engineers, the Romans, invented a new type of dam known as the *arch dam*. The "arch" in an arch dam is a (usually) concrete structure that faces upward toward the water reservoir that it creates. When that water pushes against the walls of the arch dam, it compresses the material of which the dam is made, therefore increasing the dam's resistance to water pressure.

The first arch dam was built in the Vallon de Baume in France sometime during the first century BCE. It was about 40 feet high and 60 feet long with a curvature of 73°. It consisted of two masonry walls separated by a narrow space about five feet wide (Agusta-Boularot, Sandrine, and Jean-Louis Paillet 1997; Key Developments in the History of Arch Dams 2015).

The fourth major type of dam to be developed was the *buttress dam*. The buttress dam gets its name from the use of heavy rectangular concrete structures attached to the downstream side of a dam to strengthen the resistance of the dam itself. The earliest buttress dams were built by Roman engineers in Spain to strengthen gravity or embankment dams they thought were not strong enough to survive on their own (in some cases of which they were correct, but not correct in others; see Key Developments in the History of Buttress Dams 2015). Partly because of the somewhat haphazard approach of Roman engineers to the construction of buttress dams, many authorities now claim that the earliest true dam of that type is one built in 1747 in northern Spain known as the Almendralejo (or Al-Mendralejo or Albuera de Feria or Feria) Dam (Key Developments in the History of Buttress Dams 2015).

Dam technology today is very sophisticated and makes use of all combinations of the four basic dam types, along with other modifications developed for the construction of dams in very specific locations. The largest dams in operation today exceed their earliest predecessors in size by very large factors. The largest dam currently in existence, measured by the volume of materials of which it is made, is the Syncrude Tailings Dam, an embankment dam near Fort McMurray, Alberta, Canada. This dam is just more than 290 feet tall with a length of more than 11 miles, and a volume of just more than 19,000 million cubic feet (Seminar on Safe Tailings Dam Construction 2001). By contrast, the largest dams in terms of their total height and their total reservoir capacity are, respectively, the Jinping-I Dam on the Yalong River in China, with a height of 1,001 feet, a concrete arch bridge, and the Kariba Dam (concrete arch), which forms Lake Kariba on the Zambezi River, in Zimbabwe, with a capacity of 43.3 cubic miles. The largest dams in the United States, by comparison, are (by volume of material) the Fort Peck Dam (embankment) in Fort Peck, Montana, with a materials volume of 3,390 million cubic feet, the Oroville Dam (embankment), in Oroville, California, with a height of 770 feet, and the Hoover Dam (concrete gravity arch), with a reservoir volume of 8.95 cubic miles (Dam, Hydropower, and Reservoir Statistics 2015).

Water Treatment

One might be forgiven for thinking of ancient history as a period during which early human civilizations had access to and made use of pure water resources. With relatively small populations, no industry to speak of, and, in many cases, vast water resources, early humans might be expected to have more than enough pure water with which to conduct their lives. While that view might be accurate in a general sense, there is abundant archaeological evidence that those early humans also had to deal with problems of water impurities—water pollution—that are well known to today's societies.

For example, some early Sanskrit manuscripts from the Indian subcontinent acknowledge the existence of impure water and suggest a number of techniques for remedying that problem. "It is good to keep water in copper vessels," one such manuscript declares, "and filter it through charcoal." Another remedy for impure water is to "heat foul water by boiling and exposing to sunlight and by dipping seven times into it a piece of hot copper, then to filter and cool in an earthen vessel" (Baker 1949, 1). It should be noted that during the period mentioned here—and for many centuries thereafter—no one had any idea as to what "impure" or "polluted" water might be. Awareness of non-pure water was generally related to a bad taste or smell, with little understanding that these properties might be indicators of more serious contamination of water. Nonetheless, they were apparent and important enough that humans used these signs as indications that a sample of water needed to be "purified" before being used.

A host of other methods and materials were developed down through the ages to deal with the problem of impure water. For example, the famous Greek physician, Hippocrates, a strong advocate of the curative properties of pure water, recommended the use of a device that has come to be known as *Hippocrates sleeve* for removing bad odors and tastes from impure water. The sleeve consisted of a cloth bag through which water could be poured. The bag captured the solids responsible for unpleasant odors and tastes and resulted in the release of (relatively) pure water (see an image of the Hippocrates sleeve at http://www.historicfood.com/Ypocras.htm, which shows its use for purifying both water and wine).

One of the earliest methods for dealing with a shortage of pure water was devised by Roman engineers in the third century BCE. During the earliest years of the Roman civilization, the city was able to obtain all the pure water it needed from local rivers and springs. But as the city grew in size and complexity, these sources of pure water proved to be inadequate. At the same time, the wastes generated by a growing city began to pollute those water resources. In response to this problem, the city devised a system of aqueducts, large bridge-like structures that brought clean, freshwater to the city from distant regions, the longest stretching more than 50 miles from source to the city. The first of these aqueducts was begun in the year 312 BCE. As the Roman Empire spread throughout the known world, so did the use of aqueducts until more than a thousand such structures were eventually built from Great Britain in the northwest of the empire to Turkey and the Middle Eastern region in the east (Hansen 2015a; Romaq 2015; one of the best single resource on the overall history of the development of water treatment systems currently available is Coffey and Reid 1976).

Aqueducts eventually proved to be a solution for obtaining pure water for many metropolitan areas around the world. New York City, for example, began construction on the High Bridge aqueduct in 1837 after a devastating outbreak of cholera in 1832 resulting from the use of contaminated water. The aqueduct was completed in 1848 and survives today in the form of a bridge connecting Manhattan and the Bronx (it was last remodeled and upgraded in 2015; Dwyer 2015).

From the earliest days of Christianity until the rise of the Renaissance, little new information or technology about water treatment was produced. Then, in about 1627, English scholar Sir Francis Bacon described a new way of thinking about the production of pure water: desalination. Desalination is the process by which seawater, or other saline water, is converted to pure water. In looking back over the history of the preceding millennium of scientific thought (such as it was), Bacon took note of the abundance of water in the oceans, generally unfit for human consumption, and one possible method of converting seawater to pure water that humans could use. He suggested that passing seawater through layers of sand, as occurs on beaches, might cause the removal of the salts that make seawater useless for most human uses. He devised an experiment for testing this hypothesis, an experiment that failed to confirm his hypothesis. In spite of this failure, however, Bacon brought the concept of desalination to the attention of future researchers (Bacon 1670, 1; Jesperson 1996, 7).

The realization that impure water—beyond its unpleasant odors and taste—might also possess the ability to cause disease had its origins in the historic research of Dutch microscopist Anton (or Antoni or Antony or Antonie) van Leeuwenhoek in the 1670s. Leeuwenhoek's examination of droplets of water with the microscopes he invented showed that water was never completely pure; it always contained some number and variety of impurities, such as tiny "animalcules" that either skittered through the water or spun around in circles (van Leeuwenhoek 1677). As critical as van Leeuwenhoek's research was to the understanding of water, a full explanation of the role of his tiny "animalcules" in the disease process had to await the research of Robert Koch, Louis Pasteur, and their colleagues 200 years later.

A comparable discovery of profound significance for water treatment theory and practice occurred nearly simultaneously to the development of the germ theory by Koch, Pasteur, and others. In 1854, the city of London was struck by one of the most serious outbreaks of cholera the nation had ever seen. Physician John Snow took upon himself the challenge of discovering how the outbreak had occurred and what could be done to contain it. By collecting data on the physical location of individuals who came down with the disease, he concluded that its origin was somehow associated with a pump that dispensed water from a public well on Broad Street. He proposed a simple solution to the problem: remove the pump handle. When that action was taken, citizens could no longer draw water from that well, and the cholera germs harbored (then unknown to anyone, including Snow) therein could no longer be transmitted through the population.

Snow recommended two procedures somewhat less dramatic than removing pump handles for further control of the disease. First, he said, water extracted from London wells should be passed through sand filters to remove whatever agent caused cholera. Second, all public water should be treated with chlorine, a substance known to kill bacteria and other microorganisms. With these procedures in place, the occurrence of cholera (and other waterborne diseases) was largely brought under control in London and other areas where they were introduced (Freichs 2015; Snow 1854).

By the time of Snow's discovery, one of the essential developments on which he was to depend had already been put into place. The first municipal water treatment plant had been constructed in Paisley, Scotland, as early as 1804. The plant made use of a water filtering technology developed by John Gibb, owner of a bleachery plant in Paisley. In order to get the pure water he needed for his plant, Gibb invented a filtering system consisting of sand and charcoal over which polluted water from the River Cart was passed. Gibb then sold the excess purified water he could not use to local residents, who received their water shipments by donkey cart. Shortly after Gibb's invention, a fellow resident of the city, Robert Thom, expanded Gibb's ideas in the construction of a full-scale water treatment plant, the first of its kind in history, capable of purifying River Cart water for the whole community. The Gibb–Thom concept took hold quickly and began to spread to urban areas around the world in a short period of time, with the city of Paris completing a similar system for its water supply in 1806 (Galvis 1999, 11–12; Huisman and Wood 1974, 15).

The use of chlorine to purify water had its origins in the discovery of that element by Swedish chemist Carl Wilhelm Scheele in 1774. Its disinfectant properties, however, were poorly understood for more than a century. Beginning in the mid-19th century, researchers began studying a variety of possible water purifying agents and methods, including voltaic reactions, electrolysis, the use of various oxidizing agents, and chlorine. In the United States, for example, a Philadelphia physician named Robley Dunglison suggested adding gaseous chlorine or the salts of chlorine (chlorides) to impure water in order to make it potable. "It has been proposed," he wrote, "to add to such water [marsh water] a small quantity of chlorine, or one of his chlorides, but a quantity sufficient to destroy the foulness of the fluid, can hardly fail, we should think, to communicate a taste and smell disagreeable to most individuals" (Dunglison 1835, 338). (Two technical points to be noted about Dunglison's comments and the thinking of his peers: (1) the chemical, physical, physiological, and other properties of the element chlorine are very different from chloride compounds; and (2) the harmful biological effects of impure water are not necessarily the consequence of its unpleasant odors and tastes, so eliminating these odors and tastes does not guarantee that the treated water is yet safe to drink.)

Most of these efforts at devising methods for using chlorine (and other substances) for the purification of water were generally unsuccessful during the 19th century, although they did, of course, contribute to the general body of knowledge about water purification that was developing. By the end of the century, however, technology had become sufficiently developed that large-scale chlorination plants were being developed. Probably the first of those plants was constructed at Ostend, Belgium, in 1900, although it operated for only a short period of time. Two years later, however, another such plant opened at Middelkerke, Belgium, a facility that is generally recognized as the first successful use of chlorine to purify water in the world. At maximum capacity, the plant was able to produce 1,300,000 gallons of purified water per day (Race 1918, 9).

Chlorination of water was first studied experimentally in the United States at the Louisville (Kentucky) Experiment Station for a week or two in 1896. The first full-scale municipal application of the technology, however, was not put into operation until more than a decade later when Jersey City, New Jersey, began using sodium hypochlorite to purify its water on a continuous basis. The real breakthrough in municipal chlorination of water occurred, however, with the opening of the Boonton, New Jersey, water treatment plant in 1908. When operating at maximum capacity, the plant delivered 40 million gallons of water purified with liquid chlorine to Jersey City on a daily basis (A Public Health Giant Step 2015; Safe Drinking Water, Board on Toxicology and Environmental Health Hazards. Assembly of Life Sciences. National Research Council 1980, 17–18).

Water treatment facilities are ubiquitous throughout the developed world today, although they may be less available in some developing nations. Each individual water treatment plant differs on one way or another from other water treatment plants. One of the most common models of a water treatment plant consists of three main steps: coagulation and sedimentation, filtration, and chlorination and aeration. In the coagulation process, one or more chemicals (alum is the most common) are added to raw water, forming a sticky precipitate to which dirt particles and other small solids adhere. These particles, along with larger solid materials in the raw water, are then allowed to settle out to the bottom of a vat, from which they can be removed. In the next step, the semi-purified water is passed through filters made of sand, charcoal, and/or other materials. These filters remove very small solid particles suspended in the water, some of which are responsible for the unpleasant tastes and odors present in raw water. The final step in the sequence involves the addition of a chemical, such as chlorine or bromine or one of their compounds, or another type of treatment, such ultraviolet radiation, designed to kill pathogens present in the water. The water is then delivered to a storage area, from which it can be distributed to the community. (Water treatment is a far more complex process than can be described here. For more detailed information, see Virtual Tour of a Drinking Water Plant, http://water.epa.gov/drink/tour/.)

Power Production

The collection of water for irrigation systems is by no means the only purpose for which dams are built. The other primary function of dams is as a source of power (*hydropower*) for operating mills and other types of machinery and the generation of hydroelectric power. The term *hydroelectric power* refers to electricity that is generated from the kinetic energy stored in running water.

"The Water Wheel," according to one history of machines, "is probably the oldest power driven machine not operated by men or animals." A waterwheel is a machine that converts the kinetic energy of running water into the kinetic energy of a rotating wheel and shaft. It can be used for a wide variety of purposes, such as grinding corn and other grains, crushing olives and grapes, tanning leather, making paper, forging iron, running textile machines, and operating bellows (Water Wheel 2015).

Water wheels were apparently not widely known in the earliest human civilizations of Mesopotamia and Egypt, largely because the rivers in those regions were slow-running, not possessed of enough energy to operate a waterwheel. One of the first definite mentions of a waterwheel, in fact, can be found in the writings of the Roman engineer Vitruvius (ca. 75 BCE–15 CE), who described such a device, but then noted that it was "rarely employed" by his colleagues (Hansen 2015b). The reason for this lack of interest, according to some observers, was that an abundance of human slaves and domestic animals was available for carrying out the type of work performed by the waterwheel.

Inventors faced with the challenge of designing a waterwheel that could operate on a slow-running river devised a simple solution. They constructed a dam along the river, allowing water to accumulate in the *mill pond* behind the dam. Water from the mill pond could then be released into channels leading to the waterwheel, whose power output was then considerably increased by the more rapidly running water (see, e.g., the demonstration diagrams at http://www.technologystudent.com/energy1/wtrwhll1.htm). Dam-waterwheel facilities of this type grew in popularity during the early Middle Ages. The survey taken for the Domesday Book in England in 1086, for example, found that at least 6,000 water mills were in operation, a striking figure that meant that there was one such machine for every 350 residents of the country. By 1300, that number had doubled, and it continued to rise until the middle of the 19th century, when a peak of 30,000 water mills were recorded in England. Similar numbers were reported in other countries, although the popularity of the waterwheel began to decline by 1850 as a result of the availability of other forms of power resulting from the Industrial Revolution (Smil 2008, 180–181, with many additional references at this source).

Future prospects for the development of water power in the mid-19th century—except for specialized geographic, topographic, social, economic, and other reasons—appeared dim because of the development of steam power during the Industrial Revolution. Such an approach turned out not to be the case, however, as a new and far more important use for hydropower appeared on the horizon: the generation of electricity. A key element in this new development was the discovery in 1831 and 1832 by English physicist Michael Faraday of the electric generator. The generator is a device for converting the mechanical motion of a wire within a magnetic field into an electric current. (For the principle of the electric generator, see http://www.tutorvista.com/content/physics/physics-ii/elec tricity/electric-generator.php.) Faraday's discovery prompted inventors to find ways of using the kinetic energy of running water to turn a turbine (an oversized fan) that, in turn, could then be used to turn a metal shaft inside a magnetic field to produce electrical current. The concept of a hydroelectric power plant was created. (Many good models of hydroelectric plants are available. See, e.g., https://www.youtube.com/watch?v=rnPEtwQtmGQ.)

During the last quarter of the 19th century, a number of small hydroelectric systems were put into operation, primarily for the purpose of demonstrating the possibilities of the technology. Credit for the first such system often goes to a simple hydroelectric power system installed at the Cragside country house in Northumberland, England, which was capable of lighting a single lightbulb. Similar simple systems were later put into operation in Grand Rapids, Michigan (1880); Ottawa, Ontario (1881); Dolgeville, New York (1881); and Niagara Falls, New York (1881), all producing enough electrical power for homes or small businesses (A Brief History of Hydropower 2015).

The first commercial-scale hydroelectric plant began operations on September 30, 1882, on the Fox River, in Appleton, Wisconsin. The plant was built by paper manufacturer H. J. Rogers, and it supplied enough electricity to meet the needs of his own home, his paper plant, and one nearby building, equivalent to the electric current needed to light 250 lightbulbs (The World's First Hydroelectric Power Plant 2015).

Over the next 20 years, hydropower saw an explosion of new facilities around the world, with more than 300 new plants going into operation over the period. The United States and Canada led the world in hydropower development, but significant new plants were being installed also in many other countries (A Brief History of Hydropower 2015). Construction of hydropower in the United States was motivated in particular by efforts to take advantage of the nation's enormous water reserves and to develop the vast arid regions of the West. The first of these plants to come online was the Austin Dam, near Austin, Texas, the first such plant designed specifically for the generation of hydroelectric power. The Austin plant was followed by such now-famous plants as the Niagara Falls Hydropower Plant (1895–1896), Hoover Dam (1936), and Grand Coulee Dam (1942). During the same period, the federal government also created a number of regional agencies whose purpose it was to construct dams on various river systems in the United States, including the Tennessee Valley Authority, and specialized departments for the Colorado River (Bureau of Reclamation) and the Columbia River (U.S. Army Corps of Engineers) (Energy Timelines: Hydropower 2011; Hydroelectric Power 2003).

Today, the role played by hydropower in the generation of electricity varies widely from country to country, ranging from none to 100 percent. Table 1.7 lists some of the countries that

Table 1.7   Percentage of a Country's Electricity Obtained from Hydroelectric Sources

Country	Percentage from Hydroelectric Sources
Albania	100
Angola	70.9
Australia	6.6
Austria	55.0
Bangladesh	2.0
Belgium	0.2
Brazil	80.6
Canada	59.0
China	14.8
Egypt	8.3
Germany	3.5
India	12.4
Israel	0.0
Mexico	10.8
Mozambique	99.9
Namibia	98.2
Nepal	99.9
New Zealand	51.5
Norway	96.6
Pakistan	29.9
Paraguay	100
Russia	15.7
South Africa	0.8
Spain	7.0
Sudan	75.2
Switzerland	56.8
Tajikistan	98.8
United Kingdom	1.5
United States	6.5
Yemen	0.0
Zambia	99.7

Source: Electricity Production from Hydroelectric Sources (% of Total). 2015. World Bank. http://data.worldbank.org/indicator/EG.ELC.HYRO.ZS. Accessed on July 19, 2015.

are most dependent on hydroelectric power, along with others whose production numbers may be of special interest.

Water Law

Give the essential role of water in human society, it is hardly surprising that laws associated with its ownership and use date to the earliest days of human civilization. Most of those laws fall into two general categories: ownership rights and environmental controls. By the term *water rights*, one means how the ownership of a particular water is determined. By *environmental controls*, one refers to the actions that can or must be taken or not taken to maintain a water resource in some particular condition, usually pure enough for a variety of human uses such as drinking, washing, swimming, irrigating, or using in industry.

Water Rights

Who owns the natural resources found on Earth? This question can be relatively simple for some natural resources, such as land and mineral rights. A person can purchase a parcel of land, and then he or she can be said to own that land (except in countries and/or at times when a nation declared that it owned all land within its boundaries; then one could hold "hold" or "rent" the land). The same might be said for the purchase of mineral resources buried underground. One might be able to purchase the rights to those resources and then do with them as one wishes.

But water resources are a very different matter. In the first place, water resources are often impermanent. Rivers, streams, and lakes flow freely at some times of the year or in some years, but are dry at other times. Also, water resources often have a variety of users, from people who float by and "use" part of a river for only a few minutes or hours to industries and other operations that actually remove water from a resource, which they may or may not return in the same or less quantity and quality.

For reasons such as these, rulers and governments were making laws about the ownership of water resources very early in human history. The first person to make an effort to codify previous formal and informal declarations about water rights was the Roman emperor Justinian, who, in 528 CE, ordered the publication of a compilation of all known water laws from the preceding 13 centuries. This compilation became part of the Justinian Code, one of the first comprehensive legal doctrines of modern civilization.

One of the most significant features of the Justinian Code's section on water rights was the doctrine of riparian rights. The term *riparian rights* comes from the Latin term *ripa*, for "bank," as in "river bank." The doctrine is of enormous historical significance because it has defined the way water can and cannot be used in a host of societies since Roman days, including modern water law in the United States and most other countries of the world.

With regard to riparian rights, the Justinian Code said that the water in a river, stream, lake, or ocean was part of the "public trust," in the same way that air is part of the public trust. No one can "own" these natural resources; they are and must always be available for use by the general public (What Is Public Trust? 2015). This doctrine is not quite so simple as it sounds, however. While no one could "own" part of a river or lake or seashore, one could certainly own the bank of that river, lake, or seashore and, in some instances, could own the land *under* the water up to a certain distance from the shore. According to the code:

> The public use of the banks of a river is part of the law of nations, just as is that of the river itself. All persons, therefore, are as much at liberty to bring their vessels to the bank, to fasten ropes to the trees growing there, and to place any part of their cargo there, as to navigate the river itself But the banks of a river are the property of those whose land they adjoin; and consequently the trees growing on them are also the property of the same persons.

The public use of the seashore, too, is part of the law of nations, as is that of the sea itself; and, therefore, any person is at liberty to place on it a cottage, to which he may retreat, or to dry his nets there, and haul them from the sea; for the shores may be said to be the property of no man, but are subject to the same law as the sea itself, and the sand or ground beneath it. (The Institutes of Justinian, 535 A.D. 2015)

The evolution of water rights laws following publication of the Justinian Code is far too complex to be considered in detail here. (For good discussions of this history, see Cech 2010, chapter 8; Getzler 2004; Hodgson 2004, chapter 4; Narasimhan 2008.) In general, the doctrine laid out by the code was largely adopted intact or with some modifications by other societies as they began to duplicate Justinian's efforts to codify a history of their country's laws on a variety of topics. For example, in 1256, King Alfonso X of Castile ("The Wise") directed a compilation of Spanish laws similar to that of Justinian that was eventually published in 1263 as *Las Siete Partidas* (*The Seven-Part Code* or *Seven Books of Law*). Book 3 of the code dealt with issues of property ownership and reflected, to a remarkable degree, the doctrine expressed in the Justinian Code. At one point, for example, it states that

The things that belong to all creatures who live on earth are the following, air, rain, water, and the shore of the sea. For each living person may make use of each of these things according to his need. Therefore each man may make use of the sea and its shore, fishing or sailing and doing all the things which he deems to be for his benefit. (As cited in Stone 1995, 286)

Las Siete Partidas is actually of more than historical interest in current discussions over water issues in the United States. As noted in the article just cited earlier, the legal doctrine controlling water rights issues in the southwestern United States has long been strongly influenced by the views expressed in Alfonso's document more than five centuries earlier (Stone 1995, 286–291).

Even more influential to water rights disputes in the United States has been the development of common law doctrine about water rights laws. The term *common law* refers to legal doctrines that have been established as a result of court decision rather than specific laws that have been passed by a legislature (which are known as *statutory law*). As with many features of the American legal system, the nation's current legal policies toward water use are ground to a considerable extent in the history of English common law.

Probably the best single explication of that long and complex history is an article written by T. E. Lauer, then at the University of Missouri School of Law, "The Common Law Background of the Riparian Doctrine" (Lauer 1963). In that article, Lauer traces the intricate ins and outs of the development of common law doctrine on riparian rights from what seems to be its first mention in 1187 to its impact on the American legal system in 1826. In that year, a case came before the U.S. Circuit Court for the District of Rhode Island, where it was heard before Justice Joseph Story. The case, *Tyler v. Wilkinson*, involved a complaint by a group of millowners on the Pawtucket River that an upstream competitor was diverting water from the river in such a way as to cause damage to their own operations. Justice Story wrote a long opinion that set an important precedent regarding water rights in the United States. He pointed out that simply because one owner had precedence in water use, that is, had an operation in place before his competitors, he was not allowed to withdraw enough water to disturb the operations of those competitors. "Each riparian," he ruled, "had a right to reasonable use of the water" (Lauer 1963, 60; Water Law 2015). With that decision, the first step in establishing the riparian rights of landowners in the United States was established.

Justice Story's decision in *Tyler v. Wilkinson* seemed to suggest that the legal status of water rights in the United States would essentially continue to reflect those that had been followed in Europe for nearly two millennia. Such was not, however, to be the case for very long. One of the major events that altered that scenario was the gold rush that took place in the America West (especially in California) beginning in 1848. In the frenzy that accompanied the search for gold, some traditional legal niceties were ignored. One of those "niceties" was the riparian doctrine. Gold miners began to decide on their own that the person who owned the rights to a body of water, such as a stream where he was searching for gold, was the person who got there first and started to work the stream. The new water rights doctrine soon earned the formal name of *prior appropriation*. One formal definition for the term is that "the first person who physically takes water from a stream (or underground aquifer) and places that water to some type of beneficial use" becomes the owner of that water resource. The prior appropriation doctrine has earned the slogan of "first in time, first in right" (Prior Appropriation Law 2015).

Prior appropriation allows for more than one owner of a water resource, but does not guarantee that all "owners" will actually be able to use water from a resource. For example, suppose that three individuals have prior appropriation rights to a water resource, the first with the right to the use of 10 cubic feet per second, the second with the right to 5 cubic feet per second, and the third with the right to 2 cubic feet per second. As long as the source provides 17 cubic feet per second or more, all owners will be satisfied. But suppose that the source begins to dry up and produces on 10 cubic feet per second. In that case, the second and third owners are "out of luck" and will get no water from the source.

The legitimacy of the prior appropriation doctrine of water rights was confirmed by a now-famous court case, *Irwin v. Phillips*, settled in 1855. In that case, the California Supreme Court ruled that however much the policy of the State, as indicated by her legislation, has conferred the privilege to work the mines, it has equally conferred the right to divert the streams from their natural channels, and as these two rights stand upon an equal footing, when they conflict, they must be decided by the fact of priority, upon the maxim of equity, *qui prior est in tempore potior est in jure.* ["who is there first in time is first in law."] (Hess 1917, 146)

The prior appropriation doctrine gained acceptance rapidly in the western states. Colorado became the first state to officially adopt the policy in 1872, followed by Alaska, Arizona, California, Hawaii, Idaho, Kansas, Montana, Nebraska, Nevada, New Mexico, North Dakota, Oklahoma, Oregon, South Dakota, Utah, Washington, and Wyoming (State Water Withdrawal Regulations 2015). Thus, the United States today has two very different legal systems for deciding on water rights, the riparian doctrine in the eastern and central part of the country and the prior appropriation doctrine in the western states.

Environmental Regulations

Human civilizations have probably always been accompanied by some level of air, water, and solid waste pollution. As societies became more technologically advanced (as during the Industrial Revolution), that level of pollution increased, often by significant amounts. Yet, relatively few examples of laws dealing with environmental pollution prior to the 20th century exist. One of the earliest laws sometimes cited as an example of the first water pollution law was actually written to deal with air pollution, "For punishing nuisances which cause corruption of the air near cities and great towns," passed in 1388. This law took note of the fact that

For that so much dung and filth of the garbage and entrails as well of beasts killed, as of other corruptions, be cast and put into ditches, rivers and other waters, and also many other places, within, about, and nigh unto divers cities, boroughs, and towns of the realm and the suburbs of them, that the air there is greatly corrupt and infect, and many maladies and other intolerable diseases do daily happen, as well to the inhabitants and those that are conversant in the said cities, boroughs, towns and suburbs, as to others repairing and traveling thither, to the great annoyance, damage, and peril of the inhabitants, dwellers, repairers, and travellers aforesaid . . . and if any do he shall be called before the chancellor . . . and shall be punished after the discretion of the Chancellor. (Tomlins 1811, 120–122)

Early laws such as these were extremely rare and generally largely ineffective (Newson 1992, 17–20). In fact, it was not well into the Industrial Revolution before water pollution laws became significantly more common and sometimes more effective. As just one example, the Salmon Fisheries Act of 1861 was adopted in response to pollution of many rivers and streams by a variety of industrial operations that so badly contaminated the water that downstream fishing was essentially no longer possible. The 1861 act made a number of provisions requiring industries to refrain from polluting or, at least, cleaning up the pollution of the waterways they used. This act, like many other similar to it, was also largely ineffective (Newson 1992, 19; The Salmon Fisheries Act 1861).

A roughly similar pattern for water pollution laws holds true for the United States. The first such law was the Rivers and Harbors Act of 1899, whose purpose it was to keep the nation's waterways clear of materials that would interfere with the navigation of ships. Interestingly enough, two sections of that law are still being used in lawsuits filed to promote clean waterways today, sections 10 and 13 that deal with obstructions in waterways and the dumping of materials into waterways, respectively (Kenney 2006).

A half century passed before the federal government enacted additional legislation protecting the nation's waterway, the

Federal Water Pollution Control Act (FWPCA) of 1948 (sometimes referred to as The Clean Water Act). This act did not actually provide for federal action in the maintenance of water quality in lakes, streams, and other bodies of water, focusing instead on various mechanisms to encourage the states to take such action as they felt was necessary. The FWPCA was amended a number of times, in 1961, 1966, 1970, 1972, 1977, and 1987, in attempts to improve its effectiveness in reducing pollution of the nation's waterways (Digest of Federal Resource Laws 2015).

Possibly the most significant of the many amendments made to the FWPCA were those adopted in 1972, a group of provisions now known as the Clean Water Act of 1972. One of the motivating forces driving legislators to approve this act was the series of dramatic fires that had been breaking out on Cleveland's Cuyahoga River from the early 1950s to the late 1960s. The nearly unimaginable pollution that allowed a large flowing river to catch fire inspired many ordinary citizens as well as state and federal legislators to begin calling for more aggressive federal action for the protection of the nation's waterways, one major result being the 1972 Clean Water Act (Scott 2009).

As with previous legislation, the Clean Water Act of 1972 has been updated and revised a number of times since its adoption. It continues to provide the fundamental basis for the nation's policies regarding the maintenance of water quality in U.S. rivers, streams, lakes, and other waterways.

Summary

Earth's water resources are so enormous that one wonders how there could ever be a shortage of water. But this review makes clear that there have been many times and places in human history when sufficient quantities of pure water were not readily available for human use. Over the past half century, that problem has become even more serious with a host of troublesome issues now facing the world's governments. Chapter 2 will discuss some of the most important of these issues and some of the solutions that have been proposed for those issues.

References

"Advancing the Science: Google Earth." Marine Conservation Biology Institute. http://mcbi.marine-conservation.org/what/googleearth.htm. Accessed on July 11, 2015.

Agusta-Boularot, Sandrine, and Jean-Louis Paillet. 1997. "Le Barrage et L'aqueduc Occidental De Glanum: Le Premier Barrage-voûte de L'histoire Des Techniques?" *Revue Archéologique*. 1: 27–78.

Al Ansary, A. R. 1981. *Qaryat Al-fau: A Portrait of Pre-Islamic Civilisation in Saudi-Arabia*. London: Croom Helm.

Bacon, Sir Francis. 1670. *Sylva Sylvarum or a Natural History in Ten Centuries*, 9th ed. London: Printed by J.R. for William Lee. https://archive.org/stream/sylvasylvarumorn00baco#page/n7/mode/2up. Accessed on July 17, 2015.

Baker, M. N. 1949. "The Quest for Pure Water: The History of Water Purification from the Earliest Records to the Twentieth Century." New York: American Water Works Association. Available online at http://babel.hathitrust.org/cgi/pt?id=mdp.39015007372272;view=1up;seq=1. Accessed on July 16, 2015.

Ball, Philip. 2000. *Life's Matrix: A Biography of Water*. New York: Farrar, Straus, and Giroux.

Beatty, Kelly. 2015. "Give-and-Take Origin for Earth's Water?" Sky and Telescope. http://www.skyandtelescope.com/astronomy-news/origin-of-earths-water-01022015/. Accessed on July 11, 2015.

Bice, Dave. "Modeling the Global Water Cycle." Exploring the Dynamics of Earth Systems. http://www3.geosc.psu.edu/~dmb53/DaveSTELLA/Water/global%20water/global_water.htm. Accessed on July 12, 2015.

48   The Global Water Crisis

"A Brief History of Hydropower." International
Hydropower Association. http://www.hydropower.org/
a-brief-history-of-hydropower. Accessed on July 19, 2015.

Cech, Thomas V. 2010. *Principles of Water Resources: History,
Development, Management, and Policy*, 3rd ed. Hoboken,
NJ: John Wiley & Sons, Inc.

Coffey, Kay, and G. W. Reid. 1976. "Historic Implication
for Developing Countries of Developed Countries' Water
and Wastewater Technology." Agency for International
Development. http://pdf.usaid.gov/pdf_docs/pnaad288
.pdf. Accessed on July 18, 2015.

"Dam, Hydropower, and Reservoir Statistics." 2015. United
States Society on Dams. http://www.ussdams.org/uscold_s
.html. Accessed on July 16, 2015.

"Digest of Federal Resource Laws of Interest to the U.S. Fish
and Wildlife Service." 2015. https://www.fws.gov/laws/
lawsdigest/FWATRPO.HTML. Accessed on July 23, 2015.

Dunglison, Robley. 1835. *On the Influence of Atmosphere and
Locality: Change of Air and Climate, Seasons, Food, Clothing,
Bathing, Exercise, Sleep, Corporeal and Intellectual Pursuits, &C.
&C. On Human Health : Constituting Elements of Hygiène.*
Philadelphia: Carey, Lea & Blanchard.

Dwyer, Jim. 2015. "A Stunning Link to New York's Past
Makes a Long-Awaited Return." *The New York Times.*
http://www.nytimes.com/2015/06/05/nyregion/a-stunning-
link-to-new-yorks-past-makes-a-long-awaited-return.html.
Accessed on July 17, 2015.

"Energy Timelines: Hydropower." 2011. http://www.docstoc
.com/docs/106654584/Energy-Timelines-Hydropower.
Accessed on July 19, 2015.

Fisk, Pliny. 1822. "Egypt." *Religious Intelligencer.* 7(19): 289–293.

Foster, Stephen, and Daniel P. Loucks, eds. 2006.
"Non-Renewable Groundwater Sources." Paris: United

Nations Educational, Scientific and Cultural Organization. Available online at http://unesdoc.unesco .org/images/0014/001469/146997e.pdf. Accessed on July 13, 2015.

Freichs, Ralph R. 2015. "Removal of the Pump Handle." UCLA Department of Epidemiology. School of Public Health. http://www.ph.ucla.edu/epi/snow/removal.html. Accessed on July 17, 2015.

Galvis, Gerardo. 1999. "Development and Evaluation of Multistage Filtration Plants." Centre for Environmental Health Engineering. School of Engineering in the Environment. University of Surrey. http://www.bvsde .paho.org/bvsacg/i/fulltext/galvis/galvis.pdf. Accessed on July 17, 2015.

"General Facts and Concepts about Ground Water." U.S. Geological Survey. http://pubs.usgs.gov/circ/circ1186/ html/gen_facts.html. Accessed on July 12, 2015.

Getzler, Joshua. 2004. *A History of Water Rights at Common Law*. Oxford; New York: Oxford University Press.

Grant, Roy. 2015. "Woodingdean Well." Brighton and Hove. http://www.mybrightonandhove.org.uk/page_id__6948 .aspx. Accessed on July 14, 2015.

"Groundwater: Wells." U.S. Geological Survey. http:// water.usgs.gov/edu/earthgwwells.html. Accessed on July 14, 2015.

Hansen, Roger D. 2015a. "Water and Wastewater Systems in Imperial Rome." http://www.waterhistory.org/histories/ rome/t1.html#REF. Accessed on July 17, 2015.

Hansen, Roger D. 2015b. "Water Wheels." http://www .waterhistory.org/histories/rome/t1.html#REF. Accessed on July 19, 2015.

Helms, S. W. 1977. "Jawa Excavations 1975: Third Preliminary Report." *Levant*. 9(1): 21–35.

Hess, R. H. 1917. "California Irrigation Right." *California Law Review.* 5(2): 142–159. http://scholarship.law.berkeley .edu/cgi/viewcontent.cgi?article=4084&context=californial awreview. Accessed on July 20, 2015.

Hodgson, S. 2004. "Land and Water—The Rights Interface." Food and Agricultural Organization of the United Nations. http://www.fao.org/3/a-y5692e.pdf. Accessed on July 20, 2015.

Hoekstra, Arjen Y., and Mesfin M. Mekonnen. 2011. "The Water Footprint of Humanity." *PNAS.* 109(9): 3232–3237.

"How Much Water Is There on, in, and above the Earth?" U.S. Geological Survey. http://water.usgs.gov/edu/ earthhowmuch.html. Accessed on July 12, 2015.

Huisman, L., and W. E. Wood. 1974. "Slow Sand Filtration." Geneva: World Health Organization. http://www.who.int/ water_sanitation_health/publications/ssf9241540370.pdf. Accessed on July 17, 2015.

"Hydroelectric Power." 2003. Dictionary of American History. http://www.encyclopedia.com/topic/hydroelectric_ power.aspx#1. Accessed on July 19, 2015.

"Information Center of Qanat." 2015. Internet Archive Wayback Machine. http://web.archive.org/ web/20050205102218/http://qanat.info/en/index.php. Accessed on July 15, 2015.

"The Institutes of Justinian, 535 A.D." 2015. http://faculty .cua.edu/pennington/Law508/InstitutesofJustinian.htm. Accessed on July 20, 2015.

"An Introduction to Gravity Dams." 2015. Sim Science. http://simscience.org/cracks/advanced/grav_char1.html. Accessed on July 16, 2015.

"Irrigation Handbook." 2015. Grundfos Water Services. https://us.grundfos.com/content/dam/GPU/Products/ DME/irrigation-handbook-220165.pdf. Accessed on July 15, 2015.

"Irrigation Museum." 2015. Irrigation Association. http://www.irrigationmuseum.org/exhibit2.aspx. Accessed on July 15, 2015.

Jesperson, Kathy. 1996. "Search for Clean Water Continues." *On Tap.* Summer 1996: 6–8.

Kenney, Robyn. 2006. "Rivers and Harbors Act of 1899, United States." The Encyclopedia of Earth. http://www.eoearth.org/view/article/155764/. Accessed on July 23, 2015.

Kenoyer, Johnathan M. 2011. *Ancient Cities of the Indus Valley Civilization.* Karachi, Pakistan: Oxford University Press; Islamabad: American Institute of Pakistan Studies.

"Key Developments in the History of Arch Dams." 2015. Cracking Dams. http://www.simscience.org/cracks/advanced/arch_hist1.html. Accessed on July 16, 2015.

"Key Developments in the History of Buttress Dams." 2015. Cracking Dams. http://www.simscience.org/cracks/advanced/butt_hist1.html. Accessed on July 16, 2015.

Lauer, T. E. 1963. "The Common Law Background of the Riparian Doctrine." *Missouri Law Review.* 1: 60–107.

"Law Code of Hammurabi (1780 B.C.)." 2015. http://mcadams.posc.mu.edu/txt/ah/assyria/hammurabi.html. Accessed on July 15, 2015.

McGowan, Joe. 2015. "A Visit to St. Patrick's Well." Irish Culture and Customs. http://www.irishcultureandcustoms.com/ACalend/StPatWell.html. Accessed on July 14, 2015.

Midant-Reynes, Béatrix. 2000. *The Prehistory of Egypt: From the First Egyptians to the First Pharaohs.* Oxford, UK; Malden, MA: Blackwell Publishers.

Narasimhan, T. N. 2008. "Water, Law, Science." *Journal of Hydrology.* 349(1): 125–138. http://www.osti.gov/scitech/servlets/purl/924856-9Okl1w/. Accessed on July 20, 2015.

Newson, Malcolm David. 1992. *Land, Water and Development: River Basin Systems and Their Sustainable Management*. London; New York: Routledge.

Nilsson, Jan-Erik. 2015. "Chronology and History of China." Gotheborg.com. http://gotheborg.com/chronology/index-chronology.htm. Accessed on July 13, 2015.

"Prior Appropriation Law." 2015. Division of Water Resources. Department of Natural Resources. Colorado. http://water.state.co.us/SurfaceWater/SWRights/Pages/PriorApprop.aspx. Accessed on July 20, 2015.

"A Public Health Giant Step: Chlorination of U.S. Drinking Water." 2015. Water Quality and Health. http://www.waterandhealth.org/drinkingwater/chlorination_history.html. Accessed on July 18, 2015.

Race, Joseph. 1918. *Chlorination of Water*. New York: J. Wiley & Sons, Inc. Available online at http://www.gutenberg.org/files/37389/37389-h/37389-h.htm#Fn1_14. Accessed on July 18, 2015.

Ringersma, Jacquelijn, Niels Batjes, and David Dent. 2003. "Green Water: Definitions and Data for Assessment. Wageningen, Netherlands. http://www.isric.org/isric/webdocs/docs/ISRICGreenwater%20ReviewFebr2004_.pdf. Accessed on January 17, 2016.

Roaf, Michael. 2008. *Cultural Atlas of Mesopotamia and the Ancient Near East*. New York: Facts on File.

"Romaq: The Atlas Project of Roman Aqueducts." 2015. http://www.romaq.org/. Accessed on July 17, 2015.

"Sadd Al-Kafara . . . the Oldest Dam in the World." 2015. Hydria Project. http://www.hydriaproject.net/en/egypt-sadd-al-kafara-dam/relevance9. Accessed on July 16, 2015.

Safe Drinking Water Committee. Board on Toxicology and Environmental Health Hazards. Assembly of Life Sciences. National Research Council. 1980. *Drinking Water and Health*, vol. 2. Washington, DC: National Academy Press.

Sagmit, Rosario S., and Nora N. Soriano. 1998. *Geography in the Changing World.* Manila, Philippines: Rex Book Store.

"Saline Water." U.S. Geological Survey. http://water.usgs.gov/edu/saline.html. Accessed on July 10, 2015.

"The Salmon Fisheries Act." 1861. London: "The Field" *[sic]* Office. Available online at http://babel.hathitrust.org/cgi/pt?id=hvd.hwg58z;view=1up;seq=9. Accessed on July 23, 2015.

Sarafian, Adam, et al. 2014. "Early Accretion of Water in the Inner Solar System from a Carbonaceous Chondrite-like Source." *Science.* 346(6209): 623–626.

Scott, Michael. 2009. "Cuyahoga River Fire Galvanized Clean Water and the Environment as a Public Issue." Cleveland.com. http://www.cleveland.com/science/index.ssf/2009/04/cuyahoga_river_fire_galvanized.html. Accessed on July 23, 2015.

Segrest, Michelle. 2015. "The History of Pumps through the Years." Pumps and Systems. http://www.pumpsandsystems.com/topics/pumps/pumps/history-pumps-through-years. Accessed on July 13, 2015.

"Seminar on Safe Tailings Dam Constructions." 2001. Swedish Mining Association, et al. http://ec.europa.eu/environment/waste/mining/pdf/mining_dams_seminar.pdf. Accessed on July 16, 2015.

Siebert, S., et al. 2010. "Groundwater Use of Irrigation—A Global Inventory." *Hydrology and Earth System Sciences.* 14: 1863–1880. http://www.fao.org/docrep/013/al816e/al816e00.pdf. Accessed on July 15, 2015.

Smil, Vaclav. 2008. *Energy in Nature and Society: General Energetics of Complex Systems.* Cambridge, MA: MIT Press.

Snow, John. 1854. "Mode of Communication of Cholera." UCLA Department of Epidemiology. School of Public Health. http://www.ph.ucla.edu/epi/snow/snowbook0a.html. Accessed on July 17, 2015.

Snyder, Laura J. 2015. *Eye of the Beholder: Johannes Vermeer, Antoni Van Leeuwenhoek, and the Reinvention of Seeing.* New York: W. W. Norton & Company.

"State Water Withdrawal Regulations." 2015. National Conference of State Legislatures. http://www.ncsl .org/research/environment-and-natural-resources/ state-water-withdrawal-regulations.aspx. Accessed on July 20, 2015.

Stone, Marilyn. 1995. "Las Siete Partidas in America: Problems of Cultural Transmission in the Translation of Legal Signs." In Morris, Marshall, ed. *Translation and the Law.* Amsterdam; Philadelphia: John Benjamins.

Tanksley, Arlene Kim. 2015. "Jawa Dam." Bayt.com. http:// www.bayt.com/en/specialties/q/148613/jawa-dam- is-featured-an-originally-9m-high-and-1m-wide-stone-wall- supported-by-a-50m-wide-earth-rampart-in-which- country-was-this-earliest-known-dam/. Accessed on July 16, 2015.

"Technology of Dams." 2015. International Commission on Large Dams. http://www.icold-cigb.org/GB/Dams/ technology_of_dams.asp. Accessed on July 16, 2015.

Tegel Willy, et al. 2012. "Early Neolithic Water Wells Reveal the World's Oldest Wood Architecture." *PLoS ONE.* 7(12): e51374. http://journals.plos.org/plosone/article?id=10.1371/ journal.pone.0051374. Accessed on July 13, 2015.

Tomlins, Thomas Edlyne, ed. 1811. *The Statutes at Large of England and Great Britain*, vol. 2. London: George Eyre and Andrew Strahan.

Tvedt, Terje, and Richard Coopey. 2010. *Rivers and Society: From Early Civilizations to Modern Times.* London: I. B. Tauris.

Van Leeuwenhoek, Antony van. 1677. "Observations Communicated to the Publisher by Mr. Antony van Leeuwenhoek, in a Dutch Letter of the 9th of October 1676. Here English'd: Concerning Little Animals by Him Observed in Rain-Well-Sea. and Snow Water;

as Also in Water Wherein Pepper Had Lain Infused." *Philosophical Transactions*. 12: 821–831. http://rstl .royalsocietypublishing.org/content/12/133-142/821.full .pdf. Accessed on July 17, 2015.

Violet, Pierre-Louis. 2010. "Water Engineering and Management in Early Bronze Age Civilizations." In Cabrera, Enrique, and Francisco Arregui, eds. *Water Engineering and Management through Time: Learning from History*. Boca Raton, FL: CRC Press, Chapter 2.

"Water Basics." U.S. Geological Survey. http://water.usgs.gov/ edu/mwater.html. Accessed on July 10, 2015.

"Water Law." 2015. http://ppc.uiowa.edu/sites/default/files/ uploads/water_law_senior_college_class_2_classic_and_ modern_cases.pdf. Accessed on July 20, 2015.

"Water Wheel." 2015. Machine-History.com. http://www .machine-history.com/node/575. Accessed on July 19, 2015.

"What Is Public Trust?" 2015. Flow: For Love of Water. http://flowforwater.org/public-trust-solutions/ what-is-public-trust/. Accessed on July 20, 2015.

"The World's First Hydroelectric Power Plant Began Operation September 30, 1882." 2015. America's Story. http://www.americaslibrary.gov/jb/gilded/jb_gilded_ hydro_1.html. Accessed on July 19, 2015.

"World's Largest Hand Dug Well." 2015. The Big Well. Greensburg, Kansas. http://www.bigwell.org/. Accessed on July 14, 2015.

"The World's Water." U.S. Geological Survey. http://water .usgs.gov/edu/gallery/global-water-volume.html. Accessed on July 11, 2015.

Zekster, Igor S., and Lorne G. Everett, eds. 2004. "Groundwater Resources of the World and Their Uses." Paris: United Nations Educational, Scientific and Cultural Organization. http://unesdoc.unesco.org/ images/0013/001344/134433e.pdf. Accessed on August 8, 2015.

2 Problems, Issues, and Solutions

When the well's dry, we know the worth of water.
—Franklin 1914, 627

The future political impact of water scarcity may be devastating. Using water the way we have in the past simply will not sustain humanity in future.
—Former World Leaders Call on UN Security Council to Recognize Water as a Top Concern 2012

Writing from perspectives nearly 300 years apart, Benjamin Franklin and the former Canadian prime minister Jean Chrétien deliver essentially the same message about the role of water on the planet: we ignore at our own peril the essential role of water in human life, and without appropriate action, the world is likely to face a host of water-related problems in the future. The brief history of water in human civilization provided in Chapter 1 confirms the accuracy of statements such as these. But what are the problems humans face today with regard to water quality and quantity, what are the causes of those problems, and what solutions are available for those problems?

People in developing nations often have no access to safe, fresh water. They may have to travel miles and/or wait for long periods to get the water they need for daily needs, such as drinking, cooking, and cleaning. (Sjors737/ Dreamstime.com)

Water Scarcity

Arguably, the single most important water issue facing the planet today is water scarcity. The term *water scarcity* has been defined by the United Nations as "the point at which the aggregate impact of all users impinges on the supply or quality of water under prevailing institutional arrangements to the extent that the demand by all sectors, including the environment, cannot be satisfied fully" (Water Scarcity 2014). Put more simply, perhaps, *water scarcity* refers to the condition in which there is an insufficient supply of safe freshwater to meet all the basic needs of a community, nation, or region.

The fact that people do not have access to enough water to live in safety and health may seem peculiar in developed nations, where most individuals can get all the water they want simply by turning on a faucet. But that scenario is by no means common throughout the world. The United Nations has estimated that about 2.8 billion people, 40 percent of the world population, currently exist in a state of water scarcity (Water Scarcity 2014). About 40 percent of those people (1.2 billion) exist in a condition known as *physical water scarcity*, a term first coined in a 2007 report by the International Water Management Institute. The term refers to a situation that one might first think of when discussing water scarcity, the lack of access to water because of insufficient natural resources, such as lakes, rivers, and underground reservoirs. One is likely to think of the North Africa–Middle East region as an area of physical scarcity because of the limited reserves of surface water. But other regions also qualify as physically water scarce, such as large stretches of northern India and China, southeastern Australia, and the mid-south states of the United States and adjacent regions of northern Mexico (Managing Water under Uncertainty and Risk 2012, Figure 4.10, page 125).

A second type of water scarcity is even more prevalent: economic water scarcity. The term *economic water scarcity* refers to a situation in which natural sources of freshwater may be available to a region, but insufficient efforts have been expended to make those resources available to human inhabitants of the region. For example, one might live in a developing nation where abundant freshwater from a river or lake is only a few miles away. But the government has not yet expended the money and effort to construct a piping system or other mechanism for delivering that water to that person's home. Any number of reasons can be cited for economic water scarcity, including lack of financial resources, inadequate technological knowledge, political disagreements, or simply a lack of will to carry out the work that needs to be done. Economic water scarcity is found most commonly in the world's developing regions, such as most of sub-Saharan Africa, parts of India and Southeast Asia, and the Andean nations of South America (Managing Water under Uncertainty and Risk 2012, Figure 4.10, page 125).

It perhaps goes without saying that water resources are not distributed equally around the world, so that some regions will be more water-scarce than will others. Northern Africa and the Middle East are two regions that are classically water scarce, and a recent survey found that 7 of the world's 10 nations most likely *not* to be able to meet their water demands in the near future (2035) are in this part of the world. Kuwait leads that list, with a projected water availability of 4.6 m³ (cubic meters) per person per year, followed by United Arab Emirates (13.6 m³), Qatar (21.6 m³), the Bahamas (46.9 m³), Bahrain (67.8 m³), Libya (74.3 m³), Maldives (76.6 m³), Yemen (88.8 m³), and Singapore (98.4 m³) (Mogelgaard 2015, Table 1).

The same report suggests that the number of individuals living in water-scarce or water-stressed areas will rise from a current level of about 2 billion to about 3.6 billion by 2035. (The term *water-scarce* is taken in the report to mean regions where there are fewer than 1,000 m³ of freshwater available per person per year, while the term *water-stressed* refers to a region with between 1,000 and 1,667 m³ per person per year [Mogelgaard 2015].)

Some of the most important conclusions of this report are based on an earlier study by the World Bank on the status of water resources in the Middle East and North Africa (Making the Most of Scarcity 2007). The report predicts that the amount of freshwater available to residents of this region will drop by about half from current levels by 2050. Such a scenario, the World Bank study suggests, will have "serious consequences for the region's already stressed aquifers and natural hydrological systems" (Making the Most of Scarcity 2007, xxi).

Water activists often cite a number of factors responsible for the world's current water crisis: population growth; waste of freshwater resources; contamination of lakes, rivers, and the oceans; climate change; increased urbanization; disruption of natural ecosystems; and on and on. Analyzing the water problems that humans face at any one given time and place is not easy, however, as these factors do not usually occur in isolation; instead, a multiplicity of factors are responsible for the water issues with which a community has to face.

Population Growth

The effect of population growth on water use is both obvious and fairly straightforward. Recall that the amount of freshwater available on the planet is estimated to be about 2,551,000 cubic miles (about 3.755×10^{17} cubic feet). This number represents all the freshwater available in lakes, rivers, streams, swamps, and the like, as well as water underground (How Much Water Is There on, in, and above the Earth? 2015). Then, in 1804, when the world population was about 1 billion, each person on Earth could be expected to have about 3.755×10^8 cubic feet available for his or her use. Of course, this number is purely theoretical since it varies for various locations on Earth, actual accessibility to water, and other factors. But consider the number strictly for the basis of comparison. Then, the amount of water *theoretically* available to each human on Earth over the next two centuries or more would be:

1927 (123 years later):	2 billion people	$1,878 \times 10^8$ cubic feet
1959 (32 years later):	3 billion people	1.252×10^8 cubic feet
1974 (15 years later):	4 billion people	0.939×10^8 cubic feet

1987 (13 years later):	5 billion people	0.751×10^8 cubic feet
1999 (12 years later):	6 billion people	0.626×10^8 cubic feet
2012 (13 years later):	7 billion people	0.536×10^8 cubic feet
2026 (est.; 14 years later):	8 billion people	0.469×10^8 cubic feet

(Authorities differ to some extent on the exact date of each milestone; see Current World Population 2015 and World Population 2015 for examples.)

These numbers may be too large to have much practical meaning, but they are reminders of one essential fact: the amount of freshwater on Earth is essentially constant, while the number of humans placing demands on that resource continues to grow rapidly, lately at the rate of another billion people every 12–15 years. When water shortages have historically been a problem for many regions on Earth, those problems can only be expected to grow more serious, and they may begin to develop in regions where water shortages have historically *not* been a problem.

As with other water issues, population growth is likely to affect some parts of the world to a greater extent than other parts. A 2002 report by the Population Research Bureau, for example, predicted that population increases in northern Africa and the Middle East were likely to result in a dramatic drop in the amount of freshwater available to residents of the area who, of course, would continue to rely on an essentially constant supply of water. According to that report, the average per capita supply of freshwater available to residents of the area was expected to drop from 3,645 m³ per person in 1970 to 1,640 m³ per person in 2001 to 1,113 m³ per person in 2025. Some countries would experience a more serious shortage than others, of course, with the United Arab Emirates dropping from 897 m³ per person in 1970 to 44 m³ per person in 2025, a decrease of more than 95 percent; Bahrain dropping from 455 m³ per person in 1970 to 97 m³ per person in 2025, a decrease of nearly 79 percent; and Saudi Arabia dropping from 418 m³ per person in 1970 to 59 m³ per person in 2025, a decrease of about 86 percent (Roudi-Fahimi, Creel, and De Souza 2002, Table 1, page 4).

The dramatic decrease in the availability of freshwater in many parts of the world is largely a result of other factors related to population growth. For example, with a larger population, a country must devote more land, water, and other resources to agricultural projects required to feed its additional citizens. Also, as population growth occurs, demographics tend to shift, with a larger fraction of the population moving to urban areas, where the stress placed on water resources is almost without exception more severe than it is in rural areas. Also, population growth is often accompanied by increase in industrial operations, which open up a new demand for water not present in a less populated, more rural nation. All of these changes are especially severe in the Middle East and North African regions because these regions depend so heavily on underground water resources, to a far greater extent than any other part of the world (Making the Most of Scarcity 2007, Figures 1 and 3, xxiii and xxiv, and Chapter 1).

Urbanization

An additional factor that affects water quantity and quality that almost always accompanies population growth is urbanization. The percentage of people living in rural versus urban settings has reversed dramatically over the past two centuries. Prior to 1800, the vast majority (an estimated 97%) of people lived in rural settings, and there were probably no cities with a population of more than a million people. This number began to decline, however, and by 1900, the fraction of rural residents had dropped to 86 percent (and the percentage of urbanites had risen to 14%). At this point, an estimated 12 cities worldwide had populations of more than a million (Human Population: Urbanization 2015).

This trend continued throughout the 20th century, until, by 1950, the share of urbanites had risen to 30 percent, and the number of cities with populations greater than a million had reached 83. A turning point in the rural–urban ratios occurred in 2008 when, for the first time in history, an approximately equal number of people lived in rural and urban cities. At this point, there were more than 400 cities with populations of more than a million and 19 with more than 10 million. Experts predict that by the year 2050, the split between urban and rural residents will be about 70:30 percent (Human Population: Urbanization 2015). (One of the interesting additional facts about urbanization is that it has not occurred uniformly around the world. Instead, as of 2010, 74 percent of the population in developed countries lived in urban settings, while only 44 percent of those in developing nations lived in urban settings [Human Population: Urbanization 2015].)

So why is urbanization a matter of interest or concern to those interested in water issues? Until fairly recently, there were a number of anecdotal reports about the effects of urbanization on water quality and quantity, but few scientific studies. Today that situation has changed, and specialists have a considerable amount of data to answer the question at the beginning of this paragraph.

The first thing to note is that urban land areas are significantly different from rural land areas. In rural areas, much of the natural environment—lakes, rivers, open land, trees, fields, and swamps, for example—allows for water to flow easily through the water cycle, from precipitation to surface water and groundwater reservoirs, and hence to the oceans or to underground aquifers. Urban areas, however, are generally characterized by a very different type of landscape, containing large stretches of impervious material, such as roads, highways, parking lots, driveways, and rooftops. Precipitation that falls on this type of landscape experiences a very different fate from that which falls on rural land. Instead of flowing slowly to a river, stream, or lake or slowly sinking into the ground and recharging an aquifer, urban precipitation washes quickly off impervious areas into streets and then into nearby rivers, lakes, and, ultimately, the ocean (How Urbanization Affects the Hydrologic System 2015; How Urbanization Affects the Water Cycle 2015; Urbanization and Streams 2015).

The first way in which urbanization affects water use, then, is the tendency to reduce the amount of freshwater available to an urban area as a result of precipitation. At the same time, the demand for freshwater by residents of an urban area for a host of purposes tends to place stress on whatever natural sources of water *are* available, such as rivers, streams, lakes, and aquifers. A growing population, then, often produces a greater demand for freshwater with a reduced availability of the resource from natural sources.

Urban precipitation has an effect on the quality of water also. Since precipitation runoff tends to flow more swiftly than natural rivers and streams and since much of the natural vegetation that tends to hold water in rural areas has been removed, erosion of existing waterways tends to increase dramatically. (The type of graphic that vividly illustrates this change can be found at How Urbanization Affects the Water Cycle 2015 or Urbanization and Streams 2015.) Thus, the amount of erosion on riverbanks in urban areas tends to be anywhere from 2 to 10 times as greater as it is on rural riverbanks with similar characteristics (for research on a specific example of this situation, see Neller 1988; for an overview of many studies on the issue, see Chin 2006).

Drought

One of the regular natural disasters that involve water supplies around the world is drought. From one perspective, the term *drought* is fairly easily defined as a period of time with less than normal precipitation that last for an extended period of time, such that plants are unable to grow successfully, and widespread death of animals results. But specialists in water science and other fields have pointed out that drought is actually a rather complex phenomenon with many basic aspects. In 1985, two specialists in the field of drought studies reviewed more than 150 published definitions of drought and concluded that those definitions could be classified into one of four general categories:

meteorological (based on existing weather conditions); hydrological (based on water resources); agricultural (based on effects on crops); and socioeconomic (based on the impacts of water shortage on the social, economic, political, psychological, and other aspects of a culture) (Wilhite and Glantz 1985).

However a drought is defined, there is little doubt that shortages of water primarily because of weather conditions have had some devastating effects on human societies. One of the first such droughts identified by researchers has been dated to the period from 133,000 BCE to 88,000 BCE in the region around today's Lake Malawi. Scientists have determined that the lake level dropped from than 2,000 feet during this time period, and forests and grasslands withered and died (Greenspan 2015).

Some examples of the worst droughts to have occurred in human history are the following:

- During the second millennium BCE, a severe drought apparently swept through the Middle East and Egypt, resulting in a number of very basic cultural changes, such as the widespread movement of populations, abandonment of urban centers, and the complete collapse of some national governments. Among the latter may have been the demise of the Old Kingdom in Egypt and the Akkadian Empire in Mesopotamia (deMenocal 2001; Gibbons 1993).

- In the period between about 750 and 900 CE, the Mesoamerican region (present-day Central America) experienced a series of devastating droughts that wiped out large numbers of residents of the area and disrupted the normal functioning of governments. Some experts believe that the droughts were a major, if not decisive, factor in causing the downfall of the Mayan civilization in the early 10th century, although other factors were also almost certainly involved (Gill 2000).

- Among the episodes of drought perhaps best known to Americans is the so-called dust bowl eras that lasted throughout most of the 1930s across the Great Plains region of the country. The combination of poor farming techniques and severe drought caused extensive erosion of top soil throughout the Great Plains region, turning the sky into a sometimes-permanently-opaque cloud of dust that destroyed agriculture in the region and drove hundreds of thousands of inhabitants to other parts of the country. A 2014 study by NASA found that the year 1934, in the midst of the dust bowl era, was "the single worst drought year of the last millennium" (Cook, Seager, and Smerdon 2014).

One of the primary features of current discussions about water issues around the world and in the United States is reference to the increasingly widespread appearance of drought conditions, not yet as severe as any of those mentioned earlier, but still of major concern. As an extension of the preceding list, consider a few examples from the early 21st century:

- UNICEF (originally the United Nations International Children's Emergency Fund) estimates that about 8 million residents of Ethiopia are at risk from drought conditions. About a quarter of that number is children under the age of five. Similar numbers hold of Ethiopia's neighbors, Eritrea (1.3 million at risk from drought), Somalia (with up to a million people at risk as a result of a seven-year drought), and Sudan (where 2.8 million people face food insecurity as a result of drought) (Drought Disasters 2015).

- Drought conditions in Afghanistan are responsible for the death of between 60 and 80 percent of livestock, with up to 2.5 million people also at risk of food shortages (Drought Disasters 2015).

- More than 60 percent of the soil in China's northern Shanxi Province lacks sufficient water to allow the growing of crops, with the result that a third of the province's wheat crop has been lost. An estimated 3 million people in the region are also suffering from water shortages for their personal use (Drought Disasters 2015).

- Some regions in India are suffering what officials call "the worst drought in 100 years" affecting 130 million people in 12 states (Drought Disasters 2015).
- The government of Pakistan estimates that nearly 3 million people are at risk for starvation because drought has destroyed their crops and livestock populations (Drought Disasters 2015).

Parts of the United States have experienced their own share of drought conditions over the decade ending in 2015. National, regional, and local media have carried story after story about the unusually high temperatures and low precipitation recorded in a number of states west of the Mississippi River. A report issued in early 2015 by researchers at the Indiana University and the Indiana Geological Survey, for example, has confirmed that a pattern of higher temperatures and lower rates of precipitation has been clear over the past 35 years in the upper Midwest, Louisiana, southeastern United States, and western United States, while reverse trends have been observed in New England, the Pacific Northwest, upper Great Plains, and Ohio River Valley (these conclusions do not take into account data from 2014 and 2015, however) (Ficklin, et al. 2015).

The state of California appears to have been particularly hard hit by the most recent drought. Over a period of at least four years, drought conditions have continued—and have sometimes tended to become worse—resulting in Governor Jerry Brown's having declared a drought state of emergency for California in January 2015. At that point, the governor's Drought Task Force announced the drought "one of the most severe droughts on record." The governor's declaration brought with it a number of voluntary and required programs designed to increase the extent to which individuals, communities, agriculture, and industry reduce their use of water. (More details and up-to-date information about the drought situation in California and the United States are available at California Drought 2015 and U.S. Drought Portal 2015, respectively. For images of the California drought, see California Drought Crisis 2015.)

What to Do about Droughts

Dealing with drought is clearly a problem of great concern in many parts of the world. Governments, researchers, non-governmental organizations, a variety of other groups, and ordinary citizens have attempted to find solutions that can be used with drought conditions in their own nations, in various regions of the globe, or around the world in general. These suggestions have ranged across a wide range of possibilities, from simple actions that can be taken by individuals, families, and communities, to massive infrastructure programs that may affect many thousands or even millions of people. As one might expect, recommendations differ quite substantially for developing countries, many of which have somewhat simple water access and storage systems that may consist of no more than a hand-dug well and a fairly small storage tank made of earth and/or metal, and developed nations, where millions of cubic feet of water may have to be moved for dozens or hundreds of miles to serve the water needs of millions of people in complex urban settings.

In the former situations, a number of water projects have been conceived and developed under the acronym of *WASH*, which stands for water, sanitation, and hygiene. A large body of researchers have developed, employed, and written about a variety of WASH technologies that can be used to help communities that are at risk for drought conditions or that have experienced such conditions on a regular basis in the past. One of the best available compilations of these suggestions is found in a 2010 report written by water consultant Eric Fewster, based on a variety of other reports and recommendations. Among the suggestions Fewster provides in the report are the following:

- Concrete dams, well linings, and other structures may dry out and crack as a result of drought. Solution(s): Ensure that workers learn how to make a better-quality concrete that will survive very dry conditions.

- Water becomes more saline as inflow to water resources decreases. Solution(s): Take water from a variety of sources; implement the use of solar distillation; reduce water-logging (the saturation of soil) in irrigated areas; make use of managed aquifer recharge (MAR), a system by which water is injected into the ground to increase and restore a natural aquifer.

- Reduction in precipitation and surface water resources that occurs during a drought reduces farmers' ability to grow crops. Solution(s): Make use of MAR; encourage farmers to explore crops that use less water; repair damage to water catchment and storage systems.

- Some natural and seminatural storage systems (e.g., open water reservoirs) may dry up during a drought. Solution(s): Redesign and rebuild reservoirs with greater attention to better storage of water, such as stronger concrete linings, use of more impervious rock structures; use of gutters and break walls to reduce the rate of runoff; encourage private ownership of storage facilities; make available low-cost loans for construction.

- Drought tends to cause a reduction in the water table, reducing the effectiveness of wells and boreholes of all kinds. Solution(s): Move wells or boreholes to sites with better access to aquifer; reduce water use; look for alternative sources of water; employ MAR technology to recharge aquifer.

- In some areas where drought is either a short-term or long-term issue, people may actually have to rely on vendors who deliver and sell water supplies on a regular basis, an expensive alternative for communities who are often very poor to begin with. Solution(s): Encourage governmental agencies or nongovernmental organizations to arrange for free or low-cost delivery of water or search for alternative sources of freshwater that will reduce dependence on water vendors. (An interesting U.S. example of this practice is described at Santos

2015. For additional examples of the methods that have been and can be used in developing countries to improve their access to safe freshwater, see Hays 2012. (Fewster 2010))

In addition to the many recommendations aimed at small agricultural enterprises, like those listed earlier, there is no shortage of more sophisticated, more technical, and more expensive ways of dealing with water shortages in both developing and developed countries. An example of such recommendations is the proposal to use genetic engineering to develop new types of crops that can survive on less water than their natural cousins. In 2004, researchers at the Agricultural Genetic Engineering Research Institute in Cairo, Egypt, announced that they had developed a new strain of wheat that contains a single gene from the barley plant. The engineered wheat is much more drought-tolerant than its natural cousin and can survive and thrive with a single irrigation rather than the eight required for native wheat strains (Sawahel 2004; for examples of genetic research on other crops, see also Edmeades 2008 [maize] and Karaba 2007 [rice]).

Efforts to deal with droughts on a massive scale in developed nations, such as the one that has persisted in California for an extended period of time, often require very different kinds of solutions from those recommended for simpler agricultural systems. A review of California's approach to the problem of long-term drought is an example. In 2014, in the third year of its latest drought, the state enacted a set of regulations, recommendations, and requirements designed to reduce water use in the states (Ciampa 2014). Most of these new rules were designed to *encourage* individuals, communities, industries, and agricultural enterprises to voluntarily reduce their use of freshwater over previous year levels. And, to some extent, those rules were successful with residential users having reduced their consumption of freshwater by nearly 30 percent between May 2013 and May 2015 (Individual Water Use Continues to Decline; Enforcement Efforts Grow 2015).

But the voluntary approach eventually proved a failure as a fourth year of drought began in 2015, and residential water use was still deemed too high for the state. Thus, on April 1, 2015, Governor Jerry Brown issued an executive order (the latest in a series of such orders) imposing, for the first time in the history of the state, mandatory statewide water reductions. Brown called for a reduction in water use by individuals and communities throughout the state of at least 25 percent compared with previous year totals. Some of the specific activities that were prohibited and subject to fines were using potable water to irrigate lawns and gardens in such a way as to allow runoff of the water; using potable water to wash sidewalks, driveways, and other surfaces; and using potable water for decorative water features. The penalty for such misuse of potable water was a fine of $500 per day. (State of California. Office of Administrative Law 2015. The history of gubernatorial executive orders, water board actions, and other legal activities surrounding the California drought is very complex. Probably the best resource for information on this history is California Drought 2015.)

Perhaps one of the most interesting points about Governor Brown's executive orders and actions of the state's Water Resources Control Board is that they left essentially untouched the two largest consumers of water in the state: agriculture and industry. Those two activities account for about 80 percent of all the freshwater used in the state. But the governor and his boards decided to stay with a voluntary approach to water conservation, asking agriculture and industry to find new ways to save on the water they use and adopting new water-use reports for the activities. The problem with this approach, according to one environmentalist, is that when cutting back on water use is such a major concern, "You can't leave 80 percent of the problem off the table" (Simon 2015).

The travails of California and other governmental entities attempting to deal with drought issues might easily be seen as discouragingly hopeless. But such is not the case at all, and perhaps the brightest success story in the modern world is the nation of Israel. Located in the midst of the historic Near East–North Africa arc of low-precipitation, high-temperature conditions, Israel has been faced with drought after drought during its relatively short history. Its most recent bouts with water shortages finally encouraged national planners to begin thinking seriously about long-term solutions for its drought problems. And they were successful. As of 2015, the nation not only has sufficient freshwater to meet its basic needs, but also enough more to export to neighboring countries not so well prepared for their own water shortages.

Part of Israel's success has been the result of the aggressive development and implementation of technological solutions, primarily desalination of seawater and recycling of gray (waste) water. Today, about 40 percent of Israel's potable water comes from desalination plants, with plans for that number to increase to 70 percent by 2050, and 85 percent of all household wastewater is treated and recycled (Chabin 2015; Kershner 2015).

At least equally important in Israel's success story, however, has been a change in Israeli mind-set about water itself. As Uri Shani, a former director of the Israel Water Authority, has explained, the government's first challenge was to "convince people that water is a commodity and not unlimited" (Chabin 2015). In other words, users had to recognize that taking water out of the ground, a lake, or a river was not a free activity; one had to pay for the taking and use of that water. To make its point, the Israeli government reduced the amount of water allotted for agricultural, industrial, and other uses, and then imposed a very significant tax on entities that insisted on using more than the allocated amount. Before long, water consumers learned to live with less water than they had used before, switching, for example, to crops that require less water to grow (Chabin 2015).

Climate Change and Water Resources

Drought is a fact of life for most regions of the world, more or less often, to greater or lesser degree. The consequences to humans in terms of starvation resulting from crop loses as a result of drought are well known and extensive. Having said that, drought is almost always a single event from which a community, a nation, or a region is able to recover within a matter of a few years or a few dozen years.

Climate change can also be considered to be a form of drought, but with much more profound characteristics and consequences. As defined by the Intergovernmental Panel on Climate Change (IPCC), the term *climate change* refers to "a change in the state of the climate that can be identified (e.g. using statistical tests) by changes in the mean and/or the variability of its properties, and that persists for an extended period, typically decades or longer" (Definitions of Climate Change 2007; the IPCC is an international body of climate experts created in 1988 by the United Nations Environment Programme and the World Meteorological Organization to study the world's climates and changes taking place in the climate and reporting the results of its research on this topic).

Scientists have been interested in the history, characteristics, causes, and effects of climate change for well over a century (a good introduction to the history of climate change research can be found at Introducing the History of Climate Change Science 2015). Space does not permit an extended discussion of that topic in this book, but suffice to say that the vast majority of scientists who specialize in the study of climate now believe that Earth's climate *is* undergoing a significant change and that human activities are responsible for many of those changes. In its periodic reports on the topic, the IPCC describes in great detail the evidence that is now available about climate change, the role of human activity in climate change, and some of the consequences to the planet and to human civilization that may result from climate change (see the agency's most recent report on the topic at IPCC 2014a or its summary at IPCC 2014b).

Of special interest here are the changes in water resources that are predicted by the IPCC as a result of climate change. Those changes fall into three major categories: an overall decrease in the amount of freshwater available on the planet for human consumption, an increase in the demand for freshwater among communities and regions experiencing water scarcity, and a reduction in the quality of that water.

Increased scarcity of freshwater is to be expected as a result of climate change for a number of reasons. First, as Earth's annual average temperature increases, the vast amounts of freshwater stored in glaciers, ice packs, and other frozen reserves will be reduced, a phenomenon that is already being observed in many parts of the world (Orlove 2009). Parts of the world that depend on melting ice and snow for their freshwater supplies—such as most of China, India, Pakistan, and the western United States—will begin to experience a reduction of that source of water as climate continues to warm. By some estimates, a sixth of the world's population falls into this category and will probably begin to experience water scarcity in coming decades (Parry, et al. 2007, 175).

Climate change is also expected to be accompanied by fairly dramatic changes in precipitation patterns. Those patterns will not be the same worldwide, but will vary from region to region. Current estimates suggest, for example, that rainfall is likely to increase with global warming in the Northern Hemisphere, to decrease in China, Australia, and the nation states of the Pacific, and to become even more variable than it already is in equatorial regions. The last of these estimates suggests that vast areas that are already at risk for water shortages are likely to become even more in danger of droughts and prolonged water shortages (Dore 2005).

A phenomenon related to changes in precipitation is changes in groundwater storage. It would seem obvious that increased rainfall might result in an increase in groundwater recharge. But the connection between precipitation and groundwater supplies is not so simple. In 2008, researchers at the Massachusetts Institute of Technology (MIT) attempted to predict how an increase or decrease in rainfall was likely to affect groundwater supplies. They found that the changes in groundwater were significantly greater than were precipitation rates themselves. They found, for example, that an increase in rainfall of 20 percent could result in an increase in groundwater storage of as much as 40 percent, and a decrease in precipitation of 20 percent could result in a decrease of as much as 70 percent in groundwater reserves. The conclusion, then, is that regions that already depend on groundwater for their freshwater supplies (such as most of North Africa and the Middle East) would be at risk even more if precipitation begins to decrease in the area (Ng, et al. 2010).

Yet another water resource issue associated with climate change has to do with infrastructure systems. Nearly all water sewage and control systems in existence today were built to handle relatively modest rainstorms and are overwhelmed by especially severe rainfall. But climate change models suggest that severe storms are very likely to become more common in the future, suggesting that existing systems will rapidly become obsolete in their ability to collect and move large volumes of water. Such problems will exist in developed nations, but are likely to be much more serious in developing nations, where even existing water control systems are likely to be inadequate for the effective control of storm water (Bates, et al. 2008).

Severe weather events resulting from climate change are also expected to have an impact on natural systems for controlling and distributing water. Most natural ecosystems have evolved to provide for ways of capturing and filtering water, which also act as buffers to flooding and erosion accompanying severe storms. But like human-made systems, these natural ecosystems are generally not capable of handling the input of very large amounts of water produced during storms and, instead, are likely to be damaged or destroyed by such floods (Melillo, Richmond, and Yohe 2014, Chapter 8).

At just the time that climate change is making freshwater less available to humans and the natural environment, a second concomitant change is to be expected: a growing demand for freshwater for a variety of purposes. Perhaps the most important of those greater demands will come from agriculture, which will be faced with increased average annual global temperatures and decreased reserves of freshwater and so requiring a much larger volume of water for crops by means of irrigation. One study, for example, has suggested that such factors are likely to increase the area of land requiring new irrigation systems by as much as 40 percent worldwide by the year 2080, a daunting technical, social, and political challenge (Fischer, et al. 2007).

And it will be more than crops that will need more water. The larger number of animals needed to feed a larger world population will also require a correspondingly large amount of freshwater, and any industrial developments in developed and developing nations will similarly require very large increases in the amount of water needed for their operation. Energy industries will be at particular risk of climate change conditions for a variety of reasons, one of which is the very large requirement for cooling water for most energy plants. As atmospheric temperatures and the temperature of cooling water resources (such as rivers and lakes) increase, so will the problems of coal, gas, oil, nuclear, and other types of energy facilities in obtaining water cool enough to serve a facility's needs (U.S. Energy Sector Vulnerabilities to Climate Change and Extreme Weather 2013).

A third predicted effect of climate change is a diminution in the quality of freshwater resources available for human consumption and use. This effect can be expected as the consequence of a number of climate-related changes. For example, an increase in the number and severity of storms would be expected to increase the amount of erosion of riverbanks, producing an increase in the sediment content of lakes and rivers; the overwhelming of storm and sanitary sewer systems, resulting in the backflow of garbage and other undesirable materials into rivers and lakes; the flooding of areas containing harmful or toxic materials; the leaching of fertilizers and pesticides from agricultural lands; and the pollution of freshwater resources by animal wastes washing off the land. Any one or more of these changes may also increase significantly the number and distribution of instances of waterborne diseases. Rising sea levels would also be expected to infiltrate and reduce the quality of freshwater resources near the ocean. Predicted rises in temperature alone may also have harmful effects on freshwater resources and the organisms that depend on them. Most aquatic organisms can survive in water over a limited range of temperatures, but many species would begin to die out as water temperatures begin to rise. Increased water temperature may also increase the rate of eutrophication of lakes and ponds. (Jiménez Cisneros, Oki, et al. 2014, Table 3.1 and page 237; for technical discussions of this issue, see Baba, et al. 2011; Peters 2011; for the most recent and most comprehensive information on the effects of climate change on water resources, see IPCC 2014a.)

Another View of Water Scarcity

Articles about water scarcity are now ubiquitous on the Internet, in scholarly papers, and on television and other forms of public media. Occasionally, one finds opposing statements attempting to argue that there really is no such thing as water scarcity in the world or any region of the globe. The LiveScience website on the Internet, for example, contains a posting entitled "The Water Shortage Myth" in which the author makes the simple and straightforward statement that "there is no water shortage" (Radford 2008; for similar statements, see, e.g., Biswas 2009; Koerth-Baker 2009; Zetland 2008).

Upon closer examination, these contrarian views provide a somewhat more nuanced view of the world's water problems that is based on the difference between physical scarcity and economic scarcity discussed earlier. They all point out that there are abundant supplies of water on Earth, even abundant supplies of freshwater. No one can argue, they say, that humans do not have enough water on the planet to meet their every need, even in light of population growth, urbanization, agricultural irrigation, climate change, and other factors that tend to "use up" our water supplies.

The real problem, they say, is that humans do not manage their water supplies carefully enough. In example after example, water crisis deniers describe local, state, national, or regional water systems that operate with outdated or inefficient equipment, are managed by individuals with little or no training in water management, have no long-term plan for water management and conservation, or are dysfunctional because of some other political, economic, social, or other issue. One of the world's authorities on water management, Asit Biswas, for example, has written and spoken about case after case in which Asian communities suffered from problems of "water scarcity" even when they had access to more-than-adequate physical supplies of water. The problems, he suggests, are that governments have not been willing to pay for needed upgrades or original construction of water delivery systems, they have hired inexperienced or incompetent water managers, or they have failed to take other basic steps to develop water delivery systems that ensured that people could actually receive the water resources that are physically available (This Planet Can Support Nine Billion People 2013).

One of the most common solutions for dealing with some of the problems of economic scarcity of water involves prices. Historically, economists, politicians, and other decision makers have regarded access to water as a fundamental human necessity and right. No one can live without access to water, that argument goes, so one responsibility of government is to ensure that everyone has reasonable access to the water one needs to stay alive and healthy. As a consequence of that philosophy, water usage rates in many places and at many times have been relatively low, often lower than the actual cost of piping safe, freshwater to a community.

While that argument is fundamentally correct, some critics say, it does not take into consideration the extravagant use of water for nonessential purposes that sometimes takes place in a community. Does a person or a family have the right, for example, to use large quantities of water to clean their sidewalks and driveways or to water large lawns and gardens? And do corporations have the right to build large golf courses or water features that consume huge amounts of freshwater?

In response to this argument, some experts have suggested keeping the price of reasonably moderate amounts of freshwater low in a community, while significantly increasing extravagant uses such as these. In a 2008 article on this topic, for example, economist David Zetland has recommended keeping the price of water about the same as it is now at usage rates of about 200 gallons per month for a single household, while increasing rates dramatically for usage rates greater than that amount. (For a graph showing this plan, see Zetland 2008. A number of nations around the world have now begun to implement some form of this general economic approach for better management of their water resources. An excellent summary of these plans is available at Dinar, Pochat, and Albiac-Murillo 2015.)

Another point that critics of the "water scarcity" argument make focuses on the enormous supply of water available in the planet's oceans. As noted in Chapter 1, there is about 30 times as much water in the oceans as there is in all forms of freshwater on Earth. The fundamental problem with using the oceans as a source of water, of course, is that seawater contains salts that make it unusable for nearly all purposes in which humans are interested. If there were a way of converting that seawater into freshwater, humans would have gone a long way to solving all their problems of water scarcity.

Systems of *desalination* (the removal of salts from seawater) are, of course, available and well known. Most boy and girl scouts, for example, are familiar with so-called solar stills, in which water can be purified rather simply by exposing it to sunlight in an enclosed transparent container. The problem is that desalination of water on a commercial scale is so expensive that it can be used only in circumstances in which the need is very great and a governmental entity is capable of paying to use the process to obtain freshwater. (The cost of desalinated water is almost always difficult to estimate since it varies according to the location of a plant, the type of desalination system used, and other factors. In general, desalinated water can cost anywhere from about twice that of freshwater from lakes, rivers, and other sources to ten times that cost [Eckhardt 2015; Gerbis 2015].)

As it happens, a number of countries that meet both these criteria can be found in the Middle East. Saudi Arabia, as one example, is one of the richest countries in the world in terms of its fossil fuel assets. It can easily afford the cost of building and operating desalination plants which, in 2015, supplied more than 70 percent of all potable water used in its cities and towns, as wells as most of the water used in industrial operations and water production (Water Resources 2015).

Island nations are also ripe prospects for desalination of ocean water. In many such locations, there are few or no natural lakes or rivers, and often a limited supply of rain. In such cases, desalination may be the only alternative as a source of potable water. The island of Aruba, for example, boasts one of the largest desalination plants in the world, supplying freshwater for its 39,000 residents, 1.5 million tourists, and the nation's industrial, energy, and commercial needs (Utilities 2015).

In parts of the United States, desalination is also becoming a more important source of freshwater. Between 2000 and 2010, 117 new desalination plants were built in the country, an increase of 50 percent over the preceding three decades. This brought the total number of desalination plants in the United States to 324, about 2.5 percent of the 12,500 desalination plants in the world (Leven 2013). In 2015, construction began on the largest desalination plant in the United States near San Jose, California. When completed in 2016, the plant will produce 50 million gallons of potable water each day. The cost of the desalinated water is expected to add just less than 10 percent to a citizen's water bill each month (Rogers 2014).

(A discussion of desalination technology is beyond the scope of this book, but good sources of the topic include Clayton

2015; National Research Council. Committee on Advancing Desalination Technology 2008; Shatat and Riffat 2014; Water from Water 2011.)

Water Disputes

At almost any location in the world where water resources are in short supply, disputes may arise between or among various groups, all of whom want to take advantage of river or lake water that may be the area's major source of water. When population densities are low, such disputes may never arise, or if they do, they can often be resolved without much difficulty. As population densities increase and economies become more advanced, such disputes tend to become more common and more difficult to resolve. Examples of such problems occur in many parts of the world, from arid regions in Australia to deserts in central Asia to dry regions of North Africa and the Middle East, to desiccated parts of the American West.

Water disputes arise because humans place a variety of demands on their water resources, demands such as:

- Agriculture: Growing crops and maintaining domesticated animals in arid regions are obviously difficult since large amounts of water are needed to be successful in both cases. Humans have been successful in such operations in arid regions by building dams that collect water that can then be distributed throughout irrigation systems. The largest food-producing region in the United States is the Central Valley of California, which is inherently a dry region. Agriculture flourishes there only because water from distant resources, such as the Colorado River, is piped into the region. Without that water, the Central Valley would revert to a semidesert.

- Domestic use: Cities and towns built on large lakes or rivers generally have no or few problems in obtaining the water they need for domestic use (drinking, washing, cooking, etc.), for energy production (as in power plants), for industrial operations, for recreation, and for other purposes. But municipalities built in arid regions, such as Las Vegas or Phoenix, cannot survive without having water piped in, often from hundreds of miles away.

- Energy production: Every region of the world requires the production of energy in some form or another, and the more developed the region, the greater the demand for energy. But energy production is, almost without exception, very dependent on water for heat transfer, cooling, waste removal, or other processes. When a power plant can be built on a lake or river, availability of water may not be a problem, but when it must be built on a desert in North Africa, for example, access to water becomes one of the determining factors in construction and operation costs for the facility.

- Recreation: Lakes and rivers provide a wide variety of recreational activities ranging from fishing, hiking, and camping to rafting, climbing, and wildlife viewing. In many locations, these water activities depend on the same rivers and lakes needed for agriculture, domestic water projects, power plants, and other water-using activities.

- Cultural and religious significance: For some cultures, water has a sacred meaning that is a core facet of their cultural history. As an example, some Native American tribes subscribe to creation stories in which water has a fundamental role. The Cherokee people, for example, believe that Earth at one time consisted only of water and was populated only when humans living in the sky traveled to Earth because the sky was too crowded for their survival (Native American Myths of Creation 2015). The Lakota teach that Earth was destroyed at one time by the Creating Power, who unleashed a flood of water that covered Earth. Only Kangi, the crow, survived to found a new human population, the Lakotas (Native American Myths of Creation 2015). The diversion of sacred waters for agriculture, power plants, or other reasons can, for such cultures, pose a difficult challenge to their way of life.

- Endangered species: The greater the use to which a natural source of water is put, the less hospitable that lake or river is likely to be to plants and animals that are native to it. When humans use river water, they may increase its salinity, produce greater sedimentation, introduce toxic materials, allow invasive species into the water, change its temperature, reduce stream flow, or cause other changes that are harmful to living organisms in the water. The battle between "farmers and fish" in times of limited water availability is one of the most common water disputes about which one hears today.

At one time, and still today in a few places on Earth, water disputes are rare or nonexistent. Such situations can occur when the demand for water is less than the supply, that is, when there are relatively few people, living a relatively simple life, with access to very large supplies of water. One can imagine that tribes living along the Amazon River may be unaware of "water wars" that are common on the Colorado River in the United States because they have ready access to all the water they need to meet all their needs.

But such circumstances tend to be more and more uncommon in today's world, especially during times of drought and climate change. So what are some of the kinds of water disputes that make today's headlines, and how can they be resolved?

Neighbor against Neighbor

One of the most common types of water disputes involves users who all live on the same river, up- or downstream from each other. One of the world's greatest examples of such an instance is the Colorado River in the American Southwest. The Colorado is one of the two most important water systems in the southwestern United States (the other being the Rio Grande). It rises in the central Rocky Mountains, fed by 10 major tributaries, and travels through or along the states of Colorado, Utah, Wyoming, Nevada, Arizona, New Mexico, and California until it reaches the Colorado River Delta in Mexico, between Baja

California and Sonora. (It no longer actually reaches the ocean, but runs dry in Mexico before reaching the Delta.) Its 1,450-mile path covers some of the most arid regions in the United States and, hence, is the major water resource for most of the seven U.S. and Mexican states through which it flows.

It takes little imagination to understand the problem of sorting out water rights for the river. Each individual, family, business, or municipality along the river and its tributaries hopes to be able to claim some specific amount of water for its own use each year and to have some confidence that it will actually get that water. Working out the legalities of such a system was one of the great accomplishments of American jurisprudence in the 20th century, an accomplishment achieved in 1922 with the signing of the Colorado River Compact (also known as the Law of the River) by the seven states bordering the river. The Compact assigned certain fixed amounts of water to each of the states involved, ranging from 51.75 percent of river flow to Colorado to 0.70 percent to Arizona. Terms of the Compact have been renegotiated a number of times, always in an effort to keep up with changing climate, weather, environmental, industrial, and other factors (The Law of the River 2008).

The fundamental problem with the Compact was that it started with an estimate of water flow in the river that was wildly optimistic, and that has become even less accurate over time, especially in periods of drought and climate change. So water users have legal rights to certain amounts of water in the river, but the volume of water generally does not provide for the real needs of many of its users (as an example of the current debate, see Acuna and Burke 2015).

All of which is not to say that water disputes occur only between states, large cities, companies, and large-scale agriculture. Sometimes near-neighbors can fall into dispute about the use of water resources. As just one example, a dispute arose in early 2015 when the Leonard family of Goldthwaite, Texas, decided to build a dam across the Colorado River (not the much larger Colorado River described earlier) to ensure an adequate supply of water for the family's large crop of pecan trees. The Leonards' decision was based on concerns that recent droughts and climate change might result in an insufficient supply of water for this water-hungry crop.

The Leonards' downstream neighbors, including the city of Austin, opposed the plan, fearing that it would significantly reduce the amount of water available to them, transferring the water shortage problem of the Leonards to their neighbors downstream. They also worried that other upstream water users might adopt a similar solution to possible water shortages, even further endangering the supply of freshwater to Austin and other downstream communities. As of early 2016, this particular dispute has not yet been resolved.

Fish versus Farmers

One of the most common disputes within some geographic areas is that between farmers and communities that depend on fishing. As an example, a controversy has raged for dozens of years about the use of water from the Klamath River that flows from Oregon into northern California. Historically, first rights to the use of that water have been held by Native American tribes in the area, who have traditionally depended on salmon and steelhead fishing for their own food needs as well as a source of income from their sale. For centuries, adequate supplies of water from the river were available for fishing as well as other activities downstream, such as farming and energy production. A complex system of dams was built over the years to facilitate the latter activities, a system that originally did not affect the water supply for all potential users.

As non-fishing demands increased, however, and as drought conditions began to reduce the amount of Klamath water available, disputes inevitably arose as to how all potential users could obtain the water they needed for their activities. After a tense period of some years characterized by growing animosity among users, an agreement was finally reached in which all parties agreed to give up some rights in exchange for other rights to water. A key to the agreement was the decision to remove four dams on the river, providing easier access for fish to the river, along with improvements in the river and its surrounding areas. In exchange for this improvement, Native American tribes agreed to grant greater use of the river water to other non-fishing activities, such as agriculture. Given the long-term nature of this dispute, it is still not clear as of late 2015 if this agreement will be adequate to deal with all future potential disputes about the use of Klamath River water (Rothert 2014).

Power Production versus Domestic Use

All forms of energy production require large quantities of water, sometimes for the production of steam to drive turbines and generators, and sometimes to cool operating systems, as in nuclear power plants. Depending on the method used in calculation, some sources claim that energy generation is the largest single user of freshwater in the United States, accounting for about 40 percent of the water withdrawn from lakes, rivers, and other sources (How It Works: Water for Electricity 2015). To the extent that this claim is accurate, power plants obviously pose a threat to the balanced use of river and lake waters for energy production and other purposes.

An example of the type of dispute that can erupt in such circumstances developed in Emery County, Utah, in 2012. The dispute arose when Blue Castle Holdings announced plans to construct the state's first nuclear power plant, including the withdrawal of 75 cubic feet per second of water from the adjacent Green River. As with all nuclear power plants, the water taken from the river was to be used for cooling the plant's operations and would be returned almost entirely to the Green River, albeit in a slightly modified form (increased temperature and some contamination).

Residents and groups downstream from the proposed plant site raised objections to these plans. Most pointed to the kind and level of contamination that was likely to result from the plant's use of the river water. One critic of the plan was Bob Quist, owner of Moki Mac River Expeditions, who argued that, with the power plant taking about 53,600 acre-feet per year, there was just not enough water in the river to meet all the demands placed on it. "It's bad for my business," he said, "and bad for everyone that depends on this river" (O'Donoghue 2012). Native American tribes likely to be affected by the planned power plant also raised their concerns. A spokesperson for the tribes observed that "our water is very precious. It's more precious than gold. This is our agriculture, our income, our beef, our chicken, our food" (Tribal Reps Air Concerns over Proposed Nuclear Plant 2014). As of late 2015, the Green River nuclear power plant was still in early development stages. (The complaint against the power plant can be found at Complaint and Petition for Review of Agency Action 2012.)

Power Production versus Endangered Species

As noted previously, dam construction has been enormously helpful over the centuries in managing water resources for irrigation, power production, recreational activities, and other purposes. But no dam is ever built without some amount of environmental disruption. And the larger the dam, the greater the environmental disturbance. Perhaps the greatest single example of that truism is the Three Gorges Dam on the Yangtze River near the town of Sandouping in Hubei Province, China.

A dam in this region was long dreamed of by Chinese planners as early as the rule of President Sun Yat-sen in the late 1910s. Construction did not actually begin, however, until December 1994. The dam was officially opened in 2008 and reached its planned maximum level in October 2010. By the end of 2014, the dam had become the world's largest single hydropower plant, producing 98.8 billion kilowatts of electrical energy (The World's Largest Power Plant Prevented 100 Million Tons of Carbon Emissions in 2014 2015).

The success of the Three Gorges Dam has, however, brought with it a host of disruptions that the Chinese government has largely accepted as the price for producing such a technological wonder. Among those disruptions were:

- The relocation of more than a million people previously living in the region where the dam now exists (this, and all following points, from Three Gorges Dam, Yangtze River, China 2015).
- Loss of more than a thousand archaeological sites.
- More than 1,600 mines and factories submerged by the new lake formed behind the dam.
- Accumulation of an estimated 700 million tons of sediments annually behind the dam.
- Thirteen cities, 140 towns, and more than 1,300 villages drowned by the new lake.
- The potential loss of dozens of threatened and endangered plant and animal species. Among those species are the baiji dolphin, whose lineage dates back 70 million years (and is now thought to be extinct); the Siberian crane, whose population now numbers in a few thousand; the finless porpoise, which is now found only in the Yangtze; the Chinese river sturgeon, which has survived an estimated 140 million years and is now severely endangered; along with the Chinese Tiger, the Chinese alligator, and the Giant Panda (Sanjuan and Béreau 2001/2003).

Water Use Agreements

Disputes such as those described earlier within a single state or between two or more states often seem as if they are insolvable. The stakes are often high, with people's livelihoods at risk, and most issues are fairly complicated. One of the most remarkable things about such disputes is how often they are eventually resolved to at least the grudging acceptance of all parties. The Colorado River Compact of 1922 is often mentioned as among the earliest and most successful of all such agreements in the United States, flawed as it ultimately turned out to be. But that agreement is only one of dozens of such documents accepted over the past 100 years. Similar agreements have been signed over the use of waters from the Pecos River (1948: Texas and Arkansas), Delaware River (1961: Delaware, New Jersey, New York, Pennsylvania, and the federal government), Arkansas River (1965: Arkansas and Oklahoma), and Bear River (1978: Idaho, Utah, and Wyoming) (Interstate Water Agreements of the United States 2015). Each of these agreements attempted to specify how much water could be withdrawn by each state under certain conditions.

Any number of agreements have also been reached among individuals and groups in dispute over water rights, including farmers, cattlemen, power companies, Native American tribes, environmental groups, municipalities, recreational organizations, and other interested stakeholders. The Klamath Basin Restoration Agreement of 2007 is an example of such compacts. It was adopted after a two-year negotiation among groups representing a wide variety of interests. Among the more than four dozen signatories to the agreement were the California Department of Fish and Game, the Oregon Water Resources Department, the Hoopa Valley and Yurok tribes, Humboldt and Siskiyou counties in California and Klamath County in Oregon, the Tulelake Irrigation District, the Poe Valley Improvement District, Modoc Lumber Company, Reames Golf and Country Club, Klamath Water and Power Agency, American Rivers, California Trout, Klamath Forest Alliance, and Salmon River Restoration Council (Summary of the Klamath Basin Restoration Agreement 2007; also see Ecosystem Restoration 2015).

Disputes over water use among a variety of stakeholders are hardly unique to the United States. In fact, as populations grow, states and nations become more highly developed with the ability and necessity to generate larger amounts of energy, concerns grow about the risk posed to plants and animals by water use systems, traditional farming technologies continue to be popular, and more and more disputes over water use are likely to develop. A number of groups are now studying fundamental problems of water disputes and attempting to develop methods for resolving those disputes, no matter where they may occur. One of the most successful of those groups has been a program called Water Diplomacy, developed at Harvard and Tufts universities and the MIT. The program has developed a Web site called Aquapedia that outlines a number of case studies of water disputes within and between nations with suggestions for ways of dealing with such disputes (Water Diplomacy 2015).

Transboundary Disputes

The border between the United States and Mexico is delineated for more than half its length, a distance of 1,255 miles, by the Rio Grande River. The border between the United States and Canada is marked by a series of waterways that include the St. Lawrence River at its easternmost point, through lakes Ontario, Erie, and Huron, to the western shores of Lake Superior, a total distance of 2,113 miles. The use of rivers, lakes, and other bodies of water to mark the boundary between two nations is common throughout the world. Such an arrangement has worked very well in many respects in designating the geographic area over which two adjacent countries have control. But it has not always worked very well in determining which of those two (or more) countries has control over transportation on and use of the water in those rivers, lakes, and other bodies of water. Disputes involving the disparate interests of two or more nations are known as *transboundary disputes*.

Transboundary disputes over the ownership and use of common waterways (e.g., the Rio Grande, St. Lawrence, and Great Lakes) have a very long history. Possibly, the earliest mention of "water wars" over the use of shared water resources dates to about 2500 BCE when two city-states, Lagash and Umma, went to war over access to waters from the Tigris and Euphrates Rivers in Mesopotamia (modern-day Iraq) for use in irrigation and domestic water use (Hatami and Gleick 1994). One record of the history of transboundary disputes lists 260 instances of such events dating from the Lagash–Umma dispute to the modern day (2014) (Water Conflict Chronology List 2015).

The list classifies water disputes into one of a half dozen major categories, including development dispute, military target, military tool, and act of terrorism. An example of a development dispute was the so-called Texas fence-cutting wars of the early 1880s. The period was one in which the vast resources of the American West were being explored and brought under control. One of the chief methods of claiming ownership of a piece of land was enclosing that land with a fence of barb wire, which served effectively to keep wandering cattle and traveling human scouts from entering areas where they were not welcome. The system worked well enough when the region was hit by a terrible drought in 1883, at which point many cattlemen realized their animals were cut off from water supplies by the barb-wired fences. Their solution was to attack those fences with wire cutters, allowing their animals access to the invaluable water resources they needed for their survival (Gard 1947).

Development disputes have often been associated with and/or led to military and/or related political actions. An example was the dispute over water rights in the Middle East in the mid-1960s. A decade earlier, an agreement had been hammered out between Israel and its Arab neighbors as to the use of Jordan River water, on which Israel depended heavily for its own domestic use. The so-called Unified (or Johnston) Plan provided that the less-than-friendly Arab nations where the tributaries of the Jordan flowed would allow sufficient water to reach Israel to ensure its water survival. By 1965, however, the Arab League had changed its mind and decided to divert the Hasbani and Banias Rivers that rise in Lebanon, dramatically reducing the amount of water flowing into the Jordan and, thence, into Israel. The Arab action never reached reality, however, as the Israeli military initiated an attack on Syria in response to the anticipated action by its Arab allies (Lowi 1993, Chapter 5).

Perhaps on the most bizarre examples of the use of water as a military tool in modern history were the actions of President Saddam Hussein of Iraq beginning in the mid-1990s. Frustrated by opposition of Shi'ite Muslims to his reign, Hussein decided to cut off their primary supply to freshwater in the regions southeast of Baghdad. Hussein ordered the poisoning and draining of the waters in vast marshy areas on which the local Shi'ites depended for their freshwater. Although the president's actions were met with almost universal protest by environmental groups around the world, he essentially converted these millennial-old freshwater resources into desert regions, an action that was reversed only after Hussein's removal from office during the second Iraqi War, which began in 2003 (Kubba 2011, 14–19).

Individuals and small groups of terrorists have found that disruption of water supplies can be a powerful tool for expressing their political beliefs, whether those actions actually result in serious widespread effects or are limited to frightening threats that may be almost as serious to a local population. One of the best documented examples of such a practice has come from the actions of the terrorist militia group, the Janjaweed, who have been active in Sudan and Chad for more than a decade. One mechanism the group has adopted for both psychological and military reasons is the poisoning of water wells on which local inhabitants depend by dropping dead and dismembered human and animal bodies into those wells. They have also attempted to cut off communities' freshwater supplies by blowing up the dams on which those local systems depend and destroying the implements needed to collect and use water for daily needs (Kristof 2004; Report of the International Commission of Inquiry on Darfur to the United Nations Secretary-General 2005, 235, 242, 305, 311).

Concerns about the growing potential for serious disputes over water rights have begun to grow over the past few decades at the international, national, state, and local levels. Some observers have even gone to the point of calling water the "new oil" or the "new gold" over which conflicts are likely to arise. For some time, various agencies of the United Nations have been taking note of the factors that tend to make a water war more likely, such as the fact that 148 nations lie in a region where water resources are being shared by more than one nation, and 21 of those nations lie entirely within such boundaries. The risks posed by such a condition are reflected in the fact that the past 40 years of the 20th century and the first decade of the 21st century saw more than 500 conflicts between countries over water rights, at least 37 of which involved some level of violence (Transboundary Waters 2014).

Most UN reports and other documents take a fairly optimistic view toward the resolution of water disputes, pointing to the more than 3,600 treaties and other agreements that have been signed to resolve differences over water rights. But many observers are not as sanguine about the world's ability to resolve such disputes in the future in a peaceable fashion. For example, the InterAction Council (IAC) made potential water conflicts a major focus of its 2011 meeting in Quebec City (see quotation at the beginning of this chapter). The IAC is a group of about three dozen former heads of states and other governmental entities who meet annually to discuss important international issues. Some current members include Bill Clinton, Andreas van Agt (former prime minister of the Netherlands), Bertie Ahern (former prime minister of Ireland), Gro Harlem Brundtland (former prime minister of Norway), Seyyed Mohammad Khatami (former president of Iran), John Major (former prime minister of the United Kingdom), and Amadou Toumani Touré (former president of Mali).

In its final communiqué at the completion of its 2011 meeting, IAC said that

> As global energy demands rise, the energy sector is being placed into greater competition with other water users. This will impact regional energy reliability and energy security. Until our thinking about water and energy can be

integrated, sustainability will continue to elude us. (Final Communiqué. 29th Annual Plenary Meeting 2011)

In support of this position, the group offered 17 recommendations for actions that would tend to reduce the likelihood of future conflicts over water resources, such as

- Placing water at the forefront of the global political agenda and linking climate change research and adaptation programs to water issues.
- Encouraging a discussion on water security at the UN Security Council.
- Renewing local, national, and international focus on monitoring hydrological processes and increased attention to mapping and monitoring of groundwater.
- Supporting the conservation of the world's intact freshwater ecosystems, the establishment of ecological sustainability boundaries, and investment in ecosystem restoration. (Final Communiqué. 29th Annual Plenary Meeting 2011)

Whatever international organizations such as the IAC and United Nations have to say about transboundary water disputes, the increasing possibility of active conflict over water rights has clearly caught the attention of foreign policy analysts in the United States and around the world. In the past few years, a number of articles have appeared in the professional journals in this field with titles such as "Water Wars: Forget the Islamic State. The New Conflicts of the Future Could Be Sparked by Climate Change," "The Growing Potential for Water Wars," "The Coming Water Wars," and "The World Will Soon Be at War over Water" (Clark 2013; Fergusson 2015; Harris 2014; Rousseau 2015; for a more complete discussion of this issue, see Chellaney 2013). The fundamental proposition put forward by these observers and analysts is that a growing population is leading to a more limited access to all forms of natural resources and to a degraded condition of those resources, a situation that almost inevitably will lead to conflicts in a variety of places around the world. And of all natural resources, the one that is likely to be at the center of such conflicts is water.

Some of the specific conflicts that have recently occurred, or that are likely to arise in the near future, include:

- Efforts by the new Islamic State (also known as ISIS or ISIL) to take control of the limited water resources in the nation of Iraq by seizing some of the largest dams that control the flow of the essential waters of the Tigris and Euphrates Rivers (all examples included here are from Fergusson 2015).

- Vigorous verbal disputes between ISIS and the Turkish government over claims by the former entity that the Turks are attempting to reduce the flow of the Tigris and Euphrates by diverting water through the complex system of Turkish dams that normally feed into those rivers.

- Complaints by Cambodia and Vietnam that the current dam-building program in China (and, to a lesser degree, Laos), the world's largest such endeavor, is dramatically reducing the flow of freshwater into those two downstream countries.

- Debates in certain African countries over plans to build enormous hydroelectric dams on the Congo and Nile Rivers that will produce huge amounts of electricity, often for distant countries, while disrupting and reducing the flow of freshwater to the areas immediately adjacent to those dams.

- An ongoing dispute (the longest in recent world history) between control of the Kashmir region claimed by both nations, which is essentially a battle over control of the headwaters of the Indus River, which is located in the Kashmir.

- An almost unending battle between Israel and the Palestinian Authority over control of the rivers that arise in Arab states such as Lebanon and Syria, but that provide the vast majority of freshwater needed by Israel.

Disputes over access to freshwater resources are by no means restricted to two or more nations; in many cases, they may involve two or more states, territories, communities, or other entities within a particular country. In the second decade of the 21st century, with a devastating ongoing drought spreading through much of the southwestern United States, such disputes have become almost commonplace. The usual motivation for such disputes, as always, is an increasing level of competition for a limited supply of freshwater. And while these disputes almost never risk to the level of violence, their appearance is no less significant for that fact.

As an example, consider the disputes over water rights in parts of the United States where the recently popular technology of hydraulic fracturing ("fracking") has become much more widely used in the search for and extraction of oil and natural gas reserves. This technology has dramatically revitalized the energy industry, vastly increasing the production of oil and gas in the United States, while bringing huge economic success to energy companies and to communities in which fracking has been put to use. The problem is that fracking is a water-intensive process. According to the North Dakota State Water Commission, each fracked well requires the use of about seven acre-feet of water, equivalent to about 2.2 million gallons of water (Facts about North Dakota Fracking & Water Use 2014, 5). According to one website interested in this issue, that is equivalent to the amount of water used by a city of about 35,000 people in one day (How Much Water Is Used to Frack a Well? 2014). These data make it clear how disputes over water use can arise when an energy company decides to move into an area and begins draining freshwater resources in order to conduct its operations. (For an excellent review of some of the issues involved in the dispute over fracking, see Water Wars Part One: Freshwater for Fracking Concerns Those along Devil's River 2015.)

The drought in California that extended through the 2010s also brought to the surface historic and long-lasting disputes among water users of all description, from urban and rural areas, between farmers and industrial operations, among agriculturists growing different types of crops, drawing in those with rights more than a century old to others with only recent and tenuous rights of access, involving those from water-rich parts of the state versus those from water-poor regions, and so on. Some of the specific intrastate battles that were being fought included

- As noted earlier, Governor Jerry Brown's first actions to deal with the statewide drought involved severe restrictions on the domestic use of water by private homes and communities; almost no demands were made on industries and agriculture to cut back on water use, even though these two entities make up about four-fifths of the water consumed in the state each year (Prupis 2015).

- A limited supply of water has also led to a somewhat unusual phenomenon in which farmers sometimes pitted against other farmers. Individuals who hold the oldest rights to water resources have sometimes decided to sell off all or part of the water that is due to come to them by right of appropriation. In such sales, the highest bidder gains access to some of those water rights, no matter what other factors may be involved. Neighboring farmers and often longtime friends may find themselves battling for the right to enough water to raise their crops, while watching their competitors resign themselves to a year of partial or total loss (Kreiger 2014; Skelton 2014).

- Agricultural interests may also be pitted against environmental concerns in the battle for water. Those who are concerned about the survival of a variety of wildlife plant and animal species have traditionally pointed out the need for adequate water supplies with the proper characteristics (e.g., the proper temperature) needed for many species to survive. In California, a long-running dispute has been gone on over farmers' right to sufficient water to grow their crops versus the need to divert the significant amounts of the previous freshwater to rivers and streams that are needed to keep salmon and other sport and food fish alive (Galbraith 2015).

• Another very old water dispute in California is based on the simple fact that most of the water that falls as precipitation in the state does so in its northern half, while very little precipitation falls in the southern half, where by far the majority of people live. For many years, then, the state has been faced with the problem of how to move water from areas where it is abundant, but water needs are relatively modest, to areas where water is very scarce, but water needs for urban, agricultural, and industrial operations are high. In rainy years, this problem remains one of somewhat limited concern because enough water is available for both north and south. But during droughts, the issue suddenly becomes very serious. In the early to mid-2010s, California officials began to develop plans for constructing a mammoth new pipeline designed to carry more water from the north to southern parts of the state, a plan that generally pleased residents of the south, but angered those from the northern regions (for details of that plan, see Garamendi 2015; for a historical perspective on the issue, see Olson-Raymer 2015).

Resolving Transboundary Issues

Despair over transboundary water disputes may be as inappropriate as concerns over intra-nation or intrastate controversies. In a recent review of this issue, the UN Department of Economic and Social Affairs noted that the preceding 50 years had seen only 37 actual disputes over water use compared with more than 150 treaties signed by nations originally involved in such disputes that had been able to come to agreements about their differences (Transboundary Water 2014). Interestingly enough, the first record we have of such a compact dates to the conflict between the Lagash and Umma kingdoms described earlier. Concrete evidence exists that these two nations eventually decided to call off their armed conflict over water resources and reach an agreement as to the allocation of waters from the Tigris River. The concrete evidence consists of a stone marker that summarizes the terms of the treaty and the location of the boundary between the two nations. The marker was placed at the point on the river where the boundary was to be drawn (2550 BC—The Treaty of Mesilim 2012; an interesting historical review of more than 300 treaties involving the world's great water basins can be found at Atlas of International Freshwater Agreements 2002).

A 1985 study by the Food and Agriculture Organization found that more than 3,600 treaties had been signed between two or more nations about the use of water resources, the majority involving demarcation of boundaries or navigation rights on lakes, rivers, or other bodies of water (Food and Agriculture Organization of the United Nations 1985). A more recent study of 145 water treaties found that the largest number dealt with disputes over the use of water for hydroelectric power (39%), followed by water utilization (37%), flood control (13%), industrial use (9%), navigation (4%), pollution (4%), and fishing rights (1%) (Watkins 2006, Figure 6.2, page 222).

The UN report cited earlier credits much of the success of this treaty-making to actions taken by the organization itself and other international agencies in promoting peaceful approaches to the resolution of transboundary water disputes. The key document in treaty-making history is generally thought to be the Convention on the Law of the Non-Navigational Uses of International Watercourses, adopted by the UN General Assembly on May 21, 1997, with a vote of 103 to 3. The convention required ratification by 35 states, an event that occurred only 17 years later in 2014 with ratification by Vietnam of the document. At this point in time, relatively few major powers have ratified the treaty, but it is widely regarded as providing a sound outline for the adoption of transboundary treaties on water issues (Rahaman 2009).

The general principles laid out by the convention can be found in Part II of the document. They include the following points:

- Equitable and reasonable utilization and participation: Participating states should make every effort to use water resources covered by the treaty in a reasonable fashion that is beneficial not only to themselves, but also to other signatories of the treaty.
- Obligation not to cause significant harm: Signatories to a treaty should make every effort not to cause harm to other signatories. But if such harm should occur, that country should then attempt to correct or ameliorate that harm.
- General obligation to cooperate: Signatory states should cooperate with each other "on the basis of sovereign equality, territorial integrity, mutual benefit and good faith" in order to obtain optimal use of shared water resources.
- Regular exchange of data and information: Signatory states should make every effort to share with each other hydrological, meteorological, hydrogeological, and ecological data of relevance to share waterways.
- Relationships between different kinds of uses: Unless specifically provided for, no one type of use of water resources should be regarded as more important than any other type of use (Convention on the Law of the Non-navigational Uses of International Waterways 1997).

Since 1997, the United Nations has continued to produce position papers, sponsor major conferences, and promote special days and other opportunities for concerned parties to think about and act on transboundary water issues. Among these activities have been a thematic paper, "Transboundary Water: Sharing Benefits, Sharing Responsibilities," published in 2008 (Transboundary Waters: Sharing Benefits, Sharing Responsibilities 2008); a special focus on World Water Day

2009 on transboundary issues (Shared Waters, Shared Opportunities 2009); designation of 2013 as the International Year of Water Cooperation (International Year of Water Cooperation 2013); and release in 2014 of a comprehensive document summarizing model provisions for agreements on transboundary groundwater issues (United Nations Economic Commission for Europe 2014).

Sanitation

Much of the preceding discussion has focused on the question of water scarcity and the issues that arise when adequate amounts of freshwater are not available to meet the needs of humans for a variety of purposes. But another aspect of the world's water problems remains: water quality. Millions of humans around the globe are faced with the problem of having access to water that is safe to use, a problem that may also exist alongside problems of water scarcity.

Statistics

As is the case with water scarcity, the statistics relating to water quality are very troubling. They include data such as:

- More than 780 million people around the world do not have access to safe drinking water facilities, and an estimated 2.5 billion people (more than a third of the world's population) do not have access to adequate sanitation facilities (Progress on Drinking Water and Sanitation. 2014 Update 2014, 8).
- More than 80 percent of those without access to safe drinking water and about 70 percent of those without adequate sanitation live in rural areas (Progress on Drinking Water and Sanitation. 2014 Update 2014, 26).
- About a billion people worldwide practice open defecation, a decrease from 24 percent to 14 percent worldwide between 1990 and 2012, but still far too many people as far

as experts in the field are concerned (Progress on Drinking Water and Sanitation. 2014 Update 2014, Figure 2, page 8).

• As might be expected, trends in the accessibility to sanitary facilities range widely in various parts of the world with less than half the population having such access in 46 countries. These countries are found primarily in sub-Saharan Africa and Southeast Asia and include nations such as Burkina Faso (27% of the population has access to improved sanitary facilities), Burundi (11%), Chad (22%), Eritrea (22%), Ethiopia (17%), India (32%), Kenya (24%), Laos (35%), Malawi (16%), Myanmar (33%), Nepal (17%), Nigeria (31%), Pakistan (37%), Rwanda (19%), Sri Lanka (15%), and Sudan (33%) (Progress on Drinking Water and Sanitation. 2014 Update 2014, Annex 3, pages 52–71).

Many of these statistics have been and are being compared against a set of expectations developed by the United Nations beginning in 2002 known as the *Millennium Goals*. These goals set standards for achievement in world progress in eight areas, such as eradication of hunger and poverty, reduction in child mortality, improvement of maternal health, and achievement of universal primary education. Each goal, in turn, had a number of "targets" focusing on more specific aspects of the topic. Goal 7, aimed at ensuring environmental sustainability, included Target 10, to "halve, by 2015, the proportion of people without sustainable access to safe drinking water and basic sanitation" (What They Are 2006). The most recent reports, such as the "Progress on Drinking Water and Sanitation 2014," indicate that, as of early 2015, 116 nations (out of 192 for which data were available) had met the drinking water target, 77 (out of 185 reporting) had met the sanitation target, and 56 (out of 106 reporting) had met both targets. By contrast, 40 countries were not "on target" to meet the millennium goals, 69 were not on target to meet sanitation goals, and 20 were not on target to meet both goals (Progress on Drinking Water and Sanitation. 2014 Update 2014, 7).

Disease and Death

Concerns about sanitation are not based simply on aesthetic issues, of course. People who do not have access to adequate sanitation facilities are at high risk for a wide variety of diseases, most of which are classified as *waterborne diseases*. A waterborne disease is a condition caused by a pathogen (e.g., a virus, bacterium, parasite, chemical, or other potentially harmful material) that occurs in drinking water or water used for recreation (e.g., swimming). Some of the most common waterborne diseases are listed in Table 2.1.

Table 2.1   Some Common Waterborne Diseases

Bacterial

Campylobacter

Campylobacteriosis

Chlamydia trachomatis

Cholera

Cyanobacteria

Escherichia coli 0157:H7 (also known as *E. coli*)

Legionnaires' disease

Legionella

Legionellosis

Leptospira

Leptospirosis

Mycobacterium avium complex

Mycobacterium ulcerans

Otitis externa

Pseudomonas

Salmonella

Salmonella typhi

Shigella

Shigellosis

Staphylococcus aureus

(continued)

Table 2.1 (*continued*)

Trachoma

Typhoid fever

Vibrio cholerae

Vibrio vulnificus

Viral

Adenoviruses

Astrovirus

Coxsackievirus

Dengue fever

Eastern Equine Encephalitis

Echovirus

Enterovirus

Hepatitis A

Japanese encephalitis

Meningitis, viral

Molluscum contagiosum

Norovirus

Rift valley fever

Rotavirus

Viral gastroenteritis

West Nile virus

Western equine encephalitis

Yellow fever

Parasitic

Amebiasis (CDC)

Ascariasis

Bilharzia

Cryptosporidiosis

Cryptosporidium

Cyclospora

Cyclosporiasis

Entamoeba histolytica

Fascioliasis

Fasciolopsiasis

Giardia

Giardiasis

Guinea worm disease

Helminthiasis

Hookworm

Lymphatic filariasis

Malaria

Microsporidiosis

Microsporidium

Onchocerciasis

Pinworms

River blindness

Scabies

Schistosoma

Schistosomiasis

Toxoplasma gondii

Toxoplasmosis

Trichuris trichiura (whipworm)

Chemicals

Arsenicosis

Chromium

Copper

Ethylbenzene

Fluorosis

Lead poisoning

Mercury

Methaemoglobinaemia

Nitrate

Radionuclides

Radon

Source: Condensed from Water-Related Diseases, Contaminants, Injuries by Type. 2012. Centers for Disease Control and Prevention. http://www.cdc.gov/healthywater/disease/type.html. Accessed on August 29, 2015.

Many of the diseases listed in Table 2.1 manifest themselves in a handful of very common and very dangerous symptoms, most troublesome of which may be diarrhea. Diarrhea is a condition characterized by at least three loose, and often unusually frequent, bowel movements in a day. It occurs in connection with many types of diseases of the gastrointestinal system, and in developed countries, it is often treated quite easily with no short- or long-term effects of any consequence. In most developing nations, however, diarrhea is not easily treated because the conditions causing the condition cannot be treated. As a result, a person may lose fluid very rapidly, resulting in the shutdown of major organs and death within a matter of days. Diarrhea is an especially serious problem for young children.

Experts now estimate that more than 800,000 children under the age of five die worldwide every year. This number amounts to more than 10 percent of all children in the world who die each year (Liu, et al. 2012). Nearly 9 out of 10 of all deaths worldwide of all ages are thought to be associated with diarrheal infections (Prüss-Üstün, et al. 2008, 7).

Another category of diseases of concern are called *neglected tropical diseases*, or NTDs. As their name suggests, these diseases tend to have received less attention in the past than better known and more widely studied conditions such as diarrhea and malaria. In May 2013, the 66th World Health Assembly adopted a resolution (WHA66) that called for increased attention to, research on, and treatment and prevention of 17 NTDs. Table 2.2 lists the 17 NTDs according to the four pathogens that cause them. According to the best estimates available, these diseases are endemic in 149 countries and are thought to affect more than 1.4 billion people, about one-fifth of the world's population (for a detailed description of these diseases, see Neglected Tropical Diseases 2015; for a list of additional diseases being considered for addition to those listed in Table 2.2, see http://www.who.int/neglected_diseases/diseases/others/en/).

Table 2.2   Neglected Tropical Diseases

Pathogen	Diseases
Bacterium	Buruli ulcer Leprosy (Hansen disease) Trachoma Yaws
Helminth	Cysticercosis/Taeniasis Dracunculiasis (guinea worm disease) Echinococcosis Foodborne trematodiases Lymphatic filariasis Onchocerciasis (river blindness) Schistosomiasis Soil-transmitted helminthiases
Protozoan	Chagas disease Human African trypanosomiasis (sleeping sickness) Leishmaniases
Virus	Dengue and Chikungunya Rabies

Source: Neglected tropical diseases. 2015. World Health Organization. http://www.who.int/neglected_diseases/diseases/en/. Accessed on September 5, 2015.

WASH Programs

The WASH approach of providing adequate supplies of safe water and suitable sanitation systems has been adopted by a very wide variety of national, regional, and international governmental and nongovernmental organizations over the past decade. Space does not permit a complete description of the variety of programs that have been introduced to achieve these results, but a few examples may suffice to illustrate their variety.

- The AMSHA Africa Foundation sponsors a number of WASH programs in Africa, one of which involves so-called rainwater harvesting in rural parts of Kenya. The foundation provides rainwater storage tanks called Rainwater HOGs to collect and store rainwater for use in the dry season (Rainwater Harvesting in Rural Kenya 2010).

- UNICEF has been active in developing a program called WASH in Schools, which aims to focus on providing clean water and sanitation systems for schools in many countries around the world. A number of examples of the way this program has been implemented can be found in Towards Effective Programming for WASH in Schools (2007).
- The Bangladesh Village Education and Resource Center has worked with individual and groups of villages to develop a variety of ways in which to improve their sanitation facilities without having to involve the federal government in financing or supervision of these activities (Sanitation and Hygiene Promotion 2005, 33).
- The Saniya Programme in Burkina Faso made use of a variety of approaches, including radio programs, face-to-face conversations, and traditional social events called djandjoba to educate local people about the need for handwashing and other sanitary techniques to reduce childhood diarrhea, which was epidemic in the country (Sanitation and Hygiene Promotion 2005, 68).
- In Zimbabwe, a program called ZimAHEAD has promoted WASH principles through groups known as Community Health Clubs that focus on health promotion and surveillance, sanitation, water point rehabilitation, nutrition, HIV/AIDS, and sustainable livelihoods. The director of the program, Regis Matimati, says that "while Zimbabwe falls apart, those in Health Clubs thrive" (Zimbabwe AHEAD Background 2011).
- In 1998, the Bolivian government decided to introduce on a trial basis a sewerage system originally developed in Brazil called the *condominial model*. The government invited three communities to take part in the trial, involving nearly 4,000 households. An evaluation of the program found a remarkable improvement in sanitation practices adopted by participants in the study. For example, more than half of those participants discontinued open excretion (El Alto Condominial Pilot Project Impact Assessment: A Summary 2015).

Water Pollution

Contaminated water is a core challenge for any community worldwide having to deal with problems of sanitation and hygiene. But water pollution is also an issue that extends far beyond the extensive problems confronted by WASH and similar programs. Most developed countries are satisfied when they are able to report that their water resources have become less polluted over the years as a result of their legislative, administrative, and other efforts. But such is not always the case. In the United States, for example, most measures of water have improved dramatically over the past half century. But there are exceptions. The concentration of nitrates in lake and river water in the nation, for example, has continued to rise over the past 50 years in spite of vigorous efforts by state and federal governments to bring this problem under control (increasing nitrate concentrations are largely a consequence of increased use of synthetic fertilizers in agricultural activities; Trends in Nutrients and Pesticides in the Nation's Rivers and Streams—Lessons for Understanding and Managing Water Quality 2015).

In many part of the world, however, the story of water pollution has been less encouraging. From the smallest villages in the high Himalayas to the open oceans, water pollution can often be a serious problem that affects human health and welfare as well as the natural environment. One example involves the presence of arsenic in water wells in Bangladesh.

Toward the end of the 20th century, public health officials began a campaign to encourage citizens of Bangladesh to switch from surface water to groundwater as their primary water resource. The reason for this campaign was the widespread occurrence of diarrhea among Bangladeshi children because of contaminated surface water. The program was an astonishing success, with an estimated 97 percent of Bangladeshis switching from surface water to groundwater.

Groundwater was most commonly accessed by means of traditional water wells sunk into an aquifer. What experts did not realize at the time was that underground water in Bangladesh is frequently contaminated with arsenic, a poison with significant health risks for those who ingest the element. By the early 2000s, reports began to accumulate of large numbers of Bangladeshis developing the symptoms of arsenic poisoning.

The response by international and national health agencies to this problem was to once more reeducate Bangladeshis, this time about the hazards of using arsenic-imbued water from wells and switching to other, safer sources of water. Those alternative sources consisted primarily of wells known to be free of arsenic, safe lake or river water, filtered water, or some other source of pure water. After a short period of uncertainty and distrust by the Bangladeshi population, the case for avoiding arsenic-laced water wells was made, and today, the vast majority of citizens of the country have access to safe sources of freshwater (Arsenic Mitigation in Bangladesh 2008).

A very different example of water pollution facing the world today is the so-called Great Pacific Garbage Patch (GPGP) located in the eastern and western regions of the Pacific Ocean. The GPGP was first discovered in 1997 by Charles J. Moore, who was then returning home from the Los Angeles to Hawaii TransPac sailing race (although such a phenomenon had been predicted years earlier by researchers at the National Oceanic and Atmospheric Administration). Moore noticed that the sea through which he and his crew were traveling was heavily polluted with a mass of human-made primarily plastic materials, such as bottle caps, wrapping material, bottles, bags, and toys. Researchers later discovered a second "garbage patch" in the western Pacific, off the east coast of Asia. Although no reliable estimates are available, some authorities have estimated the size of these garbage patches at a few hundred thousand to nearly 6 million square miles (Pacific Garbage Patch 2013).

Materials that form the GPGP have come from a variety of sources, about four-fifths from land-based sources (according to one estimate), and one-fifth from ships sailing across the Pacific. Dealing with this mammoth garbage dump has, for a number of reasons, proved to be a challenge, however. Some challenges are technical and involve finding ways of finding and collecting the often-minute particles that make up the GPGP, carrying those materials to land or some sea-based disposal system, and then finding a way to get rid of those materials (such as by combustion). Other challenges are social, political, and economic, and involve deciding who is responsible for carrying out these cleanup activities and who is going to pay for them (for a more detailed discussion of the GPGP issue, see Lewis 2015; Moore and Phillips 2011).

A variety of human activities result in the contamination of water supplies that harm the natural environment as well as create severe problems of water scarcity and water purity for human populations. Mining is one such activity. As only one example, one of the largest gold mines in the world is the Kumtor mine in Kyrgyzstan. This mine makes use of a number of hazardous materials in its operation, including up to 10 tons per day of a mixture of antifreeze, arsenic, copper, cyanide, explosive materials, fuels, grease, nickel, oils, sewage, uranium, and zinc. These materials make water leaving the mining district essentially unusable for any human use and very harmful to the natural environment (Moran 2012; for other examples, see Panjabi 2014).

Industrialization is also a major factor in the pollution of water resources. A common belief among economists is that industrialization is a key element in a nation's development, so that changes that represent an improvement in the life of individuals in a developing nation are almost inevitably associated with an increase in levels of pollution resulting from more and more sophisticated forms of industrialization. A frequently mentioned example is the Upper Tietê River basin in Brazil. The region is home to the largest industrial complex in Latin America, producing more than a quarter of Brazil's industrial output. Until fairly recently, the 40,000 industrial facilities in the basin returned more than 80 percent of their wastes, untreated, to the Tietê and other waterways in the basin. As a consequence, water flowing out of the basin through downstream cities and towns (including the nation's most populous city, São Paulo) was often unfit for human use and highly dangerous to the natural environment.

Widespread concern about the fate of the Tietê finally led in 1991 to action by the Brazilian government, which established the Tietê Project designed to clean up the river. As of late 2015, significant progress has been made in that direction, although industrial wastes still pose issues for the region that will require sustained efforts to overcome (Hermann and Braga Jr. 2015).

A third major factor associated with the pollution of waterways is agriculture. Traditional agricultural practices seldom result in serious pollution of rivers and lakes. But the introduction of modern agricultural practices may change that situation. Such practices include the increased use of fertilizers and pesticides and may involve much larger operations in which the production of waste materials (e.g., excreta from animals) is significantly greater than that in traditional systems. When these materials wash off the land and into rivers and lakes, they may compromise the quality of those waterways making them unfit for human consumption and use.

A study released in 2015 by the Veolia Corporation and the International Food Policy Research Institute found that pollution of waterways worldwide by agricultural activities was likely to increase significantly by 2050 as a result of a number of factors, including increased population growth that will create much greater demand for new food sources. The study found that the problem would be especially severe in northern and eastern China, and parts of India, Pakistan, and Bangladesh, but that it would be significant also in the midwestern United States, Central Europe, and central-eastern South America. As a result of these agricultural factors, the study authors concluded, "Even using the most optimistic projections, the world is on a path toward rapidly deteriorating water quality levels in many countries" (The Murky Future of Global Water Quality 2015, 3).

Conclusion

The world faces a future in which both the quantity and the quality of its water supplies are at risk, posing potentially devastating problems both for the natural environment and for human society. A growing population, continued industrialization in both developed and developing nations, modernization of agricultural practice, significant climate changes, and other factors are working together to create profound challenges for humans in coming decades. Sufficient progress has been made on a number of fronts to inspire some optimism that these problems can be solved, or at least brought under control. However, even more strenuous efforts to identify, analyze, and attack these problems will be necessary if humans are to continue to have access to reasonable supplies of adequate amounts of safe water.

References

Acuna, Alicia, and Kelly David Burke. 2015. "Colorado to California: Keep Your Hands Off Our Water." *Fox News*. http://www.foxnews.com/politics/2015/01/28/colorado-to-california-hands-off-our-water/. Accessed on August 25, 2015.

Aral, Mustafa M., et al. 2014. "Special Issue on Climate Change, Water Quality and Health." *Water Quality, Exposure and Health*. 6(1–2): whole.

"Arsenic Mitigation in Bangladesh." 2008. UNICEF. http://www.unicef.org/bangladesh/Arsenic.pdf. Accessed on September 6, 2015.

"Atlas of International Freshwater Agreements." 2002. Oregon State University. http://www.transboundarywaters.orst.edu/publications/atlas/index.html. Accessed on August 28, 2015.

Baba, Alper, et al., eds. 2011. *Climate Change and Its Effects on Water Resources: Issues of National and Global Security*. Dordrecht, the Netherlands: Springer.

Bates, Bryson, et al., eds. 2008. "Climate Change and Water." IPCC Technical Paper VI. http://ipcc.ch/pdf/technical-papers/climate-change-water-en.pdf. Accessed on August 7, 2015.

Biswas, Asit K. 2009. "Water Scarcity Is Not a Global Problem." In Haugen, David M., ed. *Global Resources.* Farmington Hills, MI: Greenhaven Press.

"California Drought." 2015. State of California. http://ca.gov/drought/. Accessed on July 28, 2015.

"California Drought Crisis." 2015. *CBS News.* http://www.cbsnews.com/pictures/californias-drought/. Accessed on July 28, 2015.

Chabin, Michelle. 2015. "Israel to California: Here's How to Save Water." *USA Today.* http://www.usatoday.com/story/news/world/2015/05/07/israel-drought-california-desalination/26923503/. Accessed on July 30, 2015.

Chellaney, Brahma. 2013. *Water, Peace, and War: Confronting the Global Water Crisis.* Lanham, MD: Rowman & Littlefield.

Chin, Anne. 2006. "Urban Transformation of River Landscapes in a Global Context." *Geomorphology.* 79(3–4): 460–487.

Ciampa, James D. 2014. "The State Board's Emergency Water Use Regulations. What You Need to Know (and Do)!" California Rural Water Association. http://calruralwater.org/pages/emergency-water-regulations/. Accessed on July 30, 2015.

Clayton, R. 2015. "Desalination for Water Supply." Foundation for Water Research. http://www.fwr.org/desal.pdf. Accessed on August 24, 2015.

"Complaint and Petition for Review of Agency Action." 2012. http://uraniumwatch.org/bluecastle_waterrights/PlaintiffComplaint_SJCD.120327.pdf. Accessed on August 26, 2015.

"Convention on the Law of the Non-Navigational Uses of International Waterways." 1997. General Assembly of the United Nations. http://legal.un.org/ilc/texts/instruments/ english/conventions/8_3_1997.pdf. Accessed on August 28, 2015.

Cook, Benjamin I., Richard Seager, and Jason E. Smerdon. 2014. "The Worst North American Drought Year of the Last Millennium: 1934." *Geophysical Research Letters.* 41(20): 7298–7305.

"Current World Population." 2015. Worldometers. http:// www.worldometers.info/world-population/. Accessed on July 25, 2015.

"Definitions of Climate Change." 2007. Climate Change 2007: Synthesis Report. https://www.ipcc.ch/publications_ and_data/ar4/syr/en/mains1.html. Accessed on August 1, 2015.

deMenocal, Peter B. 2001. "Cultural Responses to Climate Change during the Late Holocene." *Science.* 292(5517): 667–673.

Dinar, Ariel, Victor Pochat, and José Albiac-Murillo. 2015. *Water Pricing Experiences and Innovations.* Cham, Switzerland: Springer.

Dore, Mohammed H. I. 2005. "Climate Change and Changes in Global Precipitation Patterns: What Do We Know?" *Environment International.* 31(8): 1167–1181.

"Drought Disasters." 2015. UNICEF. http://www.unicef.org/ drought/drought-countries.htm. Accessed on July 28, 2015.

Eckhardt, Greg. 2015. The Edwards Aquifer Website. http:// www.edwardsaquifer.net/desalination.html. Accessed on August 24, 2015.

"Ecosystem Restoration." 2015. Reclamation: Managing Water in the West. http://www.usbr.gov/newsroom/ presskit/factsheet/detail.cfm?recordid=4. Accessed on August 27, 2015.

Edmeades, Greg O. 2008. "Drought Tolerance in Maize: An Emerging Reality." Companion Document to Executive Summary. ISAAA Briefs 39-2008. http://www.salmone .org/wp-content/uploads/2009/02/droughtmaize.pdf. Accessed on July 29, 2015.

Egan, Timothy. 2013. *The Worst Hard Time: The Untold Story of Those Who Survived the Great American Dust Bowl.* Boston: Houghton Mifflin Company.

"El Alto Condominial Pilot Project Impact Assessment: A Summary." 2015. http://www.waterfund.go.ke/ watersource/Downloads/002.%20El%20Alto%20Pilot%20 Project%20Impact.pdf. Accessed on January 17, 2016.

"Facts about North Dakota Fracking & Water Use." 2014. http://www.swc.nd.gov/pdfs/fracking_water_use.pdf Accessed on January 18, 2016.

Fergusson, James. 2015. "The World Will Soon Be at War over Water." *Newsweek.* http://www.newsweek .com/2015/05/01/world-will-soon-be-war-over-water-324328.html. Accessed on August 10, 2015.

Fewster, Eric. 2010. "Resilient WASH Systems in Drought Prone Areas." CARE Nederland. http://www.preventionweb. net/files/47729_resilientwashindroughtproneareas.pdf. Accessed on February 14, 2016.

Ficklin, Darren L., et al. 2015. "A Climatic Deconstruction of Recent Drought Trends in the United States." *Environmental Research Letters.* 10(4): doi:10.1088/1748-9 326/10/4/044009. Accessed on July 28, 2015.

"Final Communiqué. 29th Annual Plenary Meeting." 2011. InterAction Council. http://www.interactioncouncil.org/ final-communiqu-42. Accessed on August 9, 2015.

Fischer, Günther, et al. 2007. "Climate Change Impacts on Irrigation Water Requirements: Effects of Mitigation, 1990–2080." *Technological Forecasting & Social Change.* 74(7): 1083–1107.

Food and Agriculture Organization of the United Nations. 1985. "Systematic Index of International Water Resources Treaties, Declarations, Acts and Cases, by Basin," vol. 2. Legislative Study No. 34. Rome: Food and Agriculture Organization.

"Former World Leaders Call on UN Security Council to Recognize Water as a Top Concern." 2012. United Nations University. http://unu.edu/media-relations/releases/un-sc-called-on-to-make-water-a-top-concern.html. Accessed on July 25, 2015.

Franklin, Benjamin. 1914. "Poor Richard's Almanack." http://archive.org/stream/poorrichardsalma00franrich/poorrichardsalma00franrich_djvu.txt. Accessed on July 25, 2015.

Galbraith, Kate. 2015. "Threatened Smelt Touches Off Battles in California's Endless Water Wars." http://www.nytimes.com/2015/02/15/us/threatened-smelt-touches-off-battles-in-californias-endless-water-wars.html. Accessed on August 10, 2015.

Garamendi, John. 2015. "California Drought." Congressional Record. Congress.Gov. https://www.congress.gov/congressional-record/2015/6/24/extensions-of-remarks-section/article/E970-1. Accessed on August 10, 2015.

Gard, Wayne. 1947. "The Fence-Cutters." *The Southwestern Historical Quarterly.* 51(1): 1–15.

Gerbis, Nicholas. 2015. "Why Can't We Convert Salt Water into Drinking Water?" How Stuff Works. http://adventure.howstuffworks.com/survival/wilderness/convert-salt-water.htm. Accessed on August 24, 2015.

Gibbons, Ann. 1993. "How the Akkadian Empire Was Hung Out to Dry." *Science.* 261(5124): 985.

Gill, Richardson Benedict. 2000. *The Great Maya Droughts: Water, Life, and Death.* Albuquerque: University of New Mexico Press.

Greenspan, Jesse. 2015. "7 Withering Droughts." History. http://www.history.com/news/7-withering-droughts. Accessed on July 27, 2015.

Harris, Shane. 2014. Foreign Policy. http://foreignpolicy.com/2014/09/18/water-wars/. Accessed on August 10, 2015.

Hatami, Haleh, and Peter H. Gleick. 1994. "Conflicts over Water in the Myths, Legends, and Ancient History of the Middle East." *Environment: Science and Policy for Sustainable Development.* 36(3): 10–11.

Hays, Jeffrey. 2012. "Water Problems, Solutions, and Conservation in the Developing World." http://factsanddetails.com/world/cat57/sub382/item2136.html. Accessed on July 29, 2015.

Hermann, Roberto Max, and Benedito Pinto Ferreira Braga, Jr. 2015. "Case Study VI — The Upper Tietê Basin, Brazil." https://www.uvm.edu/~pbierman/classes/gradsem/2014/brazil_reading.pdf. Accessed on September 7, 2015.

"How It Works: Water for Electricity." 2015. Union of Concerned Scientists. http://www.ucsusa.org/clean_energy/our-energy-choices/energy-and-water-use/water-energy-electricity-overview.html#.Vd3zePlViko. Accessed on August 26, 2015.

"How Much Water Is There on, in, and above the Earth?" 2015. The USGS Water Science School. http://water.usgs.gov/edu/earthhowmuch.html. Accessed on July 25, 2015.

"How Much Water Is Used to Frack a Well?" 2014. Explore Shale. PennState Public Broadcasting. http://exploreshale.org/. Accessed on August 10, 2015.

"How Urbanization Affects the Hydrologic System." 2015. The USGS Water Science School. http://water.usgs.gov/edu/urbaneffects.html. Accessed on July 26, 2015.

"How Urbanization Affects the Water Cycle." 2015. California Water and Land Use Partnership. http://www .coastal.ca.gov/nps/watercyclefacts.pdf. Accessed on July 26, 2015.

"Human Population: Urbanization." 2015. Population Reference Bureau. http://www.prb.org/Publications/ Lesson-Plans/HumanPopulation/Urbanization.aspx. Accessed on July 26, 2015.

"Individual Water Use Continues to Decline; Enforcement Efforts Grow." California Drought. http://ca.gov/drought/ topstory/top-story-41.html. Accessed on July 30, 2015.

"International Year of Water Cooperation." 2013. UN Water. http://www.unwater.org/water-cooperation-2013/water-cooperation/en/. Accessed on August 28, 2015.

"Interstate Water Agreements of the United States." 2015. International Water Law Project. http://www .internationalwaterlaw.org/documents/interstate_us.html. Accessed on August 27, 2015.

"Introducing the History of Climate Change Science." 2015. Skeptical Scientist. http://www.skepticalscience.com/ introducing-history-of-climate-science.html. Accessed on August 1, 2015.

IPCC. 2014a. *Climate Change 2014: Impacts, Adaptation, and Vulnerability.* Geneva: IPCC. http://www.ipcc.ch/pdf/ assessment-report/ar5/syr/SYR_AR5_FINAL_full.pdf. Accessed on August 1, 2015.

IPCC. 2014b. "Summary for Policymakers." In: *Climate Change 2014: Impacts, Adaptation, and Vulnerability.* Part A: Global and Sectoral Aspects. Contribution of Working Group II to the Fifth Assessment Report of the Intergovernmental Panel on Climate Change. Cambridge; New York: Cambridge University Press. http://www.ipcc .ch/pdf/assessment-report/ar5/wg2/ar5_wgII_spm_en.pdf. Accessed on August 1, 2015.

Jiménez Cisneros, Blanca E., Taikan Oki, et al., eds. 2014. "Freshwater Resources." In Field, Christopher B., and Vicente R. Barros, eds. *Climate Change 2014. Impacts, Adaptations, and Vulnerability. Part A. Global and Sectoral Aspects.* Cambridge: Cambridge University Press. http://www.ipcc.ch/pdf/assessment-report/ar5/wg2/WGIIAR5-FrontMatterA_FINAL.pdf. Accessed on August 8, 2015.

Judge, Clark S. 2013. "The Coming Water Wars." *U.S. News and World Report.* http://www.usnews.com/opinion/blogs/clark-judge/2013/02/19/the-next-big-wars-will-be-fought-over-water. Accessed on August 10, 2015.

Karaba, Aarati, et al. 2007. "Improvement of Water Use Efficiency in Rice by Expression of Hardy, an Arabidopsis Drought and Salt Tolerance Gene." *PNAS.* 104(39): 15270–15275.

Kershner, Isabel. 2015. "Aided by the Sea, Israel Overcomes an Old Foe: Drought." *New York Times.* http://www.nytimes.com/2015/05/30/world/middleeast/water-revolution-in-israel-overcomes-any-threat-of-drought.html?_r=0. Accessed on July 30, 2015.

Koerth-Baker, Maggie. 2009. "Is There Really a Water Crisis?" BoingBoing. http://boingboing.net/2009/11/16/is-there-really-a-wa.html. Accessed on August 24, 2015.

Kreiger, Lisa M. 2014. "California Drought Pits Farmer against Farmer in Water Bidding Wars." http://www.dailynews.com/general-news/20140720/california-drought-pits-farmer-against-farmer-in-water-bidding-wars. Accessed on August 10, 2015.

Kristof, Nicholas D. 2004. "Dare We Call It Genocide?" *The New York Times.* http://www.nytimes.com/2004/06/16/opinion/dare-we-call-it-genocide.html. Accessed on August 9, 2015.

Kubba, Shamil A. A., ed. 2011. *The Iraqi Marshlands and the Marsh Arabs: The Ma'dan, Their Culture and the Environment.* Reading, UK: Ithaca Press.

"The Law of the River." 2008. Bureau of Reclamation. U.S. Department of the Interior. http://www.usbr.gov/lc/region/g1000/lawofrvr.html. Accessed on August 25, 2015.

Leven, Rachel. 2013. "U.S. Desalination Industry Grows since 2000: Seen as Essential to Meeting Supply Needs." Bloomberg BNA. http://www.bna.com/us-desalination-industry-n17179876105/. Accessed on August 24, 2015.

Lewis, Susan. 2015. "The Great Pacific Garbage Patch: Environmental Governance." Academia. http://www.academia.edu/4027539/The_Great_Pacific_Garbage_Patch_Environmental_Governance. Accessed on September 7, 2015.

Liu, Li, et al. 2012. "Global, Regional, and National Causes of Child Mortality: An Updated Systematic Analysis for 2010 with Time Trends since 2000." *Lancet*. 379(9832): 2151–2161.

Lowi, Miriam R. 1993. *Water and Power: The Politics of a Scarce Resource in the Jordan River Basin*. Cambridge; New York: Cambridge University Press.

"Making the Most of Scarcity. Accountability for Better Water Management Results in the Middle East and North Africa." 2007. Washington, DC: The World Bank. http://siteresources.worldbank.org/INTMENA/Resources/Water_Scarcity_Full.pdf. Accessed on July 25, 2015.

"Managing Water under Uncertainty and Risk." 2012. The United Nations World Water Development Report 4. http://www.unesco.org/new/fileadmin/MULTIMEDIA/HQ/SC/pdf/WWDR4%20Volume%201-Managing%20Water%20under%20Uncertainty%20and%20Risk.pdf. Accessed on August 8, 2015.

Melillo, Jerry M., Terese (T. C.) Richmond, and Gary W. Yohe, eds. 2014. *Climate Change Impacts in the United States: The Third National Climate Assessment. U.S. Global Change Research Program*. Washington, DC: Government Printing Office. nca2014.globalchange.gov. Accessed on August 7, 2015.

Mogelgaard, Kathleen. 2015. "Why Population Matters to Water Resources." Population Action International. http://pai.org/wp-content/uploads/2012/04/PAI-1293-WATER-4PG.pdf. Accessed on July 25, 2015.

Moore, Charles, and Cassandra Phillips. 2011. *Plastic Ocean: How a Sea Captain's Chance Discovery Launched a Determined Quest to Save the Oceans.* New York: Avery.

Moran, Robert. 2012. "Clean Water—The Price of Gold?" In Karl Weber, ed. *Last Call at the Oasis: The Global Water Crisis and Where We Go from Here.* New York: Public Affairs.

"The Murky Future of Global Water Quality." 2015. Veolia and the International Food Policy Research Institute. http://www.veolianorthamerica.com/sites/g/files/dvc596/f/assets/documents/2015/04/IFPRI_Veolia_H2OQual_WP.pdf. Accessed on September 7, 2015.

National Research Council. Committee on Advancing Desalination Technology. 2008. *Desalination: A National Perspective.* Washington, DC: National Academies Press.

"Native American—Creational Myths." 2015. http://www.bibliotecapleyades.net/mitos_creacion/esp_mitoscreacion_13.htm#menu. Accessed on August 25, 2015.

"Native American Myths of Creation." 2015. Crystal Links. http://www.crystalinks.com/nativeamcreation.html. Accessed on August 25, 2015.

"Neglected Tropical Diseases." 2015. World Health Organization. http://www.who.int/neglected_diseases/diseases/en/. Accessed on September 5, 2015.

Neller, R. J. 1988. "A Comparison of Channel Erosion in Small Urban and Rural Catchments, Armidale, New South Wales." *Earth Surface Processes and Landforms.* 13(1): 1–7.

Ng, Gene-Hua Crystal, et al. 2010. "Probabilistic Analysis of the Effects of Climate Change on Groundwater Recharge." *Water Resources Research.* 46(7): 10.1029/2009WR007831.

Oates, Naomi, et al. 2014. "Adaptation to Climate Change in Water, Sanitation and Hygiene." Water Policy Programme. Overseas Development Institute. http://www.odi.org/sites/odi.org.uk/files/odi-assets/publications-opinion-files/8858.pdf. Accessed on July 28, 2015.

O'Donoghue, Amy Joi. 2012. "Proposed Nuclear Power Plant Given Right to Use Green River Water." KSL.com. http://www.ksl.com/?sid=18942898. Accessed on August 26, 2015.

Olson-Raymer, Gayle. 2015. History 383. http://users.humboldt.edu/ogayle/hist383/Water.html. Accessed on August 10, 2015.

Orlove, Ben. 2009. "Glacier Retreat: Reviewing the Limits of Human Adaptation to Climate Change." *Environment.* http://www.environmentmagazine.org/Archives/Back%20Issues/May-June%202009/Orlove-full.html. Accessed on August 7, 2015.

"Pacific Garbage Patch." 2013. Clean Our Oceans Refuge Coalition. http://coorc.org/index.php/our-campaign/pacific-garbage-patch-what-we-will-do. Accessed on September 6, 2015.

Panjabi, Ranee Khooshie Lal. 2014. "Not a Drop to Spare: The Global Water Crisis of the Twenty-first Century." *Georgia Journal of International and Comparative Law.* 42(2): 277–424.

Parry, M. L., et al., eds. 2007. *Climate Change: Impact, Adaptations, and Vulnerability.* Cambridge: Cambridge University Press. http://www.ipcc.ch/publications_and_data/publications_ipcc_fourth_assessment_report_wg2_report_impacts_adaptation_and_vulnerability.htm. Accessed on August 7, 2015.

Peters, Norman E., ed. 2011. *Water Quality: Current Trends and Expected Climate Change Impacts.* Wallingford: IAHS Press.

"Progress on Drinking Water and Sanitation. 2014 Update." 2014. New York: UNICEF; Geneva: World

Health Organization. http://apps.who.int/iris/
bitstream/10665/112727/1/9789241507240_eng.pdf.
Accessed on August 29, 2015.

Prupis, Nadia. 2015. "In Dry California, Thirsty Oil and
Big-Ag Industries Exempt from Water Regulations."
Common Dreams. http://www.commondreams.org/
news/2015/04/03/dry-california-thirsty-oil-and-big-
ag-industries-exempt-water-regulations. Accessed on
August 10, 2015.

Prüss-Üstün, Annette, et al. 2008. "Safer Water,
Better Health: Costs, Benefits and Sustainability of
Interventions to Protect and Promote Health." Geneva:
World Health Organization. http://apps.who.int/iris/
bitstream/10665/43840/1/9789241596435_eng.pdf.
Accessed on August 29, 2015.

Radford, Benjamin. 2008. "The Water Shortage Myth."
LiveScience. http://www.livescience.com/2639-water-
shortage-myth.html. Accessed on August 24, 2015.

Rahaman, Muhammed Mizanur. 2009. "Principles of
International Water Law: Creating Effective Transboundary
Water Resources Management." *International Journal of
Sustainable Society.* 1(3): 207–223.

"Rainwater Harvesting in Rural Kenya." 2010. AMSHA
Africa. https://www.amshaafrica.org/projects-and-clients/
projects-pipeline/rain-water-harvesting.html. Accessed on
September 5, 2015.

"Report of the International Commission of Inquiry on
Darfur to the United Nations Secretary-General." 2005.
http://www.un.org/news/dh/sudan/com_inq_darfur.pdf.
Accessed on August 9, 2015.

Rogers, Paul. 2014. "Nation's Largest Ocean Desalination Plant
Goes up near San Diego; Future of the California Coast?"
San Jose Mercury-News. http://www.mercurynews.com/
science/ci_25859513/nations-largest-ocean-desalination-
plant-goes-up-near. Accessed on August 24, 2015.

Rothert, Steve. 2014. "Historic Water Agreement Reached on Upper Klamath Basin Water." American Rivers. http://www.americanrivers.org/blog/historic-water-agreement-upper-klamath-basin-water/. Accessed on August 26, 2015.

Roudi-Fahimi, Farzaneh, Liz Creel, and Roger-Mark De Souza. 2002. "Finding the Balance: Population and Water Scarcity in the Middle East and North Africa." Population Reference Bureau. http://www.prb.org/pdf/FindingTheBalance_Eng.pdf. Accessed on August 8, 2015.

Rousseau, Richard. 2015. "The Growing Potential for Water Wars." *International Policy Digest*. http://www.internationalpolicydigest.org/2015/04/12/the-growing-potential-for-water-wars/. Accessed on August 10, 2015.

"Sanitation and Hygiene Promotion." 2005. Geneva: Water Supply and Sanitation Collaborative Council and World Health Organization. http://www.who.int/water_sanitation_health/hygiene/sanhygpromo.pdf. Accessed on September 5, 2015.

Sanjuan, Thierry, and Rémi Béreau. 2001/2003. "The Three Gorges Dam: Between State Power, Technical Immensity, and Regional Implications." *Hérodote*. 102: 19–56. http://www.cairn-int.info/article-E_HER_102_0019—the-three-gorges-dam.htm. Accessed on August 26, 2015.

Santos, Fernanda. 2015. "On Parched Navajo Reservation, 'Water Lady' Brings Liquid Gold." *New York Times*. July 24, 2015: A11, 14.

Sawahel, Wagdy. 2004. "Egyptian Scientists Produce Drought-Tolerant GM Wheat." *SciDevNet*. http://m.scidev.net/global/gm/news/egyptian-scientists-produce-droughttolerant-gm-wh.html. Accessed on July 29, 2015.

"Shared Waters, Shared Opportunities." 2009. UN Water. http://www.unwater.org/wwd09/flashindex.html. Accessed on August 28, 2015.

Shatat, Mahmoud, and Saffa B. Riffat. 2014. "Water Desalination Technologies Utilizing Conventional and

Renewable Energy Sources." *International Journal of Low-Carbon Technology.* 9 (1): 1–19. http://ijlct.oxfordjournals.org/content/9/1/1. Accessed on August 24, 2015.

Simon, Evan. 2015. "California's Drought Plan Mostly Lays Off Agriculture, Oil Industries." *ABC News.* http://abcnews.go.com/News/californias-drought-plan-lays-off-agriculture-oil-industries/story?id=30087832. Accessed on July 30, 3015.

Skelton, George. 2014. "Water Fight Pits Farmer against Farmer." *Los Angeles Times.* http://www.latimes.com/local/la-me-cap-drought-20140310-column.html. Accessed on August 10, 2015.

State of California. Office of Administrative Law. 2015. http://www.waterboards.ca.gov/waterrights/water_issues/programs/drought/docs/emergency_regulations/oal_approved_regs2015.pdf. Accessed on July 30, 2015.

"Summary of the Klamath Basin Restoration Agreement." 2007. U.S. Forest and Wildlife Service. http://www.fws.gov/arcata/fisheries/reports/tamwg/2008/March10-11/Attachment5.pdf. Accessed on August 27, 2015.

Taber, Benjamen N. 2012. "Recreation in the Colorado River Basin: Is America's Playground under Threat?" Colorado College. https://www.coloradocollege.edu/dotAsset/c1d0b548-4350-4be7-b0a5-8de6692b973b.pdf. Accessed on August 25, 2015.

"This Planet Can Support Nine Billion People." 2013. *The European.* http://www.theeuropean-magazine.com/916-biswas-asit/917-the-right-to-water. Accessed on August 24, 2015.

"Three Gorges Dam, Yangtze River, China." 2015. Eng. 125CS. http://www.coe.montana.edu/ee/rmaher/engr125_fl06/Three%20Gorges%20Dam.pdf. Accessed on August 26, 2015.

"Towards Effective Programming for WASH in Schools." 2007. Delft: IRC International Water and Sanitation

Centre. http://www.unicef.org/wash/files/TP_48_WASH_ Schools_07.pdf. Accessed on September 5, 2015.

"Transboundary Waters." 2014. International Decade for Action "Water for Life" 2005–2015. http://www.un.org/ waterforlifedecade/transboundary_waters.shtml. Accessed on August 9, 2015.

"Transboundary Waters: Sharing Benefits, Sharing Responsibilities." 2008. UN Water. http://www.unwater .org/downloads/UNW_TRANSBOUNDARY.pdf. Accessed on August 28, 2015.

"Trends in Nutrients and Pesticides in the Nation's Rivers and Streams—Lessons for Understanding and Managing Water Quality." 2015. U.S. Geological Survey. http://water.usgs .gov/nawqa/headlines/nut_pest/TrendsBriefingSheet.pdf. Accessed on September 6, 2015.

"Tribal Reps Air Concerns over Proposed Nuclear Plant." 2014. *Moab Sun News*. http://www.moabsunnews.com/ news/article_12ab0c62-2875-11e4-a5e8-001a4bcf6878 .html. Accessed on August 26, 2015.

"2550 BC—The Treaty of Mesilim." 2012. http://www .duhaime.org/LawMuseum/LawArticle-1313/2550-BC— The-Treaty-of-Mesilim.aspx. Accessed on August 27, 2015.

United Nations Economic Commission for Europe. 2014. "Model Provisions on Transboundary Groundwaters." http://www.zaragoza.es/contenidos/medioambiente/ onu/1314-eng_Model_Provisions_on_Transboundary_ Groundwaters.pdf. Accessed on August 28, 2015.

"Urbanization and Streams: Studies of Hydrologic Impacts." 2015. U.S. Environmental Protection Agency. http://water .epa.gov/polwaste/nps/urban/report.cfm. Accessed on July 26, 2015.

"U.S. Drought Portal." 2015. National Integrated Drought Information System. https://www.drought.gov/drought/. Accessed on July 28, 2015.

"U.S. Energy Sector Vulnerabilities to Climate Change and Extreme Weather." 2013. U.S. Department of Energy. http://energy.gov/sites/prod/files/2013/07/f2/20130716-Energy%20Sector%20Vulnerabilities%20Report.pdf. Accessed on August 7, 2015.

"Utilities." 2015. Aruba Economic Affairs. http://www .arubaeconomicaffairs.aw/index.php?option=com_content& task=view&id=29&Itemid=42. Accessed on August 24, 2015.

"Water Conflict Chronology List." 2015. Pacific Institute. http://www2.worldwater.org/conflict/list/. Accessed on August 9, 2015.

"Water Diplomacy." 2015. http://waterdiplomacy.org/. Accessed on August 27, 2015.

"Water from Water—Desalination." 2011. YouTube. https:// www.youtube.com/watch?v=2XMRlFMJB-g. Accessed on August 24, 2015.

"Water Resources." 2015. Royal Embassy of Saudi Arabia. https://www.saudiembassy.net/about/country-information/ agriculture_water/Water_Resources.aspx. Accessed on January 18, 2016.

"Water Scarcity." 2014. International Decade for Action "Water for Life" 2005–2015. http://www.un.org/ waterforlifedecade/scarcity.shtml. Accessed on August 8, 2015.

"Water Wars Part One: Freshwater for Fracking Concerns Those along Devil's River." 2015. Our Texas Water. http://ourtexaswater.org/file/video/water-wars-part-one-freshwater-fracking-concerns-those-along-devils-river. Accessed on August 10, 2015.

Watkins, Kevin, et al. 2006. *Human Development Report 2006: Beyond Scarcity: Power, Poverty and the Global Water Crisis.* New York: United Nations Development Programme. http://www.undp.org/content/dam/undp/

library/corporate/HDR/2006%20Global%20HDR/HDR-2006-Beyond%20scarcity-Power-poverty-and-the-global-water-crisis.pdf. Accessed on August 27, 2015.

"What They Are." 2006. Millennium Project. http://www.unmillenniumproject.org/goals/index.htm. Accessed on August 29, 2015.

Wilhite, Donald A., and Michael H. Glantz. 1985. "Understanding the Drought Phenomenon: The Role of Definitions." *Water International*. 10(3): 111–120.

"World Population. Historical Estimates of World Population." 2015. U.S. Census Bureau. http://www.census.gov/population/international/data/worldpop/table_history.php. Accessed on July 25, 2015.

"The World's Largest Power Plant Prevented 100 Million Tons of Carbon Emissions in 2014." 2015. *Business Insider*. http://www.businessinsider.com/afp-chinas-three-gorges-dam-breaks-world-hydropower-record-2015-1. Accessed on August 26, 2015.

Zetland, David. 2008. "The Water Shortage Myth." *Forbes*. http://www.forbes.com/2008/07/14/california-supply-demand-oped-cx_dz_0715water.html. Accessed on August 24, 2015.

"Zimbabwe AHEAD Background." 2011. http://www.africaahead.org/2011/04/zimbabwe-ahead/. Accessed on September 5, 2015.

Introduction

Water, sanitation, and hygiene issues involve a wide variety of scientific, technological, social, psychological, economic, political, and other questions. Various individuals have a variety of viewpoints about one or more of these questions. This chapter provides interested parties with an opportunity to express their own stands on one or more of these issues. The positions expressed here are those of the writers only, and not necessarily those of the author or others involved with the production of this book.

Follow the Money
Trudy E. Bell

Disputes over water use often present challenging problems for third-party observers. Are the facts presented by both sides true? Are they being presented in the proper context? Is important information being withheld from neutral observers? How much weight should be given to one person's views compared with the views of others? A recent example of such a situation has been the drought crisis in California that has extended over at least four years. What factors are responsible for this drought, and what steps should be taken to resolve the crisis?

One of the world's largest bodies of fresh water, the Aral Sea, has been decreasing in size for years, ensuring dramatic changes in the lifestyles of people who live near it. (Vladimir Borodin/Dreamstime.com)

It is often up to individual citizens and taxpayers to slice through hype, get to the facts, and come to independent conclusions. But how? How can a person determine what statements are true, or evaluate what proposed options for technology or policy are wise—or outright dangerous? Here are some suggestions for dealing with such situations.

Frame the question carefully. For any given issue, ask: how will different choices actively help California at large—all its people and all its environment, including its rivers and groundwater aquifers—not just for right now but also for years into the future? Is any choice under consideration a high-stakes gamble with California's water resources just on a hypothetical chance that in the future enough snow or rain might fall in the mountains for long enough to recharge rivers and aquifers? Or does the choice actually conserve and use wisely the dwindling precious supplies we already have, in recognition that the future might well be dryer yet?

Look at the entire picture. On the water supply side, many technological solutions have been proposed to relieve stress on groundwater by tapping other sources of water undrinkable in their normal state, including desalination (drinking from the Pacific Ocean by removing salt from seawater) and direct and indirect potable reuse (drinking from the toilet by purifying sewage). Other proposed solutions include building more water storage facilities or canals.

But addressing water supply is only half the problem. The other half of the problem is water demand. Even if urban water use—which is only 20 percent of California's human consumption of water—went to zero, agricultural water use remains the elephant in the room. Yet, addressing the laws and public policies of water rights and water use, especially for agriculture, has been called a political "third rail"—meaning instant political electrocution for any legislator approaching the whole subject. One indication that water use has passed into the realm of the political are billboards along interstate I-5 and other roads throughout the southern Central Valley bearing such messages as: "No Water = No Jobs" and "Get the Delta pumps and people working" and "Is growing food wasting water?" and "Stop the Congress-Created Dust Bowl."

Research numbers, and be aware of the quality or reliability of various sources of information. Political Web sites, like the roadside billboards, are trying to persuade you of one particular viewpoint over another. But if you are seeking objective facts to make up your own mind, consult official U.S. or California government statistics or peer-reviewed university scientific information or analyses. Be thorough in your research, where several knowledgeable experts may draw different conclusions from the same data, ask why—are the data incomplete?

Do your own arithmetic to check assertions and numbers, and to investigate their original context to see whether data were misrepresented. Benjamin Disraeli famously observed that there are three types of lies: lies, damned lies, and statistics. To alert yourself to ways numbers can be visually misrepresented, check out How to Lie with Statistics, a short, funny, and insightful book by Darrell Huff first published in 1954 and still in print (Huff 1993). Digging deeper into numerical data may also reveal to you whether any important truth was actually omitted.

Follow the people. Pay attention to the names of people who head up companies or serve on their boards of directors, and compare those names with the names listed as consultants on city, county, or state boards appointed to examine and evaluate various proposals. If a company representative is also on a panel evaluating the merit of a proposed technology or service offered by that company, ask: could there be a conflict of interest? Might the company be trying to steer the panel to choosing its own particular solution rather than objectively evaluating all the proposals? Query the head of the panel or ask about that at a public meeting.

Ask tough questions about the winners and losers resulting from any proposed technology or public policy. Who will be paying the bills (taxpayers? private investors?)? What will they be getting for that money (if anything)? Who will benefit or profit from the investment (the company? taxpayers? private investors)? Will there be any losers from the investment if it succeeds (taxpayers? California's groundwater aquifers)? What about if it fails?

Research political assertions. Return for a moment to the roadside billboards, especially the one that asks "Is growing food wasting water?" The answer the billboard wants you to conclude is: "Of course not." But a bit of savvy digging can lead you to realize otherwise about certain crops—especially if the crop demands a lot of water and can be raised without irrigation elsewhere in the country (e.g., research alfalfa and cattle) or is a luxury food primarily exported for profit rather than being a staple food consumed domestically (research almonds). At the scale of California's agricultural industry and prodigious groundwater use, such exports amount to exporting vast volumes of California's precious groundwater, draining its aquifers for profit.

Think long term. Companies look at the bottom line of their balance sheets just for the current quarter or the current year. But what about next year? And the year after? What if the drought continues? Long-term climate models point to an overall dryer climate for California in the future. Moreover, scientists examining tree rings of centuries-old blue oak trees can trace California climate patterns long before paper weather records started to be kept in the late 1800s and have found evidence of past "megadroughts" lasting a decade or more. What if similar megadroughts recur in the years ahead?

Remember. In the chilling words of Gray Brechin, visiting scholar at the Department of Geography at the University of California, Berkeley, "when there's no water—well, there's no water" (Martin 2015).

References

Huff, Darrell. 1993. *How to Lie with Statistics*, reissue edition. New York: W. W. Norton.

Martin, Glen. 2015. "Groundwater Zero: We're Worried about the Drought. But Not as Worried as We Should Be." Cal Alumni Association. http://alumni.berkeley.edu/california-magazine/just-in/2015-05-27/groundwater-zero-were-worried-about-drought-not-worried-we. Accessed on October 30, 2015.

Trudy E. Bell, MA, is a former editor for Scientific American *and* IEEE Spectrum *magazines and former senior writer for the University of California High-Performance AstroComputing Center. She has written, coauthored, or edited a dozen books, written several hundred articles on science and technology for national magazines, and edited a dozen reports for the Union of Concerned Scientists.*

Aral Sea
John R. Burch Jr.

The Aral Sea is located within the borders of Kazakhstan and Uzbekistan. Its basin extends into Afghanistan, Iran, Kyrgyzstan, Tajikistan, and Turkmenistan. Fed primarily by the Syr Dar'ya and Amu Dar'ya Rivers, the Aral Sea was the fourth-largest lake in the world as recently as 1960. Due to a combination of expanded irrigation and climate change, the lake has shrunk dramatically. By 2007, the Aral Sea was approximately 10 percent of its former size. The Aral Sea's dramatic decline has yielded catastrophic effects on the local environment and the region's human population.

Before its precipitous decline commenced, the Aral Sea's brackish waters were inhabited by more than 30 fish species that supported a booming fishing industry. The local ecosystem also supported an abundance of flora and fauna. Although farmers were already using the waters of the Aral Sea's basin for irrigation, it was not at a scale that significantly affected the amount of water flowing into the lake. In 1960, the basin's waters were irrigating approximately 11 million acres of land. During the 1960s, the Union of Soviet Socialist Republics (USSR) began to construct unlined canals to divert water from both the Syr Dar'ya and Amu Dar'ya Rivers to bring irrigation to desert lands for agricultural purposes. In addition, reservoirs were created on those river systems to impound large amounts of water. The construction of the canals and reservoirs deprived the Aral Sea of water that was required to compensate for water lost through evaporation. By 1990, the basin's waters were irrigating more than 17.5 million acres of land. The loss of all that water resulted in the Aral Sea not only shrinking, but also having its ecosystems destroyed. As the water volume declined, its salinity increased significantly, resulting in the loss of all but six of the fish species that had once supported the fishing industry. The flora and fauna that had thrived in the wetlands that surrounded the Aral Sea had likewise begun to disappear. The 319 species of birds that had once resided in the basin had been reduced to 160. Mammal species had declined from 70 to 32. Desertification set in as the waters receded. Shipping centers such as Aralsk and Moynak had their harbors lose their water. The exposed expanses of seabed were, and are, rich in salt, agricultural chemicals, and other contaminants. Windstorms carry the dust from the seabed to far locales, leading to severe health problems for many people. Respiratory, liver, and kidney ailments are common, as are cancers affecting the esophagus and throat (Micklin and Aladin 2008).

The USSR treated the decline of the Aral Sea as a state secret for decades. It was not until 1985, under Mikhail Gorbachev's glasnost policy, that the desiccation of the lake became known internationally. By the end of that decade, what had once been a single lake had become two: the Small Aral, also known as the Northern Aral, and the Large Aral. Soviet scientists hatched a grand plan to divert waters from rivers in Siberia to help replenish the Aral Sea, but the collapse of the USSR in 1991 thwarted that initiative. The newly independent Kazakhstan took the responsibility of restoring the Small Aral. It constructed an earthen dike in the early 1990s to control the outflow of water to the south. The dike eventually failed, but while it held, the water level increased and salinity declined. Kazakhstan, with funding assistance provided by the World Bank, constructed a stronger earthen dike that included a gated concrete dam. Since its completion in 1985, inflows from the Syr Dar'ya River have allowed the Small Aral to increase in size and depth. The corresponding drop in salinity has allowed some fish species to once again thrive.

The Large Aral continues to disappear. In 2007, it became three distinct bodies of water. One area is a gulf region that will eventually disappear. All hope is not lost for the eastern and western basins, which are presently connected by a narrow channel. The fate of those two bodies of water will depend on the decisions of the countries that utilize the waters from the Amu Dar'ya River for irrigation. If they allow more water from the river to flow into the Large Aral, then that body of water can possibly begin to recover to a certain extent. Otherwise, it will continue to shrink, and its water will become so saline that the only organisms that will be able to live in it are bacteria. Unfortunately, the political will to improve the flow of water from the Amu Dar'ya River to the Large Aral is not manifesting itself in the countries that are dependent on the river for irrigation, as their expansion of irrigation projects continues unabated.

Reference

Micklin, Philip, and Nikolay V. Aladin. 2008. "Reclaiming the Aral Sea." *Scientific American*. 298(4): 64–71.

Additional Bibliography

Kostianoy, Andre G., and Aleksey N. Kosarev, eds. 2010. *The Aral Sea Environment*. New York: Springer-Verlag.

Micklin, Philip. 2010. "The Past, Present, and Future Aral Sea." *Lakes & Reservoirs: Research & Management.* 15(3): 193–213.

Micklin, Philip, Nikolay V. Aladin, and Igor Plotnikov. 2011. *Destruction of the Aral Sea: Anatomy of an Environmental Disaster.* New York: Springer.

Synnott, Mark. 2015. "Sins of the Aral Sea." *National Geographic.* 227(6): 114–131.

Zonn, Igor S., et al., eds. 2009. *Aral Sea Encyclopedia.* New York: Springer-Verlag.

Dr. John R. Burch Jr., dean of Library Services at Campbellsville University, is the author or coauthor of seven books, including Water Rights and the Environment in the United States: A Documentary and Reference Guide *(ABC-CLIO, 2015). His book* The Encyclopedia of Water Politics and Policy in the United States *(Congressional Quarterly Press, 2011), coedited with Steven L. Danver, was named an Outstanding Academic Title in 2012 by CHOICE: Reviews for Academic Libraries.*

Desalination and Reuse: Facing a Global Water Crisis with Alternative Technologies
Roberto Molar Candanosa

It's easy to take water for granted in developed countries. Flushing a toilet in Europe or showering in the United States consumes more water than what is available to hundreds of millions of people in developing countries (United Nations Development Programme, 2006). Ameliorating the stress caused by water scarcity is crucial for sectors including sanitation, agriculture, and manufacturing. For example, considering the water and food a chicken needs to live—as well as the amount of water needed to grow that food—it takes about 20 gallons of water to produce a single egg (USGS 2015). These numbers make water an invaluable treasure that will likely become a top commodity over other key natural resources, like petroleum (Dumaine 2014).

In light of the water crisis, alternative technologies could be part of the solution. Two of the most common methods for water management include seawater desalination and water reuse. This essay will review the main advantages of these technologies while considering possible concerns associated with their processes.

Desalination

Earth's oceans offer a virtually unlimited supply of water. Experts estimate that seawater will be a crucial water source for regions under water stress (Sood and Smakhtin 2014). However, our bodies cannot process excessive amounts of salt, and drinking seawater would eventually be fatal (NOAA 2014). Fortunately, new developments in purification technology and renewable energy will continue to make desalination a promising solution to mitigate water scarcity (Sood and Smakhtin 2014).

Desalination technologies use mainly two methods to yield freshwater: distillation and a special form of purification known as reverse osmosis (Khawaji et al. 2008). Desalination by distillation removes salt by boiling water, capturing the vapor, and cooling it down, which changes the water vapor into a liquid and salt-free phase. On the other hand, distillation by reverse osmosis works by pressurizing saltwater through a permeable membrane, leaving behind the salts and the water combining with freshwater in a different compartment (OAS 1997).

Desalination plays an important role for communities near coasts, with some reports estimating desalination technologies yielded about 25 km^3 of freshwater worldwide in 2010 (Sood and Smakhtin 2014). However, continuing to use these technologies can be difficult due to the high costs of powering desalination plants. The only countries that have used desalination are affluent nations or those under high water stress and where energy is less expensive (Sood and Smakhtin 2014). These countries include Saudi Arabia, the United Arab Emirates, Algeria, Libya, Australia, Spain, and the United States, but the alarming trends in water scarcity could push other countries to invest in desalination (Sood and Smakhtin 2014; USGS 2014).

The future for water desalination technologies may seem favorable, but the water industry also needs to consider potential environmental impacts related to the process. While only about 1 percent of desalination plants use renewable energy, a most worrying environmental concern is desalination's effect on marine life (Lattemann and Höpner 2008; Sood and Smakhtin 2014). For instance, seawater intake screens in desalination plants can draw marine organisms along with seawater or disrupt organisms and minerals settled in the seabed. On the other hand, desalination can disturb marine ecosystems when plants release hot salts, minerals, and other by-products of the desalination process back into the ocean. These discharges can have deadly repercussions for some marine organisms (Lattemann and Höpner 2008).

Lattemann and Höpner (2008) present measures to minimize desalination's environmental impacts. To avoid sucking larger organisms (e.g., turtles or fish) into a desalination plant, water intake pressures and intake screen size should be considered. Similarly, intake and discharge structures should be placed away from the coasts to minimize harm to smaller organisms (e.g., plankton). Concentrates discharged back into the ocean should be diluted, treated, and cooled down to avoid disrupting marine environments. Further, locations of desalination plants should be chosen strategically to minimize distribution pipelines that would disturb terrestrial ecosystems.

Graywater Treatment

Desalination seems like an obvious solution to mitigate water scarcity, but it's not the only option. Water scarcity also can be ameliorated in part with alternative methods, like graywater reuse. Graywater is wastewater from sinks, showers, and laundry—excluding water containing feces and urine from toilets, also known as blackwater. Experts estimate that graywater accounts for about 75 percent of the water wasted in household tasks (Ghaitidak and Yadav 2013). Technologies to treat it are becoming popular worldwide for functions such as irrigation and flushing toilets. The United States, Japan, and Australia are pioneers of graywater reuse, with nations such as Germany, the United Kingdom, and Spain following along (Domènech and Saurí 2010).

Ghaitidak and Yadav (2013) review graywater treatment techniques, which range from preliminary ones that remove small materials to advanced ones that remove suspended soils, biodegradable organics, and other dissolved contaminants. Coagulation and flocculation mix graywater rapidly to neutralize the negative charges of the dissolved contaminants, making contaminants form a clumped mass that can be more easily removed. Another treatment technique, known as constructed wetlands, uses plants, soils, and microorganisms within them to remove suspended solids, metals, and toxic organics. Graywater filtrations, on the other hand, can effectively remove viruses and parasites using gravels and sand.

More complicated systems for graywater reuse include rotating biological contactors. This system rotates filters partially submerged in graywater to expose microbes to the atmosphere, a process that degrades organic contaminants. On the other hand, microfiltration membrane bioreactors use membrane filtration systems to remove organics and contaminants, while sequencing batch reactors use bacteria to eat and transform dissolved organics into suspended solids that can be more easily removed (Ghaitidak and Yadav 2013).

The advantages of graywater reuse need to be considered cautiously, especially because contaminants in graywater can give rise to pathogens. Reuse by constructed wetlands, as well as coagulation and flocculation techniques, may be unable to remove certain organic contaminants. Similarly, some systems using porous membranes to filter water could fail when trying to remove microorganisms smaller than their membrane's pores (Ghaitidak and Yadav 2013).

Pathogens, microbes, and other contaminants in poorly treated graywater pose serious health and environmental concerns. Humans should be concerned with disease transmissions from drinking or eating food possibly irrigated with contaminated water. Similarly, some types of sodium left in water can disturb soil and make it less suitable for plants. Also, a most critical risk of graywater reuse is contaminating groundwater, since pollutants could penetrate the soil and contaminate underground water reserves (WHO 2006).

Feasible Water Solutions

In conclusion, desalination and graywater reuse could play key roles in ameliorating the water crisis. While graywater reuse may not always yield drinking water, some reuse technologies could be used simultaneously for functions such as sewage or irrigation. Also, developments in renewable energy could make large-scale desalination more feasible option in the future, as long as preventive measures ensure safety for marine environments. Overall, the amount of saltwater on Earth makes desalination technologies an attractive alternative for water resources engineering and management, and reusing graywater could minimize overusing valuable freshwater supplies.

References

Domènech, Laia, and David Saurí. 2010. "Socio-technical Transitions in Water Scarcity Contexts: Public Acceptance of Greywater Reuse Technologies in the Metropolitan Area of Barcelona." *Resources, Conservation and Recycling*. 55(1): 53–62.

Dumaine, Brian. 2014. "What Is Water Worth?" *Fortune*. 169(7): 94–100.

Ghaitidak, Dilip, and Kunwar Yadav. 2013. "Characteristics and Treatment of Greywater—A Review." *Environmental Science & Pollution Research*. 20(5): 2795–2809.

Khawaji, Akili D., Ibrahim K. Kutubkhanah, and Jong-Mihn Wie. 2008. "Advances in Seawater Desalination Technologies." *Desalination*. 221(1–3): 47–69.

Lattemann, Sabine, and Thomas Höpner. 2008. "Environmental Impact and Impact Assessment of Seawater Desalination." *Desalination*. 220(1–3): 1–15.

National Oceanic and Atmospheric Administration (NOAA). 2014. "Can Humans Drink Seawater?" National Ocean Service. http://oceanservice.noaa.gov/facts/drinksw.html. Accessed on October 12, 2015.

Organization of American States (OAS). 1997. "Source Book of Alternative Technologies for Freshwater Augmentation in Latin American and the Caribbean." International Environmental Technology Centre. http://www.oas.org/dsd/publications/Unit/oea59e/ch20.htm#TopOfPage. Accessed on October 12, 2015.

Sood, Aditya, and Vladimir Smakhtin. 2014. "Can Desalination and Clean Energy Combined Help to Alleviate Global Water Scarcity?" *Journal of the American Water Resources Association*. 50(5): 1111–1123.

United Nations Development Programme. 2006. "Human Development Report 2006, Beyond Scarcity: Power, Poverty and the Global Water Crisis." http://hdr.undp.org/sites/default/files/reports/267/hdr06-complete.pdf. Accessed on October 15, 2015.

United States Geological Survey (USGS). 2015. "How Much Water Does It Take to Grow a Hamburger?" The USGS Water Science School. http://water.usgs.gov/edu/activity-watercontent.html. Accessed on October 4, 2015.

United States Geological Survey (USGS). 2014. "Saline Water: Desalination." The USGS Water Science School. http://water.usgs.gov/edu/drinkseawater.html. Accessed on October 4, 2015.

World Health Organization (WHO). 2006. "Overview of Greywater Management: Health Considerations. http://applications.emro.who.int/dsaf/dsa1203.pdf. Accessed on October 1, 2015.

Roberto Molar Candanosa is a graduate student of science and technology journalism at Texas A&M University and has a bachelor's in English. He uses what he learned about the rhetoric of style to help bridge the gap between science and the public, passionately thinking about the environment and the rest of the universe.

Balancing Supply and Demand on the Colorado River
Hannah Holm

Both cities and agriculture in the southwestern United States rely heavily on the Colorado River, but an imbalance between supply and demand puts the whole system at risk. Bringing supply and demand into balance will require significant changes in the way water is used, but is vital for the future of the region. Fortunately, both governance structures and cultural shifts offer hope for non-traumatic adaptation to a potentially drier future in the river basin.

Introduction

The Colorado River is the great river of the southwestern United States. Tributary streams collect snowmelt in the high mountains of Colorado and Wyoming and carry life-giving water to the Colorado and Green Rivers, which wind their way through desert valleys and canyons before merging downstream from Moab, Utah. The enlarged Colorado then pauses behind Glen Canyon Dam, which forms Lake Powell, before plunging into the Grand Canyon and providing many a rafter a wild ride before calming again in Lake Mead, which was created by Hoover Dam. Beyond Lake Mead, the waters of the river flow in many different directions through canals to farms and cities in California, Arizona, and Mexico, as well as trickling along its own diminished channel toward Mexico's Sea of Cortez.

The Colorado River is not a big river in terms of its length or volume. It is only the fifth longest in the United States, and its average annual flow is dwarfed by the Mississippi and Columbia Rivers (Jacobs 2011, 7).

Despite its small size, the Colorado River is extremely important. The river and its tributaries provide water for almost 40 million people and 2.2 million hectares of agricultural land. This includes areas outside the natural drainage of the river, including Denver and Colorado's eastern plains, which get their Colorado River water from tunnels under the Continental Divide. Salt Lake City, Albuquerque, and Los Angeles are other cities outside of the Colorado River's drainage that receive some of its water (BOR 2012). From farms, the water travels even further: about two-thirds of the winter vegetables eaten in the United States are grown in California's Imperial Valley with water from the Colorado River, so you could say the whole country relies on it (Meadows 2012). In addition to its practical human uses, the waters of the Colorado River and its tributaries provide sustenance and habitat for wildlife and wild beauty for boaters and anglers.

The Challenge

Since the early 2000s, cities and farms have taken more water out of the Colorado River basin than has come into the basin through rain and snow. This is partly due to drought and partly due to the volume of demands on the river (BOR 2012). So far, the giant reservoirs of Lake Mead and Lake Powell have cushioned the impact of this imbalance, but this cannot continue forever: if use continues to exceed supply, the reservoirs will eventually run dry.

Global climate models indicate that flows in the river could diminish even further during the coming decades, and hotter temperatures will increase evaporation rates and the amount of water plants need to grow (BOR 2012). It is also possible that some years could be wetter than previously observed, but it is hard to predict when those may occur.

While the future water supply in the basin is hard to predict and impossible to control, water use can be controlled. Controlling it is complicated, however, by the fact that water use is governed by many different people and organizations in seven U.S. states and two Mexican states. Everyone wants to make sure they continue to get their fair share, and the amount allocated on paper is more than the amount nature provides. When the U.S. Bureau of Reclamation surveyed states in 2011 on how much water they thought they would need in coming decades, all predicted increases, largely due to anticipated population growth (BOR 2012).

Moving toward Solutions

Fortunately, the recent past provides indications that water use can indeed be curtailed without major social or economic upheaval. Forecasts aside, actual water use in the basin is beginning to decline, even as populations and economic activity continue to increase. It is important to understand why use is decreasing and what can be done to push it down even further in order to ensure that both the human and natural systems that rely on the Colorado River and its tributaries flourish into the future.

Water use has begun to decline partly because of agreements negotiated between water users, and partly because of changes in behavior by individuals and organizations. On the negotiation side, the states and major water users that share the Colorado River have negotiated guidelines for managing Lake Powell and Lake Mead and how to handle shortages. These agreements lay out what reservoir levels will trigger an official shortage and what reductions in water deliveries will occur in what order if levels continue to drop. Negotiations have also resulted in new ways of sharing water and getting "credit" for use reductions that can be banked in Lake Mead, helping everyone stay ahead of an official shortage (Kempthorne 2007).

The desire to stay ahead of a shortage has also helped drive new agreements between different water user groups. For example, Southern California cities have paid farmers to fallow some of their fields some of the time, taking turns, so the cities can use water that would otherwise have grown crops while still keeping the farmers in business (MWDSC 2013).

Farmers throughout the basin are also getting increasingly precise with water management, upgrading irrigation infrastructure and improving soil health in order to maximize production while decreasing losses to evaporation and thirsty weeds. These efforts are particularly important, because agriculture consumes approximately 70 percent of the water consumed in the Colorado River basin (BOR 2012).

In cities, it is becoming increasingly clear that growing populations don't have to increase water use. Water use trends have sharply diverged from population and economic growth trends in many southwestern cities (Fleck 2015). This is partly a result of more efficient appliances and improved water management by municipalities, but it's also partly a result of a cultural shift, where large green lawns are becoming less desirable and people feel a shared sense of responsibility to be stewards of their water resources.

These trends are encouraging, but they are so far not enough to drop water use below the reliable supply in the basin. Water users throughout the basin will need to continue to enhance their commitment to doing their part to support the whole

Colorado River system for that system to be able to continue to support the vibrant cities, agriculture, and natural wonders that define the region.

References

Cohen, Michael, with Juliet Christian-Smith and John Berggren. 2013. "Water to Supply the Land: Irrigated Agriculture in the Colorado River Basin." Pacific Institute. May 2013. http://pacinst.org/wp-content/uploads/sites/21/2013/05/pacinst-crb-ag.pdf. Accessed on September 30, 2015.

Fleck, John. 2015. "Decoupling Water Use from Growth, the New Mexico Example." Blog post. August 8, 2015. http://www.inkstain.net/fleck/2015/08/decoupling-water-use-from-growth-the-new-mexico-example/. Accessed on October 1, 2015.

Jacobs, Jeffrey. 2011. "The Sustainability of Water Resources in the Colorado River Basin." The Bridge: Linking Engineering and Society. Winter 2011. Published by the National Academy of Engineering. https://www.nae.edu/File.aspx?id=55285. Accessed on September 30, 2015.

Kempthorne, Dirk. 2007. "Record of Decision: Colorado River Interim Guidelines for Lower Basin Shortages and the Coordinated Operations of Lakes Powell and Mead." December 2007. U.S. Department of the Interior. http://www.usbr.gov/lc/region/programs/strategies/RecordofDecision.pdf. Accessed on September 30, 2015

Meadows, Robin. 2012. "Research News: UC Desert Research and Extension Service Celebrates 100 Years." *California Agriculture*. 66(4):122–126. October–December 2012. http://californiaagriculture.ucanr.edu/landingpage.cfm?article=ca.v066n04p122&fulltext=yes. Accessed on October 1,2015,

Metropolitan Water District of Southern California (MWDSC). 2013. "Palo Verde Land Management, Crop Rotation and Water Supply Program . . . at a Glance." http://www.mwdh2o.com/PDF_NewsRoom/6.4.2_Water_Reliability_Palo_Verde.pdf. Accessed on October 1, 2015.

United States Bureau of Reclamation (BOR). 2012. "Colorado River Basin Supply and Demand Study." http://www.usbr.gov/lc/region/programs/crbstudy.html. Accessed on September 30, 2015.

Waterman, John. "The American Nile." *National Geographic.* http://www.nationalgeographic.com/americannile/. Accessed on September 30, 2015.

Hanna Holm is coordinator of the Ruth Powell Hutchins Water Center at Colorado Mesa University.

Not Just Schoolyard Gossip: The Dirty on Water, Disease, and Education in Africa
Emily Myers

What can students in Africa teach us about the global water crisis? Examining the reasons why children in poor African countries miss school reveals the frightening extent of the global water crisis. The combination of disease, inadequate water systems, poverty, gender norms, and human biology often produces barriers to attending school for many students.

Malaria is a mosquito-borne disease and top killer of children in Africa. Unmanaged pools of standing water function as breeding grounds for malaria-carrying mosquitoes. A study from Kenya estimated that children miss 11 percent of school because of malaria—that is, if they do not die from it first (Midzi et al. 2011, 2). Children who survive multiple bouts with malaria often demonstrate poorer cognitive abilities than their peers (Midzi et al. 2011, 2). Children miss a significant proportion of their education because, if they are out sick with malaria, and if they recover, these children return to school unable to optimize their learning.

People cannot adequately clean their faces without reliable access to clean water, creating conditions perfect for the development of trachoma (McCauley et al. 1990, 1233). Trachoma is a contagious bacterial eye infection that may leave people blind after suffering repeated infections (Water Related Diseases 2015). A study conducted in Tanzania found that children are unable to clean their faces, putting themselves at risk for trachoma, when (1) water sources are located too far from their homes and (2) they fear wasting the water they do have on something seemingly trivial (McCauley et al. 1990, 1236). Children miss school because they are home sick with trachoma or they come to school and spread the disease to their classmates. They may later develop blindness after recurrent infections, another barrier to learning.

Less than half of all schools in eastern and southern Africa have sufficient water supplies or sanitation facilities, further highlighting the severity of the global water crisis (Water, Sanitation and Hygiene 2015). It is not uncommon for students without access to soap and water to simply wipe their hands on the walls of the school latrines to clean themselves (Freeman, et al. 2015, 8). This practice exposes other students to additional pathogens, putting them at risk for illnesses that may keep them out sick from school (Freeman et al. 2015, 8). Research has also found that the dirtier a school bathroom is, the less likely a student is to use it (Dreibelbis et al. 2013, 463). Some scientists postulate that some children avoid going to school altogether because the bathrooms, if the school even has them, are too dirty to use (Dreibelbis et al. 2013, 463).

The global water crisis has a particularly harsh impact on African girls and their educations. In several African countries, such as Zambia, Lesotho, Malawi, Kenya, Mozambique, and Ethiopia, 25 percent of the population spends more than 30 minutes walking to collect water (Gender and Water, Sanitation and Hygiene [WASH] 2015). In these nations, people generally consider collecting water to be a woman's chore (Dreibelbis et al. 2013, 463). Girls are absent from school more than boys, likely because their lengthy water-gathering tasks cause them to miss school (Dreibelbis et al. 2013, 463). If impoverished African communities had running tap water in each home, girls would be able to stay in school rather than being compelled to complete domestic chores.

When girls enter adolescence, they confront another barrier to continuing their education. Schools often lack proper bathrooms or do not have enough bathrooms to split them by gender (Water, Sanitation, and Hygiene 2015). When girls begin menstruating, their schools do not have the facilities necessary that allow them to care for themselves with the privacy they require (Water, Sanitation, and Hygiene 2015). When girls are confronted with this embarrassing dilemma, they often skip school or drop out completely.

Providing impoverished communities across Africa with safe water systems will enable children to stay in school and better their futures. The dilemma is not that solutions are lacking; knowledge of what constitutes a strong water system and waterborne disease prevention exists. So what does the world still have to learn about resolving the global water crisis? Financing and implementing these solutions remain the greatest challenges to promoting universal access to secure, clean water. The global water crisis must be addressed to ensure every individual's right to education and health.

References

Dreibelbis, R., et al. 2013. "Water, Sanitation, and Primary School Attendance: A Multi-Level Assessment of Determinants of Household-Reported Absence in Kenya."

International Journal of Educational Development. 33(5): 457–465.

Freeman, M, et al. 2015. "Associations between School- and Household-Level Water, Sanitation and Hygiene Conditions and Soil-Transmitted Helminth Infection among Kenyan School Children." *Parasites & Vectors.* 8(412): 1–13.

"Gender and Water, Sanitation and Hygiene (WASH)." 2015. UNICEF. http://www.unicef.org/esaro/7310_Gender_and_WASH.html. Accessed on October 6, 2015.

McCauley, A., et al. 1990. "Changing Water-Use Patterns in a Water-Poor Area: Lessons for a Trachoma Intervention Project." *Social Science & Medicine.* 31(11): 1233–1238.

Midzi, N, et al. 2011. "Knowledge, Attitudes and Practices of Grade Three Primary Schoolchildren in Relation to Schistosomiasis, Soil Transmitted Helminthiasis and Malaria in Zimbabwe." *BMC Infectious Diseases.* 11(169): 1–10.

"Water Related Diseases." 2015. WHO. http://www.who.int/water_sanitation_health/diseases/trachoma/en/. Accessed on October 6, 2015.

"Water, Sanitation and Hygiene." 2015. UNICEF. http://www.unicef.org/esaro/5479_water_sanitation_hygiene.html. Accessed on October 1, 2015.

Emily Myers earned her BA in anthropology, with minors in Spanish and public health, from the University of Minnesota. Presently, she studies global health at Emory University for her MPH in Atlanta, Georgia. She looks forward to combining her passions for writing and traveling with her goal of enhancing health globally as a future public health professional.

A Water Riot
Katherine Ann Stanfill

The Millennium Development Goals written by the United Nations set clear goals for the world to strive toward in addressing the need for sustainable access to safe drinking water and basic sanitation (Goal 7: Ensure Environmental Sustainability 2015). In the Dominican Republic, progress has been made, yet overall, the numbers remain poor. "In 2009, 48.1% of tested public water supply sources had measurable amounts of fecal coliforms" (Dominican Republic Poverty Assessment 2006). In addition, there are great disparities between the public water supplies dependent upon geographic location. There is broad progress in coverage throughout the country, but deficiencies in water supply and sanitations services remain for poor underserved populations (Health in the Americas 2012 Edition 2012). The southern region of the Dominican Republic near the Haitian border is home to a population that is vulnerable to the poor health outcomes associated with a lack of access to an improved water source. This community has become the focus of a nongovernmental organization (NGO) that I had the privilege of working with during the summer of 2015.

The organization installs water systems in schools and provides educational programming to the children. Complete with a local staff and commitment to long-term sustainability, the nonprofit is well on their way to challenge the current state of water crisis within the country.

In each of the local communities where the nonprofit works, there is a water supply piped in by the local government. This infrastructure of pipes extends into most homes where there is a faucet. As noted earlier, however, this water is often not safe to drink. The country's water infrastructure could obviously still use some work. This gap is common in countries where nonprofits find their role, such as the one I was working with for the summer.

One day, as we were heading to a rural community to run educational programming, our schedule quickly deviated from the typical. We arrived at the school, but as soon as our pickup truck was parked within the school's gate, there was a frisky shuffle of people, the unquestionable sense that something was not right. I quickly went to the upper deck of the building and from there had a safe vantage point for observation. I had a clear view of the one paved road that passes through this town, a highway of sorts that is the only means of transportation connecting to other neighboring communities. A group of locals had pulled large trees across the pavement, making it physically impossible for any vehicles to pass through. Our truck had been the last vehicle to have proceeded. Quickly, the protesting locals put out tires and set them on fire, causing a smoke screen. They also scattered large rocks to further discourage any efforts to skirt around the blockades. Teenage boys seemed to make up the predominant component of the crowd. Interestingly enough, and to my bewilderment, an elderly woman with a cart of fruit slowly and nonchalantly meandered through the area of disturbance, with no one paying the slightest amount of attention. She was safe, as there was nothing that the protestors wanted from her. Others from the community were intrigued, some finding further off vantage points like myself, others getting closer to the action. Other than a few bottles being thrown and shouting, hardly anyone wanted to confront these teenage boys, who now each had machetes in their hands, T-shirts wrapped around their heads, leaving only their eyes to be seen, and anger brimming out of their actions.

Some contextual elements help one comprehend the odd situation. This community's water system, which was supposed to be the government's responsibility, had not been operational for several days. A broken main community pipe combined with the current drought meant that there was no water coming through the government's pipes, and there was no water in the street canals. A lack of attention on the government's part and the lack of expertise to fix it within the community led to the problems. Even the nonprofit's water systems were dependent upon the community waters being piped in for filtration. A couple of days without water leaves people desperate. Cooking, bathing, sanitation, hydration are all immediate concerns when there is no water. Systemically, over time, the lack of water affects education, ability to work, and interpersonal relationships. The seriousness of this community's situation compounded over the course of about a week, leading the protestors to take desperate actions to get their water back. Unfortunately, these communities have learned that their problems will be addressed only if they make their concerns known to the right people. And so that means that protestors stage a riot, for as long as necessary, until one of the cars coming down the highway happens to be someone of enough importance. They are waiting for the kind of person that has the ability to take action toward fixing the community's water problems and bring an end to the riot. In the meantime, everyone else had no choice but to sit and watch.

Water crises such as the one described here are affecting daily lives in the Dominican Republic as it affected mine that day. Our team got safely back to the office at the end of the day after an extra two hours of driving to circumvent the riot. At the weekly staff meeting, discussions revealed that nothing would be said or done about the riot we observed. Any comments made had the potential to lead to questions by the nonprofit's board of directors in the United States, which could have led to withdrawal of funding. And so the riot went unmentioned, and with the realities not to be discussed, the severity of the crisis was swept under the rug. While it is imperative that funding continues to further efforts for new water systems and water education, not speaking on the real issues and situations at hand that the field staff face leads to the lack of acknowledgment of the depths of the global water crisis. The broken system shall remain.

References

"Dominican Republic Poverty Assessment: Achieving More Pro-Poor Growth." 2006. Report no. 32422-DO. World Bank. http://www-wds.worldbank.org/external/default/ WDSContentServer/WDSP/IB/2006/11/30/000090341_ 20061130091611/Rendered/PDF/32422.pdf. Accessed on October 16, 2015.

"Goal 7: Ensure Environmental Sustainability." 2015. Millennium Development Goals and Beyond. http:// www.un.org/millenniumgoals/environ.shtml. Accessed on October 15, 2015.

"Health in the Americas 2012 Edition: Country Volume, Dominican Republic." 2012. Pan American Health Organization. http://www.paho.org/Saludenlasamericas/ index.php?option=com_docman&task=doc_view& gid=127&Itemid=. Accessed on October 16, 2015.

Katherine Ann Stanfill is completing her Master of Public Health at Emory University in Atlanta. Originally from Ohio, she completed her undergraduate degree in biomedical science and Spanish at The Ohio State University. Driven by her faith, she is passionate about working toward improving international health care from a scientific approach.

Rural Water Supply Challenges in Developing Countries
Ivanna Tan

There has been significant progress in enabling sustainable access to safe drinking water and basic sanitation for the world's population since the Millennium Development Goals were established in 2000. However, there are regional and urban–rural disparities, with rural coverage in developing countries lagging significantly behind. According to the WHO/UNICEF Joint Monitoring Programme 2015 report, of those still without access to improved drinking water sources, 80 percent live in rural areas, and the majority of them are from sub-Saharan Africa and the developing economies of Asia (World Health Organisation 2015).

One of the key drivers of this situation is poverty. Extreme poverty is concentrated in developing countries and is still a largely rural phenomenon, where the rural poor often live in sparsely populated remote areas and fragile contexts. Hence, rural populations are able to afford only small sums for improved water provision and cannot pay for full water utility cost recovery due to the large proportion of poor households in rural areas. Additionally, developing countries have limited public funds to enable water infrastructure coverage and usage subsidies for the very poor.

Rural areas also tend to suffer from a lack of other basic services such as transport infrastructure and electricity, increasing the difficulty of water infrastructure and service delivery as well as reducing potential economies of scale of centralized water systems. This results in significantly higher capital and recurring costs that further strain available financial resources.

To ensure communities are able to obtain sufficient and affordable water supplies throughout the design lifetime of the infrastructure, both the physical infrastructure and the water services have to continue to function reliably and safely. It is insufficient to focus on just the short-term delivery of water facilities like wells, pumps, reservoirs, and treatment systems. The delivery of attendant water services like repairs and regular maintenance, monitoring of water usage and quality, and tariff collection are equally important.

Reports on water point failures in the past years have shown that a significant percentage of rural water systems actually fail in a short period of time (Improve International 2015), belying the rosy statistics of increased access to water for the rural poor. Breakdowns are a normal occurrence for any facility. It is when facilities are not fixed in a timely manner or cannot be repaired that communities then become adversely affected and are unable to obtain the benefits associated with the infrastructure.

Such failures can be caused by hydrological issues, where the initial water source selection was not properly conducted or when subsequent unexpected changes in the hydrology of the location lead to patchy or insufficient water supplies. Poor design and construction of the water system can also lead to premature failure of the facility. In most cases, however, failures have largely been attributed to issues with water service delivery rather than physical failure. The underlying causes of these failures—lack of financial resources (for operating expenditure), low technical capacities, and poor institutional structures—are prevalent in the rural areas of developing countries and pose significant challenges in increasing sustained rural water access.

The water infrastructure management model promoted and widely implemented by aid agencies and governments has been a community-managed one, deemed as best suited for application in rural developing country contexts. However, at the community level, low levels of education and a lack of technical knowledge often lead to communities having difficulty carrying out repair and maintenance work. Such user organizations also tend to suffer from poor investment planning that often cause the financial failure of water supply systems.

Rural water facilities that are unable to depend on user tariffs to cover maintenance and operation costs and which must instead rely on non-water tariffs and public subsidies have been shown to perform more poorly, with few instances of success. Depending on water tariff revenues, however, is not without its challenges. Tariffs rely on adoption and usage rates, which in turn are affected by whether communities, who are used to obtaining "free" water, recognize the economic value of water as well as their willingness and capacity to pay for the services. The enforcement and collection of tariffs also pose significant challenges for community organizations that are resource strapped and that lack formal recognition from local governments.

Moreover, the decentralized administrative structures that are common in most developing countries often mean that local governments do not have the technical and organizational capacities and resources to manage local water resources and infrastructure. Regulations to govern such organizations as well as legal acknowledgment of their roles and responsibilities are typically absent, and even where they exist, enforcement is weak, resulting in low accountability.

Despite these numerous challenges, sustainable rural water access in developing countries is achievable. It just needs deeper and continued community engagement, increased capacity building of both communities and local governments, and prioritization of resources by governments and increased philanthropic investments.

References

Improve International. "Statistics on Water Point Failures." https://improveinternational.wordpress.com/handy-resources/sad-stats/. Accessed on October 29, 2015.

Kanbur, R., Rhee, C., and Zhuang, J. 2014. "Inequality in Asia and the Pacific: Trends, Drivers, and Policy Implications." *Asian Development Bank e-Quarterly Research Bulletin.* 5(2).

Lockwood, H., and Smits, S., 2011. *Supporting Rural Water Supply: Moving towards a Service Delivery Approach.* Rugby, UK: Practical Action Publishing.

World Health Organisation. "Key Facts from JMP 2015 Report." http://www.who.int/water_sanitation_health/monitoring/jmp-2015-key-facts/en/. Accessed on October 28, 2015.

Ivanna Tan works at Lien AID, an international nonprofit dedicated to enabling Asia's rural poor gain sustainable access to clean water and sanitation. Her interest lies in water and land management systems, and resource reuse. She is currently pursuing her master's degree in sustainable development.

Remediation of the Buffalo River
Andrew Van Alstyne

This essay looks at the history of remediation efforts in the Buffalo River. The city of Buffalo played a central role in U.S. economic development in the 19th century. When construction of the Erie Canal was completed in 1825, Buffalo became a major shipping hub between East Coast ports and the Great Lakes. By 1900, Buffalo was the eighth-largest city in the country. Beyond shipping, Buffalo would come to play a key role in many industries, including grain, steel, lumber, and manufacturing. As population grew, the city was unable to develop adequate infrastructure to meet demand. By the 1960s, the combination of shipping, industry, and population resulted in the Buffalo River becoming one of the most polluted rivers in the United States. A 1968 government report noted that "residents who live along its backwaters have vociferously complained of the odors emanating from the river and of the heavy oil films. In places the river's surface is a boundless mosaic of color and patterns resulting from the mixture of organic dyes, steel mill and oil refinery wastes, raw sewage, and garbage" (Federal Water Pollution Control Administration 1968).

The river first received federal attention in the 1960s after a local conservationist, Stanley Spisiak, brought President Lyndon Johnson, along with other leading state and national political figures, on a boat tour of the river. In Spisiak's description of the meeting, he said, "I showed him a bucket of sludge from the Buffalo River and gave him a big spoon to stir it with . . . [President Johnson responded] 'don't worry, I'll take care of it'" (quoted in Sanders 2012). Over the course of the 20th century, there were sustained efforts to clean up the Buffalo River, most notably as part of the Great Lakes Water Quality Agreement (GLWQA) between the United States and Canada.

In 1987, the GLWQA was updated to develop a three-stage Remedial Action Plan (RAP) model as well as to include a requirement for public involvement. Stage One RAPs focused on defining impairments present in local areas of concern (AOCs). Stage Two identified the best possible course of action, and Stage Three involved documenting impairments that had been removed. Over the next decade, government officials, industry, and local citizens worked diligently to develop the RAP documents, though efforts slowed by the mid-1990s.

Through developing the Stage One and Two plans, the collaborative process between stakeholders has been widely recognized as the most successful of any U.S. AOCs. While the New York State Department of Environmental Conservation was the lead party in developing the action plans, it worked closely with citizens, industry, and local governments. In explaining the ability to work together, a citizen participant told me that it "really comes down to connecting with people. Not necessarily connecting with the agencies, but finding people you can work with and understanding their perspective, not just being antagonistic about your different beliefs" (Personal communication with author).

In the early 2000s, two federal laws, the Great Lakes Legacy Act and the Great Lakes Restoration Initiative, provided hundreds of millions of dollars for cleaning up the Great Lakes. The availability of resources and increasing political pressure to make tangible improvements led to another wave of GLWQA actions. The Buffalo AOC led the way in a new approach: citizen leadership. Unlike the earlier era, where citizens were a partner at the table, in the 2000s, citizen organizations have increasingly played a more central planning and leadership role. One of the primary reasons for this change is that state environmental agencies have faced significant budget cuts and often no longer have the staffing necessary for overseeing projects on this scale.

In Buffalo, the Buffalo Niagara Riverkeeper (originally the Friends of the Buffalo River) is now the lead party in the AOC. The organization was originally founded in 1989 by citizen participants in the RAP in order to build connections between the local community and the river. During its time in charge, Riverkeeper has expanded citizen participation, worked successfully with businesses to clean up local brownfields, and won numerous federal grants to fund major cleanup projects on the river. Its time in charge has also transformed the organization. A leader in the organization told me, "We went from an all-volunteer board with one part-time staff . . . [to now, when] our full-time paid staff now is about 15 or 16 not to mention all of the volunteers and interns and stuff" (Personal communication with author).

Beyond its success at cleaning up environmental problems like contaminated river sediments and industrial brownfields, Riverkeeper is also working to make the river a community resource. One example of this is its contribution to the development of the Inner Harbor. This project has transformed the abandoned grain elevators and brownfields at the mouth of the river into a site for concerts, outdoor movies, recreation, and economic development.

Praise for Riverkeeper's leadership is universal. A government employee captured this in our conversation: "As far as Riverkeeper taking over, it's made the whole thing a more worthwhile process" (Personal communication with author). In recent years, Riverkeeper has also become the lead party for the Niagara River AOC, hence the name change from Friends of the Buffalo River to Buffalo Niagara Riverkeeper. The organization's success has become a model for the Great Lakes as a whole, as NGOs are increasingly playing leadership roles in local remediation.

References

Federal Water Pollution Control Administration. 1968. "Lake Erie Report: A Plan for Water Pollution Control." United States Department of Interior. http://nepis.epa.gov/Exe/ ZyNET.exe/500016O5.txt?ZyActionD=ZyDocument& Client=EPA&Index=Prior%20to%201976&Docs=&Query= &Time=&EndTime=&SearchMethod=1&TocRestrict=n& Toc=&TocEntry=&QField=&QFieldYear=&QFieldMonth=& QFieldDay=&UseQField=&IntQFieldOp=0&ExtQField Op=0&XmlQuery=&File=D%3A%5CZYFILES%5CIN DEX%20DATA%5C70THRU75%5CTXT%5C00000 006%5C500016O5.txt&User=ANONYMOUS&Password= anonymous&SortMethod=h%7C-&MaximumDocuments= 1&FuzzyDegree=0&ImageQuality=r75g8/r75g8/x150y 150g16/i425&Display=p%7Cf&DefSeekPage=x&Searc hBack=ZyActionL&Back=ZyActionS&BackDesc=Resu lts%20page&MaximumPages=1&ZyEntry=1. Accessed on January 18, 2016.

Sanders, Bruce. 2012. "A Retrospective on Stanley Spisiak: A Man with a Mission." Defense Video & Imagery Distribution System. http://www.army.mil/ article/89945/A_retrospective_on_Stanley_Spisiak__a_ man_with_a_mission/. Accessed on October 19, 2015.

Andrew Van Alstyne is an assistant professor of sociology in the Department of History, Sociology & Anthropology at Southern Utah University. He earned his PhD in sociology at the University of Michigan, where he studied public participation in Great Lakes remediation programs. His current research focuses on water scarcity in southwestern Utah.

Responding to Global Changes:
The Water Quality Challenge –
Prevention, Wise Use and Abatement

www.worldwaterweek.org

WORLD WATER WEEK
WORLD WEEK
20 Years

4   Profiles

Introduction

Progress in dealing with the world's water, sanitation, and hygiene (WASH) problems is, to a large extent, the result of endless labors on the part of individuals and organizations that devote vast amounts of time, energy, and financial resources to these efforts. A complete list of such individuals and organizations is well beyond the scope of this book. But it is possible to mention a sample of those individuals and organizations who have contributed to solving at least some share of the WASH problems that humans face today.

Perry Alagappan

Alagappan was named the winner of the 2015 Stockholm Junior Water Prize for his invention of an inexpensive and effective device for removing heavy metal contaminants from industrial waste water, making it safer for use as drinking water and for other domestic purposes. The award consisted of a trip to Sweden to receive the award, a $10,000 cash award, a crystal trophy, and a $5,000 cash award for his high school to promote water research and other science, technology, engineering, and mathematics (STEM) research projects at the school.

Alagappan explained that his research arose out of a trip to India three years earlier with his parents. There he saw firsthand

Guidance in helping the world's populations understand the scope and significance of our global water crisis is often in the hands of respected experts such as Rita R. Colwell. (Bertil Ericson/AFP/Getty Images)

the results of people having to access water from rivers and streams that were already heavily contaminated with waste products from electronics production and other forms of manufacturing. Given the rapid rate of industrialization in the country, it seemed only reasonable to expect that this problem would continue to be more serious and that more and more lives would be at risk from the contaminated water.

Alagappan's device consisted essentially of a filter made of quartz wool on which were deposited carbon nanotubes. Up to 99 percent of contaminants in industrial waste water passing through these filters was removed by the filter. The device can be manufactured commercially at an approximate cost of $20 per unit, or about one-fifth the cost of the best available existing water purification device for use with heavy metals.

Alagappan had invented the device while he was still a student at Clear Lake High School, in Houston, Texas, where he later graduated as salutatorian of his class. During his senior year, Alagappan was also a guest researcher in the laboratories of Andrew Barron in the Department of Chemistry at Rice University, in Houston. A full description of Alagappan's project is available online at Water Environment Federation, http://w.weftec.org/PublicInformation/page.aspx?id=284, see "Full Paper."

Alagappan's parents are both engineers, and he has credited them with encouraging and promoting his own interest in science and research. After graduation, he planned to matriculate at Stanford University to continue his studies in science and engineering.

American Water Works Association

URL: http://www.awwa.org/

The American Water Works Association (AWWA) claims to be "the largest nonprofit, scientific and educational association dedicated to managing and treating water." Founded in 1881, the organization currently has more than 50,000 members from the United States and around the world. The organization dates its history to March 29, 1881, when a group of 22 men representing the water industry from Illinois, Indiana, Iowa, Kansas, Kentucky, and Tennessee met at Engineer's Hall on the campus of Washington University, in St. Louis, to form an association "for the exchange of information pertaining to the management of water-works, for the mutual advancement of consumers and water companies, and for the purpose of securing economy and uniformity in the operations of water-works." Those principles guiding the association for nearly a hundred years until a new constitution adopted in 1976 included a somewhat refined form of those general objectives. Today the association focuses on four major goals:

Advancing the knowledge of the design, construction, operation, water treatment and management of water utilities and developing standards for procedures, equipment and materials used by public water supply systems;

Advancing the knowledge of the problems involved in the development of resources, production and distribution of safe and adequate water supplies;

Educating the public on the problems of water supply and promoting a spirit of cooperation between consumers and suppliers in solving these problems; and

Conducting research to determine the causes of problems of providing a safe and adequate water supply and proposing solutions thereto in an effort to improve the quality and quantity of the water supply provided to the public.

At the time of its formation, there were fewer than a thousand public water supply systems operating in the United States. Today, there are more than 50,000 such systems. As the size and scope of water treatment systems has developed over more than 130 years of AWWA's existence, so has the complexity of the organization created to deal with water issues. Today, the association consists of five major levels of organization: leadership and staff, sections, councils, divisions, and committees. The leadership of the association consists of a board of directors that meets twice a year and sets general policy for the organization; executive committee that carries out board policies in the interim between board meetings; and a general staff who are responsible for the day-to-day operations of the association. The 43 AWWA sections are geographical regions that allow much of the association's business to be carried out in such a way as to meet with individual member's specific interests and concerns. The sections often correspond to state boundaries (e.g., the Michigan, Indiana, and Ohio sections), while others encompass more than one state (e.g., the Western Canada, Pacific Northwest, and Mexico sections). Each section operates under its own bylaws, elects its own officers, and meets at least once a year in conferences that range in size from a few hundred to more than 2,000 participants.

The six AWWA councils have been created by the board of directors and are designed to deal with broad, general issues with which the association is concerned, as suggested by their names, the International, Manufacturers/Associates, Public Affairs, Standards, Technical and Educational, and Water Utility councils. The eight divisions have been created to deal with specific areas of water management with which members might be particularly interested. Those divisions focus on distribution and plant operations, engineering and construction, management and leadership, small systems, water conservation, water quality and technology, water resources, and water science and research.

To some extent, much of the association's day-to-day operations takes place through more than 250 committees that deal with very specific topics in which individual members are interested. The subject of such committees ranges from organisms in water and finance, accounting, and management to source water protection and horizontal and vertical line shaft pumps to coagulation and filtration and disinfection systems. Each committee is led by a chairperson elected by committee members and is supported by a staff person from the AWWA central office. Most committees meet at least once a year at the annual meeting, but tend to conduct their business by e-mail rather than through regular face-to-face meetings.

The association sponsors a number of major conferences each year, the largest and most important of which is the annual conference attended by about 11,500 participants in 2015, 640 of whom came from 42 foreign countries. In addition to the annual conference, AWWA sponsors major meetings on specialized topics, such as (for 2016) biological treatment, membrane technology, financial management, potable refuse, sustainable water management, water infrastructure, utility managements, water loss, and water quality technology. AWWA also operates an extensive number of educational programs including ACE Online, a collection of podcasts of previous conference sessions for those who had been unable to attend the meetings themselves, webinars on a variety of specific water-related topics, and self-paced distance learning courses on topics such as introduction to the utility, basic supervision, hiring employees and rules, management responsibilities, and management styles.

The AWWA Web site is an invaluable source of basic information on a large number of topics associated with the collection, storage, and management of water resources. Some of the topics for which information is available are asset management, backflow prevention and cross connection control, climate change, cyanotoxins, desalination, drought, groundwater, how water works, small systems, source water protection, wastewater, wastewater collection systems, water conservation, and water loss control. These Web pages are available to the general public, upon registration at the AWWA Web site (http://www.awwa.org/resources-tools/water-knowledge.aspx).

AWWA has two regular publications, a scholarly journal of research and news, *Journal AWWA*, and a monthly magazine dealing with news of interest to the industry, *Opflow*. In addition, the association publishes a number of industry standard publications, manuals of practice, reports, books, digital downloads, and other publications of interest to professionals in the field and/or the general public.

John Briscoe (1948–2014)

Briscoe was an environmental engineer who was born in South Africa but spent most of his life working in a variety of water-related programs in Bangladesh, Mozambique, Brazil, the United States, and other countries. He was awarded the 2014 Stockholm Water Prize for his ability to combine "world-class research with policy implementation and practice to improve the development and management of water resources as well as access to safe drinking water and sanitation." Briscoe died at his home in Poolesville, Maryland, on November 12, 2014, only a few months after receiving the Stockholm award.

Briscoe was born on July 30, 1948, in Brakpan, South Africa. His father worked at a stock exchange, and his mother managed an orphanage and day care center. Brakpan is a gold and uranium mining town at the edge of a very arid region in South Africa. Growing up in this setting, Briscoe was later to say, gave him an especially firsthand understanding as to what it meant to live in an area where water scarcity was an everyday fact of life. After completing his secondary education, Briscoe enrolled at the University of Cape Town, from which he received his BS degree in civil engineering in 1969. He then continued his studies at Harvard University, which granted his MS and his PhD degrees in environmental engineering in 1972 and 1976, respectively.

In his curriculum vitae, Briscoe notes that he spent his life working at a variety of organizations concerned with issues of water and economic development, including a number of major universities, such as Harvard University and the University of North Carolina; a major international public health research institution (the Cholera Research Laboratory, now the International Center for Diarrheal Diseases Research); a nongovernmental organization (OXFAM); government water management agencies (South Africa and Mozambique); and the World Bank. His detailed list of jobs illustrates this diverse range of activities, which included three months working for the South African electricity company, ESCOM, on the construction of thermal power stations; three months with the John Mowlen Company, in the building of the King George Dock in Hull, England; one year as a planning engineer at the Department of Water Affairs in South Africa; one year as a research scientist at the Harvard University School of Public Health; two years as an epidemiologist at the Cholera Research Laboratory in Bangladesh; two years as a water engineer at the National Directorate of Water in Mozambique; two years as senior economist for the Brazil Department of the World Bank; five years as chief of the Water and Sanitation Division of the World Bank; and eight years as senior water advisor at the World Bank. At the time of his death, Briscoe was Gordon MacKay Professor for the Practice of Environmental Engineering and director of the Harvard Water Initiative.

Briscoe was author, coauthor, or editor of eight books, including *Water for Rural Communities: Helping People Help Themselves* (with David de Ferranti, 1988); *India's Water Economy: Bracing for a Turbulent Future* (with R.P.S. Malik, 2006); *Handbook on Water Resources Development and Management in India* (with R.P.S. Malik, eds., 2007); and *Pakistan's Water Economy: Running Dry* (with Usman Qamar, 2007). He was also the author or coauthor of 120 peer-reviewed papers and book chapters.

In addition to the Stockholm award, Briscoe received a number of other honors, including the University of Cape Town Medals in Hydraulics, Hydrology, Transportation, Highways, Soil Mechanics and Thesis; City of Cape Town Gold Medal as Best Graduating Engineering Student at the University; South African Steel Institute Award for Best Structural Design; Harvard University Clemons Herschel Prize, Grande Medalha de Inconfidencia from the government of Brazil, President's Award of the International Water Association, and Stroud Prize for Excellence in Water.

Jimmy Carter (1924–)

An important feature of many WASH programs involves the reduction or elimination of so-called neglected tropical diseases (NTDs). The term refers to a group of communicable diseases that occur primarily in tropical and subtropical countries among an estimated 1 billion people. They include conditions such as Chagas disease, dengue fever, guinea-worm disease (dracunculiasis), yaws (endemic treponematoses), leishmaniasis, leprosy (Hansen disease), river blindness (onchocerciasis), and schistosomiasis. In the late 1980s, the Carter Center, in Atlanta, Georgia, took on the task of eliminating one of these diseases, guinea-worm disease. At the time, the disease affected an estimated 3.5 million people worldwide, and little research had been done on the prevention or treatment of the condition. Thirty years later, in 2015, experts estimated that only 126 cases of guinea-worm disease remained in the world. It was on its way to being only the second communicable disease (after smallpox) to be completely eradicated from the Earth. Credit for accomplishment of this impressive feat goes primarily to the Carter Center and its founder, former U.S. president Jimmy Carter. Carter decided in the late 1980s to make guinea-worm disease a target of his organization's efforts after visiting Africa and seeing firsthand the devastation caused by the disease. For his efforts in this area, Carter was named one of the "Heroes of Water" by *Impeller* magazine in 2012.

James Earl Carter Jr. (generally known as "Jimmy") was born in Plains, Georgia, on October 1, 1924. His mother was Bessie Lillian Gordy Carter, a registered nurse, and his father was James Earl Carter Sr., a farmer and a businessman who ran a general store. In 1928, the Carters moved from Plains to the nearby town of Archery, a community consisting largely of African Americans. Although James Carter Sr. still believed in segregation of the races, he allowed his son to befriend his neighbors regardless of their skin color. Young Jimmy became an entrepreneur at a young age when he began growing peanuts on an acre of land that his father had given him. He conducted his business while attending Plains High School, from which he graduated in 1941.

After graduation, Carter matriculated at Georgia Southwestern College in nearby Americus. He regarded his time at Southwestern primarily as preparation for his real ambition, obtaining an appointment to the U.S. Naval Academy in Annapolis, Maryland. Thus, he focused on the courses at Southwestern that would allow him to qualify for the Naval Academy and not necessarily for graduation from Southwestern. Finally, in 1943, Carter obtained his appointment to the Naval Academy, from which he graduated in 1946. After receiving his commission, Carter was assigned to the battleship USS *Wyoming*, in Norfolk, Virginia. A month after receiving his assignment, he was married to Rosalynn Smith, with whom he was eventually to have four children, John, James III (Chip), Donnell, and Amy.

In 1948, Carter was accepted at the submarine officer training school at New London, Connecticut, setting the path he had decided to follow in the navy. After assignments in Honolulu and San Diego, Carter returned to New London in 1952, where he had been accepted as a member of Admiral Hyman Rickover's new nuclear submarine program. At the completion of the program, Carter was assigned to the USS *Seawolf,* one of the first U.S. nuclear submarines.

At this point in his life, Carter seemed set on a career in the U.S. Navy, with the possibility of significant advances up the career ladder. His future was interrupted, however, with the death of his father on July 23, 1953. After agonizing over his choices, Carter finally decided to resign his commission in the navy in order to return to Georgia and take up the running of his father's business. He left the navy with an honorable discharge on October 9, 1953, and returned to Plains.

For the next decade, Carter struggled with the peanut business in Plains, dealing with a variety of economic and environmental issues that nearly brought the business to bankruptcy.

As he struggled with the business, Carter also became involved with dramatic political changes occurring around him as a result of the U.S. Supreme Court's 1962 *Baker v. Carr* case, in which the court affirmed the now famous "one-man, one-vote" policy for all elections in the United States. The decision led to the opening of elections in Georgia that had previously been controlled by a handful of influential individuals. Carter decided to run for the state senate at the last moment and, when votes had been counted, appeared to have lost the race. A recount found that questionable voting had occurred and that instead of losing by 139 votes, he had actually won by 831 votes. Carter took his seat in the Georgia senate on January 14, 1963.

Carter was reelected to the state senate in 1964, but began to think of higher offices even before his second term ended. In 1966, he announced that he had decided to run for the U.S. House of Representatives, although he soon changed his mind and decided to run for governor of Georgia instead. Carter lost that election and returned to the peanut farm in Plains. But he had announced to his supporters that he would be back and, in fact, he ran for governor again in 1970, this time successfully. A month before completing his first term as governor (Georgia governors are allowed to serve only one term), Carter announced that he was running for president of the United States in the 1976 election. At the time, he was virtually unknown nationally and was thought to have no chance of success. He pursued an aggressive campaign, however, and was elected 39th president of the United States on November 2, 1976.

Carter served only one term as president, being defeated in a landslide by Ronald Reagan in 1980. He then returned to Plains, but began a second career that has involved a wide array of political and humanitarian activities, including visits to almost every part of the world to encourage fair elections and humane treatment of all groups of individuals. In 2002, Carter received the Nobel Peace Prize in recognition of his efforts "to find peaceful solutions to international conflicts, to advance democracy and human rights, and to promote economic and social development."

CH2M

CH2M received the 2015 Stockholm Industry Water Award "for developing and advancing methods to clean water, and increasing public acceptance of recycled water." The company was formed in 1946 by three graduates of Oregon State College (now Oregon State University), in Corvallis, Holly Cornell, Jim Howland, and Burke Hayes, and one of their civil engineering professors, Fred Merryfield. The name they originally chose for their business, Cornell, Howland, Hayes, and Merryfield, was later changed to the current shortened version consisting of the initials of their last names.

Initially formed to "tackle important problems with technology, creativity, and ingenuity," the firm took on a broad range of construction, consulting, design, and management problems. But it became particularly involved with water problems early in its history. For example, they were hired in 1965 to take on the task of helping to redesign the South Lake Tahoe (California) Public Utility's wastewater treatment plant. The existing plant was unable to keep up with rapid developments taking place around the lake, and its water treatment system was unable to continue providing potable water to its customers. CH2M developed new technology to solve this problem, technology that it claims "became a model for many tertiary advanced wastewater treatment facilities" that were later built in many parts of the world. (Tertiary wastewater treatment is the final phase of purification that makes water safe for domestic uses.)

Today, CH2M has expanded far beyond its modest beginnings with the capacity to take projects of virtually any size and any complexity anywhere in the world. It works with governmental agencies at all levels on construction, transportation, environmental, nuclear, energy, industrial, and water problems.

Some current examples include the construction of the new 20 Fenchurch Building on the shores of the Thames River in London; the revitalization of the Anacostia Waterfront region in the Washington, DC, area; the expansion of the Metrolinx Rapid Transit system in Toronto, Canada; and the design and planning of the Business Bay project in Dubai, United Arab Emirates. The range of capabilities the company now claims is extensive, including the design, production, operation, and maintenance of federal facilities and infrastructure; electronics manufacturing systems; commercial and industrial zones; conveyance and storage systems; bridges, tunnels, pipelines, and terminals; roads; urban development and regeneration projects; nuclear waste systems; refining plants; aviation programs; sports complexes; chemical systems; and all forms of water management, delivery, storage, and treatment systems.

As indicated by the 2015 Stockholm award, CH2M is still intimately involved in a variety of water projects. One current example was the design, construction, operation, and maintenance of the Aqua Nueva Water Reclamation Facility in Pima County, Arizona. The challenge there was to find ways of producing enough clean water in one of the most arid regions of the country to meet all of the growing needs of the county, a problem solved by the design and construction of a plant able to reclaim water that would otherwise be returned as unusable to the environment. Another water project currently under way is the Thames Tideway Tunnel being built for a distance of 25 kilometers under the city of London. The purpose of the tunnel is to collect untreated sewage discharges that are currently being dumped directly into the Thames and deliver those discharges to a new wastewater treatment plant where they will be purified for domestic use.

Today CH2M employs more than 20,000 people to serve 5,000 clients in more than 50 countries with a positive impact on more than 10,000 individual communities. The company takes special pride in its efforts to promote diversity within its ranks, with 11 network groups established to promote the special interests of groups such as women, blacks, Hispanics, those with disabilities, LGBT employees, and veterans. It claims to have redistributed $440 million to local minority-, women-, and veteran-owned businesses in the United States.

In 1991, CH2M established the CH2M Foundation (now known as the CH2MHill Foundation) with the purpose of providing support for STEM programs at the high school and college levels. In 2013, the foundation expanded its mission to include the promotion of sustainable communities and the volunteer work of CH2M employees. The foundation's three major programs currently are Engineers without Borders, whose 15,900 members work with communities to find appropriate solutions for water supply, sanitation, energy, agriculture, civil works and structures; Water for People (W4P), which is attempting to find sustainable solutions to communities without access to safe water supplies; and Bridges to Prosperity, which works to bring health care, education, and markets to communities in remote areas of the world.

Rita R. Colwell (1934–)

Rita Colwell was awarded the 2010 Stockholm Water Prize for her research on waterborne diseases and their impact on human health worldwide. As early as the 1960s, she began studying the *Vibrio cholera* bacterium, which is responsible for one of the world's most serious infectious diseases, cholera. She found that the bacterium could survive in a dormant state and be revitalized when environmental conditions became hospitable to that reawakening. The discovery meant that cholera remained a problem in areas where no outbreak was occurring and that prevention techniques were essential to prevent the bacteria from emerging from its dormant state, once more causing a resurgence of the disease. More recently, she has been particularly interested in the relationship between climate change and the spread of waterborne diseases. Her research in the Bay of Bengal, for example, has demonstrated that rising ocean temperatures have a direct and measurable effect on the number of cholera cases being reported in the region.

Rita Rossi was born in Beverly, Massachusetts, on November 23, 1934. She was the seventh of eight children born to Louis and Louise Di Palma Rossi. Her father was an Italian immigrant who had started his own construction company in Beverly, and her mother was a homemaker who was eager to have her children all receive the best possible education. After completing her primary and secondary education in Beverly, Rossi matriculated at Purdue University, from which she received her degree in bacteriology in 1956. Although she had planned to go on to medical school, she decided instead to continue her studies at Purdue in order to stay with her boyfriend of the time, Jack Colwell. She eventually married Colwell in May 1956, gaining her master's degree in genetics two years later. She then continued her studies in marine biology at the University of Washington, where she received her PhD in the field in 1961.

After receiving her doctorate, Colwell remained at Washington as research assistant professor, a post she held until 1964. She was concurrently a guest research scientist at the National Research Council of Canada, in Ottawa, from 1961 to 1963. In 1964, Colwell was offered a position as assistant professor at Georgetown University, in Washington, DC. She was promoted to associate professor and given tenure two years later, but decided to leave Georgetown in 1972 to accept an appointment as professor of microbiology at the University of Maryland at College Park. She has maintained her affiliation with Maryland ever since, currently serving as distinguished university professor of computational biology. Colwell also currently holds the titles of distinguished university professor at Johns Hopkins University Bloomberg School of Public Health, senior advisor and chairman emeritus at Canon U.S. Life Sciences, Inc., and president and CEO of CosmosID, Inc.

Throughout her academic career, Colwell has been involved in a host of governmental and nongovernmental activities involved in issues related to marine biology, waterborne diseases, and environmental issues in general. She became associated with the U.S. Environmental Protection Agency as a consultant in 1975 and continued to serve in a variety of other positions with the agency for most of the rest of her career. She has also served as the director of the Sea Grant College at Maryland (1981–1982), the director of the Center for Environmental and Estuarine Studies at Maryland (1981–1982), a member of the research advisor committee of the National Science Board (1983–1990), and the founding director and later president of the Center for Marine Biotechnology at Maryland. From 1998 to 2004, Colwell also served as the 11th director of the National Science Foundation.

Colwell's list of honors and awards is very long and includes 55 honorary doctorates from academic institutions around the world. She is also the recipient of the Order of the Rising Sun, Gold and Silver Star, from the government of Japan; the 2006 National Medal of Science; and the 2010 Stockholm Water Prize. She is the author, coauthor, and editor of 17 books, including *Oceans and Health: Pathogens in the Marine Environment* (with Shimshon Belkin, 2004; 2010); *Global Change and the Human Prospect: Issues in Population, Science, Technology and Equity* (with Thomas F. Malone, 1992); *The Door in the Dream: Conversations with Eminent Women in Science* (with Elga Wasserman, 2000); and *Vibrios in the Environment* (1984). Colwell has also published more than 700 scholarly papers in peer-reviewed publications.

Eugene Gangarosa (1926–)

Eugene Gangarosa is an authority in waterborne diseases who has been involved in WASH issues for more than a half century. During his early career, he was especially interested in the etiology of intestinal infections and, in 1959, published an important study on the causes of cholera. The results of that study led Gangarosa to become interested in methods for preventing and treating cholera, especially rehydration therapy. He is sometimes thought of as the father of the field of tropical (or environmental) enteropathy, a condition characterized by the occurrence of frequent intestinal infections, commonly caused by continual oral–fecal contact, especially in young children. In addition to his field research, Gangarosa and his wife, Rose, have been influential philanthropists in creating and promoting institutions to encourage research and education in the field of WASH programs. In the 1980s, he was involved in the creation of the Emory University School of Public Health, where he is now professor emeritus. In 2004, he was also responsible for the creation of the Center for Global Safe WASH at Emory, a joint project of Emory, the Centers for Disease Control and Prevention (CDC), the Carter Center, CARE, and the Georgia Institute of Technology. In 2005 and 2011, the Gangarosas funded two academic chairs at Emory's Rollins School of Public Health. Since 1994, the couple has also funded and led the Gangarosa International Health Foundation, for the purpose of providing access to safe water for the estimated 2 billion people worldwide who currently do not have that access.

Eugene John Gangarosa was born in Rochester, New York, on August 7, 1926. He attended the University of Rochester, from which he received his AB, MS, and MD degrees in 1950, 1955, and 1954, respectively. He completed his internship at Tripler General Hospital, in Honolulu, in 1955–1956 and his residency at the Walter Reed General Hospital, in Washington, DC, in 1957–1959. While at Walter Reed, he specialized in the study of epidemiology, training that he later continued at the Epidemic Intelligence Service of the CDC from 1964 to 1966.

Gangarosa's first academic appointment was as assistant professor of medicine and microbiology at the University of Maryland School of Medicine (1961–1964). During that period, he was also the director of the Pakistan Medical Research Center of the University of Maryland International Center for Medical

Research and Training in Lahore (1962–1964) and chief of the Epidemic Intelligence Service epidemiology program (1964). In 1965, Gangarosa began a long relationship with the CDC by accepting an appointment as chief of the Enteric Disease Branch of the Bacterial Diseases Division, a post he held until 1968. He then became director of the Bacterial Diseases Division from 1968 to 1978. Concurrently with this appointment, he also served as an adjunct professor of cellular and molecular biology at the Medical College of Georgia (1976–1978).

In 1978, Gangarosa returned to academia as dean of the faculty of health sciences and professor of public health at the American University of Beirut, where he remained until 1981. He then accepted an appointment at the Emory School of Medicine, where he served as a professor and director of the master of public health program from 1983 to 1989 and interim director of the division of public health from 1989 to 1990. In 1990, Gangarosa officially retired from his post at Emory and was named professor emeritus, a title he continues to hold.

This listing does not begin to adequately describe the variety of posts that Gangarosa has held during his long and busy career. He has, for example, been a consultant to the World Health Organization (WHO) and the World Bank, a member of the WHO expert advisory panel on bacterial diseases, consultant to the U.S. Surgeon General, medical and research consultant to the first of Pathogen Control Associates, Inc., and consultant to the U.S. Department of Agriculture foodborne disease control program.

During his academic career, Gangarosa published more than 120 peer-reviewed papers in scholarly journals, as well as 24 chapters in books on enteric and related diseases and disorders. In 1978, Gangarosa was awarded the CDC Medal of Excellence, the agency's highest award for distinguished scientific contributions. In 1980, he was appointed a fellow of the American College of Physicians and, in 1991, was recognized with the Thomas Jefferson Award, Emory's highest award, given to a faculty member who has contributed most to institutional development. He has also received the University of Rochester's Humanitarian Award, the American Public Health Association's Distinguished Lectureship award, and the Wade Hampton Frost Award.

Ros Gangarosa has had a distinguished career in education herself, as a teacher of piano and English at both secondary and college levels. She also served as principal of the Lahore American School during the period that her husband was also employed in Pakistan. She has also worked with Eugene on a variety of philanthropic projects at Emory.

Peter H. Gleick (1956–)

Gleick is one of the best known and highly respected authorities on water issues in the world today. In 1987, he cofounded with two generally unnamed "colleagues" the Pacific Institute (PI), whose complete and legal name is the Pacific Institute for Studies in Development, Environment, and Security, located in Oakland, California. Gleick is now the president of the institute. His Web page on the institute's Web site credits Gleick with refocusing the topic of water from one restricted largely "from the realm of engineers to the world of social justice, sustainability, human rights, and integrated thinking." The same site credits Gleick with producing the first analysis of climate change on water resources, some of the earliest research on water-based conflicts, and defining the basic needs of humans for water and the right of humans to have access to water. In 2003, Gleick was awarded one of the prestigious MacArthur fellowships for his work in the field of water issues.

Peter Henry Gleick was born in New York City on December 24, 1956, to Donen and Beth Gleick. His father was an attorney and his mother, the author of children's books. He attended public school in Manhattan, but experienced a fascination early in his life for the natural world, which was not necessarily on display in the urbanized New York City area. He spent much of his free time as a boy and young man walking through Central Park, visiting Nantucket Island with his parents, and attending science camp in northern Michigan as a teenager. His first specific interest in water issues appears to have been encouraged when he was 16 and attended a National Science Foundation summer program at the University of Southern California. His lifelong interest in the environment seemed already predetermined during these early years.

Gleick matriculated at Yale University in the fall of 1974, where he pursued a degree in engineering and applied science. After earning his BS in that field in 1978, he enrolled at the University of California at Berkeley, from which he received his MS and PhD degrees in energy and resources in 1980 and 1986 respectively. While still studying at California, he held a number of jobs in the field of environmental science, including deputy assistant to the governor of California in the state's Energy and Environment Office, research associate in the Energy and Resources Group at the University of California, and research and teaching associate at the University of California and the Lawrence Berkeley Laboratory. Shortly after receiving his doctorate, he cofounded the PI, with whom he has been associated ever since.

Gleick is the author, coauthor, and editor of 10 books, including *Water in Crisis: A Guide to the World's Fresh Water Resources*, *Bottled and Sold: The Story Behind Our Obsession with Bottled Water*, and *A 21st Century U.S. Water Policy*. He has also been involved in the production of the biennial report on freshwater resources, *The World's Water*. He is also the author or coauthor of more than a hundred journal articles, peer-reviewed reports, book chapters, and other professional publications.

In addition to his MacArthur fellowship, Gleick has been honored with one of the 2007 Top Environmental Achievement Awards of the Environment Now Foundation, the 2008 "Benny" award of the Business Network Ethics group of South

Africa, the United States Water Prize of 2011, the 2011 Ven Te Chow award of the International Water Resources Association, an award as a "Water Hero" for 2012 by the Xylem Corporation, and the first Lifetime Achievement Award of the Silicon Valley Conservation association for 2013.

Gleick's list of public and professional service positions covers more than a page of his curriculum vitae and includes posts such as member of the editorial boards of the publications *Global Change and Human Health*, *Encyclopedia of Global Change*, *Encyclopedia of Life Support Systems*, *Environment and Security*, *Water Policy*, *Climatic Change*, and *Environmental Research Letters*; member of the board of directors of the Environmental Science and Policy Institute, International Water Resources Association, Middle East Water Information Network, and Blue Planet Network; and member of a number of other organizations, such as the American Association for the Advancement of Science Atmospheric and Hydrospheric Sciences Section, California Energy Commission Public Interest Energy Research project, the Gulbenkian Foundation Think Tank on Water and the Future of Mankind, and American Geophysical Union Hydrology Section Water and Society Technical Committee.

In 2012, Gleick was accused of being involved with documents originating with the Heartland Institute, an organization that has raised doubts about climate change in the past. He left office briefly while this claim was being investigated and returned to office after he was cleared of any wrongdoing by an independent investigator. (See "Climate Scientist Peter Gleick Admits He Leaked Heartland Institute Documents, http://www.theguardian.com/environment/2012/feb/21/peter-gleick-admits-leaked-heartland-institute-documents and "Peter Gleick Reinstated after Investigation into Heartland Papers, http://articles.latimes.com/2012/jun/07/local/la-me-gs-peter-gleick-reinstated-after-admitting-obtaining-heartland-papers-20120607, both accessed on September 28, 2015.)

Global Water Partnership

URL: http://www.gwp.org/en/

Global Water Partnership (GWP) was founded in 1996 by a consortium consisting of the World Bank, the United Nations Development Programme, and the Swedish International Development Cooperation Agency. The impetus behind the creation of GWP dates to the 1992 International Conference on Water and the Environment, held in Dublin, which completed its sessions with the adoption of a document, the Dublin Statement on Water and Sustainable Development, which set forth the principles by which water programs should be developed in order to make available a sustainable and accessible source of water for the world's population. Plans for the development of an international water management agency progressed over the next four years, especially at the United Nations Conference on Environment and Development, held in Rio de Janeiro, in that year. GWP finally became a reality at an August meeting of the principals in Stockholm and a second meeting of the technical committee in Windhoek, Namibia, in November.

The theoretical principle on which the work of GWP is based is called Integrated Water Resources Management (IWRM), a working principle that was developed over a number of years during the early stages of the organization's development. It can be defined as a process that involves the development of land, water, and other resources in such a way as to "maximise economic and social welfare in an equitable manner without compromising the sustainability of vital ecosystems." IWRM is, therefore, a holistic approach to water management that takes account of not only the need for economic development and the best interests of human welfare, but also the continued survival of the natural environment.

Participation in GWP is open to all organizations that accept the general principles embodied in IWRM. As of late 2015, the organization had established 13 regional partnerships, 85 country partnerships, and 3,051 individual partnerships located in 178 countries. The distribution of these partnerships was as follows: Caribbean (22 nations, 92 individuals); Central Africa (6, 164); Central America (7, 184), Central and Eastern Europe (12, 161), Central Asia and Caucasus (9, 161), China (1, 100), Eastern Africa (10, 211), Mediterranean (25, 86), South America (10, 303), South Asia (7, 530), Southeast Asia (10, 249), Southern Africa (12, 323), and West Africa (15, 274). The most common individual partnerships were those with nongovernmental organizations and area networks (37% of all individual partnerships) and governmental or other types of public organizations (26%), followed by research and educational institutions (16%), private sector companies (13%), professional organizations (3%), international organizations (2%), and other types of organizations (3%).

GWP takes a number of approaches in attempting to achieve its general objectives. It is, first of all, an advocacy agency that attempts to inform governmental agencies and other decision-making groups of the nature of water problems the world is facing and the ways in which nations and communities can deal with those problems. GWP also acts as a coordinating agency that brings together stakeholders involved in the resolution of specific water management problems in a given area. The organization also provides access to such group to the technical resources that are available for dealing with a variety of water management issues. Some examples of the type of projects carried out by GWP are the following:

- The nation of Botswana adopted its first Water Act in 1968, but it soon became evident that the act was inadequate for dealing with the country's serious and ongoing water shortage problems. The government eventually turned to the GWP for advice and assistance in the drafting of a new and revised water plan, which was eventually adopted in 2013. The new plan appears far more likely to help the government in dealing with its ongoing water problems.

- The severity of water and sanitation problems in Karachi, Pakistan, with a population of more than 18 million, was being recognized as early as 2000, but little progress was being made in solving these problems. In 2007, a local water partnership was established by the Hisaar Foundation, a charitable organization working for water and food security. The foundation requested assistance from GWP, which provided a model for dealing with problems similar to those faced by Karachi, along with help in setting up a coordinating committee and organizing meeting. The agency also provided some seed money for initial projects in meeting the city's water and sanitation needs. These efforts eventually resulted in the formation of partnerships that are realizing some success in attacking the city's water and sanitation issues.

- Growing concerns over climate change has led to the creation of a number of programs designed to ensure sustainability of water supplies in regions especially at risk for reduction in water resources. In 2011, GWP became part of an effort to assess and develop water resources at risk from climate change in the Lake Cyohoha catchment area between Burundi and Rwanda. GWP's involvement included the identification of structural problems that were inhibiting the cooperative development of water resources, as well as identifying and coordinating the many groups with interest in resolving the climate change water issues in the region.

- As in many arid regions, water use issues have existed for generations in the Zarafshan River basin region of Uzbekistan. Such issues have become more serious only in recent years, and local officials finally decided to form a partnership with GWP to find ways of dealing with these issues more efficiently. They sought assistance from the organization in development programs to educate residents of the area of the importance of water management, to develop technical expertise in improving water management programs, and to plan for future developments to improve the resiliency of water resources from the Zarafshan.

An especially useful feature of the GWP Web site is its Tool Box section, which contains a number of suggestions ("tools") that can be used in solving water management issues, case studies showing how such tools have been used in the past, a summary of the critical challenges faced in the area of water management worldwide, and some issues that cut across specific water management problems, such as gender, youth, and financing. The Web page also contains an excellent collection of relevant publications.

Groundwater Foundation

The mission of the Groundwater Foundation is to educate the general public so as to ensure a sustainable supply of pure groundwater for future generations. The organization was founded in 1985 by Susan S. Seacrest, a homemaker living in Nebraska's Platte Valley. A year earlier, Seacrest had read an article about the potential contamination of groundwater in the region's aquifers and wondered whether such a possibility might be related to the ongoing digestive problems being experienced by her young son. She decided to contact a researcher quoted in the article, Dr. Dennis Weisenberger, who encouraged her to learn more about groundwater issues and to consider actions she could take in support of that valuable resource. "Never one to shy from a challenge," as she wrote in her 2000 review of the foundation's history, she moved forward with her own research on groundwater, leading to her 1985 action in creating the Groundwater Foundation.

The Groundwater Foundation is a membership organization, open to all individuals interested in the goals and activities of the association. Membership dues account for only 5 percent of the organization's income; however, the remainder coming from grants (56% of all income in 2013), supporters and contributions (32%), and other sources (7%). Among its current sponsors and supporters, the foundation lists the U.S. Geological Survey, the Nebraska Department of Environmental Quality, the Nebraska Environmental Trust, Archer Daniel Midlands, the Aspegren Foundation, The Cooper Foundation, Disneyland, ExxonMobil, Nebraska Public Power District, Olsson Associates, Teledyne Isco, Valley Irrigation, and the Valmont Foundation.

The foundation has also developed a working relationship with a number of groups through programs designed to carry out its educational mission. In addition to a number of sponsors and supporters, the list of partners includes groups such as 1 percent for the Planet, Community Services Fund, Girl Scouts Spirit of Nebraska, Marshfield Utilities, National Ground Water Association, Nebraska Pharmacists Association, Nebraska Public Power District, Nonprofit Association of the Midlands, Science Olympiad, Senninger Irrigation, Southern Nevada Water Authority, the U.S. Environmental Protection Agency, and the U.S. EPA Water Sense program.

The Groundwater Foundation sponsors a wide variety of events for individuals and communities, with the goal of promoting better understanding of groundwater issues. Some examples include:

- Science Olympiad events, in which Olympiad participants select a project related to groundwater issues suggested by the foundation that they can submit for their project.

- The Girl Scouts' "Let's Keep It Clean" program, in which members of the Girl Scouts can complete groundwater projects, through which they can earn a variety of uniform patches.

- Groundwater Guardian, a program through which the foundation recognizes communities of all types for local groundwater education and protection activities, and provides tools, resources, and motivation.

- Groundwater Guardian Green Sites, which focuses on green spaces, such as golf courses, parks, educational and business campuses, for implementing groundwater-friendly practices as part of site maintenance.
- Nebraska Wellhead Protection Network, a foundation-managed program that brings together agencies and organizations that help communities develop and implement plans for the protection of wellhead installations in Nebraska.
- Growing Groundwater Awareness, a project in which the foundation works with individual communities to develop programs to educate their citizens about groundwater issues and work toward the implementation of sustainable groundwater use. Examples of successful programs are available on the foundation's Web site.
- National Conference, a biennial meeting that brings together supporters, partners, members, constituents, and the general public to learn and share groundwater education and protection experiences.

The foundation produces two regular newsletters, "The Aquifer," a quarterly publication that contains current groundwater news, along with news about foundation events, programs, project, and other information; and "Recharge Report," a bimonthly electronic newsletter that also features water news and news about foundation affairs. Of special interest to those interested in groundwater issues are two sections on the organization's Web site providing useful information on such topics, "Get Informed" and "Kids' Corner."

Thomas Hawksley (1807–1893)

Hawksley was widely regarded during the second half of the 19th century as one of the two most eminent water engineers in the world. He was credited with the invention of a number of devices for the control of water storage and management, as well as the design of water distribution systems for most of the major cities of England after about 1850. A recent biography of Hawksley in *Water World* magazine called him "one of the greatest 19th-century water engineers," although the same article bemoans the fact that he is "virtually forgotten" by water engineers and historians today.

Thomas Hawksley was born on July 12, 1807, in Arnold, Nottinghamshire, England, to John and Mary (Whittle) Hawksley. He attended Nottingham Grammar School until the age of 15, at which time he was articled (became an apprentice) to Edward Stavely, an architect and surveyor in Nottingham. At the completion of his apprenticeship, Hawksley himself became a partner in Stavely's firm, then to become known as Stavely, Hawksley, and Jolland. The firm specialized in water projects, although they also took on a number of jobs involving the construction and installation of gas supply projects.

In addition to operating his own business at Stavely, Hawksley, and Jolland, Hawksley was employed by the Trent Waterworks Company, which was responsible for supplying water to his hometown of Nottingham. (The company was later reorganized as the Nottingham Waterworks Company.) His first assignment with Trent was the construction of an additional water supply system for the delivery of water to Nottingham, a task he undertook at the age of 23.

A major focus of much of Hawksley's early work was the design of systems that could keep the water it delivered pure from contamination that would result in the spread of contagious diseases such as cholera. He was faced with that problem early on in his career when cholera struck his hometown of Nottingham in 1832, apparently at least partly as a result of water pipes that were unable to keep out the organisms causing the disease. In attempting to deal with this problem, Hawksley designed a number of system components that fit more tightly and that could be used more easily so as to make the system completely watertight and impenetrable to cholera and other disease-causing organisms. He was so successful in these efforts that his systems were widely recognized as being responsible for saving very large numbers of lives in England during a major outbreak of cholera in 1848–1849. By that time, he had been responsible for the design and installation of water systems in most of England's major cities and towns, including Liverpool, Sheffield, Leicester, Lincoln, Leeds, Derby, Darlington, Oxford, Cambridge, Sunderland, Wakefield, and Northampton. In addition to water delivery system, Hawksley became involved in the construction of dams and reservoirs in which community water supplies were collected and store. He was also involved with the construction of sewage and drainage systems in a number of cities and towns, although not to the extent of his work with water systems.

By some accounts, Hawksley's most notable invention was a water tap that could seal a pipe tightly with a simple turn of the handle. The device superseded an earlier model of tap in which the handle was turned only a quarter turn, failing to produce the tight seal needed to protect the system from contamination. Hawksley's device was at first regarded as unworkable because of the mechanical constraints it placed on the system. He was able to work through these constraints, however, eventually producing a product that many people in the world take as a given without a second thought, a reliable flow of pure water at a simple turn of a tap.

Hawksley was also involved with the design and construction of natural gas delivery systems and served as an engineer for the Nottingham Gas Light and Coke Company simultaneously with his work at the Nottingham Waterworks Company for a period of more than 50 years. Later in life, he also served as the first president of the Institution of Gas Engineers and Managers from 1863 to 1866. He was also elected president of the Institution of Civil Engineers from 1872 to 1873. The English Institution of Mechanical Engineers still holds an annual lecture, the Thomas Hawksley Lecture, and awards an annual gold medal in his honor.

Hawksley died at his home in Kensington, London, on September 23, 1893. He was the progenitor of a family that would remain affiliated with water projects for many generations. His son, Charles Hawksley (1839–1917), grandson Kenneth Phipson Hawksley (1869–1924), and great grandson, Thomas Edwin Hawksley (1897–1972), all became notable water engineers in their own right.

Michael R. Hoffmann (1946–)

Hoffmann was awarded a $400,000 grant in 2011 by the Bill and Melinda Gates Foundation for research on a self-contained, solar-powered toilet that can be used by communities that currently have no access to any other type of toilet facilities. Hoffmann's toilet looks not that different from the portable toilets that are seen at construction sites, outdoor festivals, and other settings, but it operates on a very different principle. The toilet is powered by a photovoltaic panel that provides the energy needed to break down water and waste products produced in the toilet to hydrogen gas and other products. The hydrogen gas is then stored in hydrogen fuel cells that can be used to produce energy on demand, as during the evening when there is no sunlight. Hoffmann predicts that a single such toilet would be able to serve about 500 people per day. Test toilets currently cost about $2,000 each, but that cost can be significantly reduced when the toilets are produced in volume, one goal of the Gates grant.

Michael Robert Hoffmann was born in Fond du Lac, Wisconsin, on November 13, 1946. He attended Northwestern University, from which he received his BA in 1968, and Brown University, where he earned his PhD in 1974. He completed his postdoctoral studies in environmental engineering at the California Institute of Technology (Caltech) from 1973 to 1975. At the completion of his postdoctoral studies, Hoffmann accepted an appointment as assistant professor of civil and mining engineering at the University of Minnesota, where he was promoted to associate professor in 1978. In 1980, Hoffmann was invited to return to Caltech and become associate professor of environmental science and engineering. He has remained at Caltech ever since, gaining promotion to full professor in 1986 and then being named James Irvine Professor of Environmental Science in 1996, a title he continues to hold. Hoffmann also served as dean of graduate studies at Caltech from 2002 to 2008.

Hoffmann's research has covered a wide range of topics in chemistry during his academic career, including atmospheric chemistry, chemical kinetics, catalytic oxidation and reduction, photochemistry, photocatalysis, nanotechnology, sonochemistry, photo-electrochemistry, pulsed-power plasma chemistry, environmental water chemistry, and microbiology. He has long been interested also in the practical applications of his research in real-life situations where people's health and lives depend on improving their access to safe water and sanitation systems. His invention of the solar-powered toilet is the most recent result of this line of research.

Hoffmann is the author or coauthor of more than 300 peer-reviewed publications and the holder of seven patents based on his research. His honors include an NCAA Athletic Scholarship in track and field (1964–1968), the Alexander von Humboldt Prize (1991), E. Gordon Young Creative Advances Award (1995), ACS Creative Advances in Environmental Science and Technology Award (2001), Jack Edward McKee Medal of the Water Environment Federation (2003), and Alexander von Humboldt Foundation Senior Scientist Award (2004). He has also held a number of honorary teaching and research positions, such as the Lady Davis Distinguished Lecturer at Hebrew University in Jerusalem (1996), Davis Distinguished Lecturer at the University of New Orleans (2001), Dodge Distinguished Lecturer at Yale University (2002), Johnston Distinguished Lecturer at the University of California at Berkeley (2003), R. Gordon Distinguished Lecturer at the University of Toronto

(2003), Distinguished Visiting Scholar at Tsinghua University, Beijing (2008), Innolec Lecturer at Masaryk University, Brno, Czech Republic (2008), Distinguished Lecturer at National Taiwan University, Taiwan (2008), Erudite Distinguished Scholar, State of Kerala, India (2010), and Distinguished Visiting Chair Professor, National Taiwan University, Taipei (2010). Hoffmann has been elected a fellow of the International Union of Pure and Applied Chemistry (2000) and a member of the National Academy of Engineering (2011).

International Water Resources Association

The International Water Resources Association (IWRA) is a non-profit, non-governmental network of experts from a variety of fields who are interested in all aspects of water resource issues. The organization was created in 1971 largely through the efforts of Chinese American hydraulic engineer Ven Te Chow, then professor of civil and hydrosystems engineering at the University of Illinois. At the time of its origin, IWRA had 195 individual members, two corporate members, and five institutional members.

A major factor in the formation of IWRA was planning then in progress for the First World Water Conference, "Water for the Human Environment," scheduled to be held in Chicago. The conference was a huge success, with attendees from 62 countries offering 175 papers on many aspects of the conference topic. Professor Chow was elected president of the association and served in that post until 1979. The first publication produced by IWRA was a newsletter called "Water International." In 1975, that publication was reconstituted as a professional journal with the same name. Professor Chow also served as the first editor-in-chief of the journal.

Throughout its history, the primary activity of IWRA has been the World Water Congress, held (usually) every three years in a different location. The 15th World Water Congress was held in Edinburgh, Scotland, on May 25–29, 2015, and the 16th congress is scheduled to be held in Cancun, Mexico, from May 29 to June 2, 2017. Over the years, the organization has continued to expand the number and variety of its activities.

Early on in its history, IWRA took steps to emphasize the international character of its mission. It established so-called geographic committees, whose goal it was (and is) to focus on water-related issues of special concern to specific countries or regions. Currently, four such committees are in existence, committees for China, India, Japan, and Oceania. The association also began outreach campaigns to and programs with a number of nongovernmental organizations, such as The World Bank, the International Development Bank, the WHO, the Organization of American States, and the United Nations Environment Programme.

Another step forward occurred in 1994 with the formation of the World Water Council (WWC). This organization was created at the suggestion put forward by leaders of a number of disparate national, regional, and international water organizations as a way to "unite the disparate, fragmented, and ineffectual efforts in global water management," according to the IWRA Web site. The founding committee of the council held its first meeting a year later, marking the origin of a major international advocate for water policy worldwide.

IWRA sponsors no events other than the World Water Congress and produces only one other publication, a newsletter, "IWRA Update." The association does offer a number of awards annually, Crystal Drop Award for individuals or organizations that have made laudable contributions to the improvement of the world's water situation; the Ven Te Chow Memorial Award and Lecture, in honor of the association's first president; the IWRA Distinguished Lecture Award; the Water International Best Paper Award, based on "originality, innovation, technical quality, and contribution to water resources management"; the Award for Excellence in Water Resources Management, which recognizes regional, national, or local institutions that have exhibited sustained excellence in water resources management; and the Young IWRA Member Scholarship Award, which recognizes a member under the age of 33 for an outstanding contribution to the management of water resources.

John L. Leal (1858–1914)

Leal was an American physician who is credited with being the first individual to recommend the use of chlorine for the large-scale purification of a municipal water treatment facility.

During the late 19th century, the city of Jersey City, New Jersey, like many urban areas at the time, experienced a number of widespread occurrences of waterborne diseases, such as typhoid fever and diarrhea, which resulted in hundreds or thousands of deaths and hospitalizations. In an effort to deal with this problem, the city contracted with Jersey City Water Supply Company to construct a new facility to provide safe and pure water to the municipality. After the new plant had been built, it was discovered that the plant failed at certain times of the year, such as on days following major storms. On those occasions, the water passing out of the plant was contaminated with bacteria and other disease-causing agents. As a consequence of this defect, the city sued the water company, refusing to pay the cost of construction.

Called in as an expert witness by the water company, Leal suggested a simple "fix" for the problem. He proposed adding water solutions of chloride of lime (calcium hypochlorite; $Ca(ClO)_2$) to water passing through the plant as a way of killing bacteria and producing safe and pure water. Leal based his suggestion on a procedure he had long practiced as health officer in Paterson, New Jersey. The city approved Leal's suggestion, and a model plant was built to test the chlorination hypothesis. The plant worked as Leal had predicted, the city dropped its suit against the water company, and chlorination as a way of purifying water spread rapidly across the country over the next decade.

John Laing Leal was born in Andes, New York, on May 5, 1858. Leal's father was John Rose Leal, a physician who served in the Civil War. During the siege of Charleston (South Carolina) Harbor in 1863, Leal became seriously ill, probably with amoebic dysentery, caused by drinking contaminated water. The senior Leal suffered from the condition over the next 19 years, and his death was probably a result of the disease.

When Leal was nine years old, his family moved to Paterson, where Leal was to spend the rest of his life. He attended the Paterson Seminary before matriculating at Princeton College (now Princeton University) in 1876. He earned his BA and MA degrees from Princeton in 1880 and 1883 respectively. Leal then continued his studies at the Columbia College of Physicians and Surgeons, where he received his MD degree in 1884.

After completing his studies at Columbia, Leal returned to Paterson to open a private practice. This phase of his life did not last very long as he accepted an appointment as city physician for Paterson only two years later, in 1886. He continued his affiliation with the city of Paterson for the rest of his life, serving as health inspector in 1891 and health officer from 1892 to 1899, when he became an advisor to the East Jersey Water Company. In 1911, toward the end of his life, Leal was invited to return to public service as president of the Paterson Board of Health, a post he held until his death at the age of 56 on March 13, 1914, in Paterson.

In 2013, the board of directors of the AWWA voted to establish a new award in Leal's honor. The award is now given annually to an individual or organization that has made "a notable and outstanding public health contribution to the water profession."

Sidney Loeb (1917–2008)

Loeb is generally credited with developing (along with Canadian researcher Srinivasa Sourirajan) the process of reverse osmosis of seawater, currently the most popular industrial method of desalination. Reverse osmosis is a process by which pressure is applied to seawater, forcing it through a semipermeable membrane in order to remove particles of materials (such as ions of sodium, potassium, calcium, and chlorine) that make the water unsuitable for human consumption. The process is referred to as *reverse* osmosis since it acts against the normal process of osmosis that occurs when solutions of two different concentrations are placed on opposite sides of a semipermeable membrane. Loeb and Sourirajan's research resulted in the rapid development not only of a new and effective method of water desalination, but also of a technology that had a host of other applications, as in the beverage, food, drug, chemical, and biochemical industries.

Sidney Loeb was born in Kansas City, Missouri, on May 13, 1917. His family moved to Chicago when he was only two years of age, a city where he was to spend his early years. After completing his primary and secondary education, he enrolled at the University of Illinois, from which he received his BS degree in chemical engineering in 1941. He then moved to Los Angeles, where he spent 20 years working in the fields of petrochemicals, rocket motors, and nuclear reactors before deciding to return to school to continue his education. To do so, he entered at the University of California at Los Angeles, where he earned his MS and PhD degrees in chemical engineering in 1959 and 1964, respectively. It was during this period that he worked with fellow graduate student Sourirajan to develop the modern system of reverse osmosis with their doctoral advisor Samuel Yuster. In 1964, Loeb and Sourirajan received a patent for "High flow porous membranes for separating water from saline solutions."

A year after receiving their patent, Loeb was hired by the city of Coalinga, California, to design a small reverse osmosis desalination plant for the community. The plant went into operation in June 1965, producing 20 cubic meters of fresh drinking water per day, an insignificant amount from a practical standpoint, but an important step in validating the industrial validity of the new technology.

Shortly after his success with the Coalinga plant, Loeb was invited to build a similar facility for the Negev Institute for Arid Zone Research at Beersheba, Israel. The plant began operation in 1967, producing 200 cubic meters of potable water for the Kibbutz Yotvata community near Beersheba. Loeb then accepted an offer to remain at the Negev Institute (later to become a part of the Ben Gurion University of the Negev) to become professor of chemical engineering and to continue his research on reverse osmosis desalination, a post he held for 15 more years. During this time, Loeb continued to develop improvements in his reverse osmosis process, always motivated by his understanding and appreciation of the need to find new and more efficient ways of producing clean water in regions where that resource was not already readily available.

Loeb retired from active research and teaching in 1986. He died at his home in Omer, Israel, on December 11, 2008.

Millennium Water Alliance

The Millennium Water Alliance (MWA) is a 501(c)(3) non-profit organization whose purpose it is to find ways of delivering safe water and sanitation systems to individuals and communities who currently do not have access to such resources. The organization was formed in 2003 by a consortium of nongovernmental organizations working in the field of safe water and sanitation for developing nations. The immediate impetus for the group's creation was a public statement by then secretary of state of the United States Colin Powell's intention to "reduce by half, the proportion of people without access to safe and affordable drinking water and sanitation" by the year 2015. The goal was achieved two years early through the efforts of groups such as MWA, which then went on to focus on additional goals of safe water and sanitation for the world's poorest communities.

MWA currently consists of members, most of whom have their headquarters in the United States. They are Aguayuda, Catholic Relief Services, Global Water, IRC International Water and Sanitation Centre, Living Water International, Water.org, Water4, Water Missions, CARE, Food for the Hungry, HELVETAS Swiss, Lifewater, Pure Water, Water Aid, and W4P. Funding for MWA's programs comes from a variety of governmental, industrial, and charitable organizations, including the Coca-Cola Foundation and the Coca-Cola Foundation Africa, the Conrad N. Hilton Foundation, Global Environment and Technology Foundation, Craigslist Foundation, U.S. Department of State, P&G, U.S. Agency for International Development (USAID), and the Wallace Genetic Foundation.

MWA currently operates five major programs, each of which is funded by a specific partner or group of partners. For example, the Kenya program is designed to provide safe WASH programs for rural regions of that country and is funded primarily by the USAID. Other programs include the Ethiopia program (funded by the Hilton Foundation), Latin America program (Coca-Cola Latin America and the FEMSA Foundation), A-WASH program, and the Circuit Rider program, designed to support small water supply systems in a diverse collection of countries that includes the United States, Canada, Honduras, Guatemala, El Salvador, Belize, Haiti, Nicaragua, El Salvador, and Costa Rica.

In addition to WASH programs such as these, MWA carries on an ambitious and active program of advocacy for WASH efforts in the United States and other countries around the world. The goal of this program is to better inform decision- and policy-makers of the need for better WASH activities in developing nations, provide more information about the types of technology and economic programs that are available, tell success stories from MWA and other organizations' efforts in the field, and offer advice and consultations for new efforts in developing countries. The organization understands and bases its advocacy efforts on the reality that national and state governments are ultimately responsible for the success of most

WASH programs, but that specific efforts must be based on the needs and desires of individual communities.

Peter Morgan (1943–)

Morgan is an English-born environmentalist who is now a citizen of Zimbabwe, winner of the 2013 Stockholm Water Prize. The prize was awarded for "his work to protect the health and lives of millions of people through improved sanitation and water technologies." A number of devices have been invented over the decades to make safe water and efficient sanitation more readily accessible to people in developing countries. The problem often is that these devices are too expensive for most communities and individuals to make use of. Morgan's inventions have been designed to overcome this limitation, to provide simple water systems, inexpensive toilets, and other devices that are cheap and easy to use as well as meeting the needs of those without access to such resources.

One such device is the Blair ventilated pit latrine (also known as the VIP [for ventilated improved pit] toilet system), which has now become the most commonly available toilet in the country of Zimbabwe. About a half million of the devices are currently in use in the nation. The latrine operates on the principle that sunlight heating the top of the unit causes an upward draft through the structure, removing odors and insects that would otherwise make the latrine unpleasant and unhealthy to use. Morgan invented the system in the 1970s when the Blair Research Laboratory was part of the then Rhodesian Ministry of Health. (For a diagram and explanation of the structure's operation, see http://www.bellatrines.co.nz/how_it_works.html.) Another of Morgan's inventions is a so-called bush pump that is made of simple, inexpensive materials that can be easily assembled without expensive equipment and specialized knowledge. (For detailed information about and illustrations of the pump, see http://www.rural-water-supply.net/en/implementation/public-domain-handpumps/bush-pump.)

Peter Roger Morgan was born on October 2, 1943, in Wellingborough, England. He attended the Romford Royal Liberty Grammar School in Essex, where he received "A" level passes in botany, zoology, chemistry, and physics. He then entered the University of Hull, from which he received his BSc degree in zoology in 1964 and his PhD in marine biology in 1968. At the suggestion of his doctoral advisor, Morgan then accepted an appointment as research fellow in limnology at the University of Malawi, studying the fish and fisheries of Lake Chilwa, near the city of Zomba. By the end of that assignment, Morgan was beginning to feel an affinity to Africa, and he stayed on as a medical research officer at the Blair Research Laboratory in Zimbabwe, a post he held from 1972 to 1990. He then stayed on as an advisor to the Ministry of Health. In 1993, Morgan was appointed the first chairman of the Mvuramanzi Trust, a nonprofit, nongovernmental organization that he cofounded and which was established to deal with water and sanitation needs of the country of Zimbabwe not then being met by other programs. At the same time, Morgan accepted an appointment as the director of Aquamor, a small Zimbabwe-based company for research and development of water and sanitation projects in developing countries. Morgan left his post at Mvuramanzi in 1996, but continues to be affiliated with Aquamor.

In addition to his research and development activities, Morgan has long been involved in a variety of professional associations. He has served as the editor of the *Zimbabwe Science News*, president of the Zimbabwe Scientific Association, member of the Medical Research Council of Zimbabwe, and member of the Management Board of the Zimbabwe Institute of Water and Sanitation Development. He is the author of two books, more than 100 scholarly papers, and 66 editions of the *Blair Research Bulletin*. In addition to the Stockholm Water Prize, he has been honored with the 1976 P.H. Haviland Award of the Zimbabwe Institution of Engineers; 1983 Zimbabwe Scientific Association Gold Medal Award for outstanding scientific research; 1986 Certificate of Distinction of the Research Council of Zimbabwe; 1986 International Inventors Award, presented by the king of Sweden; 1997 Paul Harris Fellow of the Rotary Foundation of Rotary International; 2009 AMCOW AfricaSan Award for Technical Innovation in Sanitation; and 2012 RWSN Award for Lifetime Services to Rural Water Supply. In 1991, he was awarded an MBE (Most Excellent Order of the British Empire) by Queen Elizabeth II.

Pacific Institute

The PI is a nonprofit research institution devoted to the study of global water issues and the development of proposals for the creation of policies for the sustainable use and management of global water resources. The institute's full and legal name is the Pacific Institute for Studies in Development, Environment, and Security. PI was founded in 1987 by environmentalist Peter Gleick and two colleagues with the purpose of "creat[ing] a healthier planet and sustainable communities." Among the many directions in which that mission statement may have led, the institute has chosen to deal with water issues and most recently, and in particular, on the interrelationship of those issues with global climate change. The organization's offices are located in Oakland, California, and its operating budget in 2014 was about $2.25 million. Gleick continues to serve as president of the organization.

On its Web site, PI outlines the general approach it uses in attacking the problems in which it is interested. The primary elements of that approach include:

- *Improving understanding*, by providing decision-makers with the information they need to make and carry out appropriate policies. This information may come in the form of reports, briefings, fact sheets, curricula, tools, conferences, other types of materials, and training sessions designed for target audiences.

- *"Releasing trapped knowledge,"* a process by which information generally known to the academic and other specialized communities is made available to workers in the field and the general public.

- *Partnering with other organizations,* which may include groups from the smallest community groups to international nongovernmental organizations and the United Nations. A sample of the groups with which PI currently partners includes the Alliance for Water Efficiency, California Urban Water Conservation Council, Ditching Dirty Diesel, Oakland Climate Action Coalition, Oxfam America, and World Vision.

- *Developing "practical innovative solutions, management incentives, and economic drivers"* for groups in the private and public sectors by providing information on "best practices" for dealing with a variety of problems.

- *Initiating and participating in problem-solving activities that involve a variety of groups* by suggesting methods by which stakeholders with a wide variety of opinions can come to consensus.

- *Promoting justice and democratic decision-making,* a process achieved by bringing new and diverse voices to the discussion of a topic.

- *Conducting extensive outreach,* which goes beyond simply publishing reports and other useful materials to include making sure that those materials actually reach the people and groups for whom they were intended.

Much of the institute's work focuses on a number of currently important issues that, as of late 2015, included: The Human Right to Water; Sustainable Water Management—Local to Global; Corporate Water Stewardship; Environmental Health and Justice; Empowering People and Communities; Climate Change Vulnerability and Resilience; Water and Poverty; Water and Conflict; Water-Energy Nexus; and Water, Food, and Agriculture. Detailed information about each of these topics is available on the PI Web site at http://pacinst.org/issues/. The Water and Poverty section, as an example, provides additional information on subtopics such as Mobile Phone Solutions for Water, Sanitation, and Hygiene (WASH); Community Choices System; Climate Change Resilience in Developing Countries; Multiple-Use Water Services; Water Quality; Green Jobs and Water; Water and Environmental Justice; and Recognizing the Human Right to Water.

A particularly interesting and useful service provided by the institute is the "Tools" section of its Web site. This page contains a number of resources that individuals and groups can use to deal with a number of common water-related problems. The recommended tools are also arranged in a variety of ways, such as tools by issue, tools for water managers, tools for business, and tools for community action. Some examples of the kinds of tools that are available are californiadrought.org, a Web site that provides a host of information on the California drought that can answer questions about the drought and provide suggestions for dealing with various aspects of the drought; River Friendly Calculator, a tool designed in particular for residents of the Sacramento area to help them maintain their environment, while reducing their carbon footprint; WECalc, a program designed to help homeowners calculate their own domestic water use and find ways of reducing that use; WeTap, which serves as a guide to public drinking water locations; The World's Water Series, a collection of biennial reports on the status of the world's water resources; and Water Conflict Chronology, a summary of disputes over water resources locally and regionally that have taken place throughout recorded history.

Bindeshwar Pathak (1943–)

Pathak is sometimes known as "the million toilet man" in recognition of the change he has brought to India in reducing the rate of open defecation in the nation. The practice of open defecation has a very long history in India and other parts of the world, where an estimated 1–2 billion people still practice this unhygienic act. According to Indian tradition, for example, one should not defecate in the vicinity of a place where people live; instead, they should go off some distance, dig a hole, and then cover the hole with dirt, leaves, and other materials. This tradition arose, of course, untold centuries before anyone knew about the way in which diseases are spread by open defecation. And since old traditions do not die easily, many people in India and other developing nations of the world prefer to continue the practice of open defecation, especially when they know nothing about the health consequences of such an act.

One of the most outspoken and successful of critics against open defecation, certainly in India, and probably in the world, is Bindeshwar Pathak. Pathak was born on April 2, 1943, in Rampur, Bihar state, India, to an upper-class family belonging to the Brahmin caste. He learned very early about the strict divisions that exist among castes in India, especially the disregard in which the lowest castes, the so-called untouchables, are held. The story is told that, as a child, he accidentally came into contact with an untouchable woman. As punishment for this event, his grandmother forced him to eat cow dung as a way of understanding how completely unacceptable such an act is. The punishment apparently had an opposite effect, however, as it caused Pathak to think about the level of degradation in which the lower castes were forced to live and the simple, healthy features of modern life from which they were excluded, safe sanitation being one.

After completing his secondary education, Pathak matriculated at Patna University, in Patna, Bihar, from which he received his bachelor's degree in sociology (1964), master's degrees in sociology and English (1980), a doctorate in English (1985), and another doctorate in English literature (1994). Even at this early age, he was thinking and writing about sanitation issues, two of his qualifying papers being on "Liberation of scavengers through low cost sanitation" for his doctorate and "Eradication of scavenging and environmental sanitation in India: a sociological study" for his sociology degree.

Pathak's earliest experience with a social movement came in 1968 when he volunteered to work with the Bhangi-Mukti (scavengers' liberation) Cell of the Bihar Gandhi Centenary Celebrations Committee. The general group had been formed in honor of the work of Mahatma Gandhi and the specific committee, to find ways of liberating the Bhangi (toilet-cleaners) from their unpleasant tasks. The cell selected Pathak to conduct a survey of the problem and come up with ideas for improving the sanitation facilities then generally available to all but the highest castes in India. Pathak later reflected that he was "totally unprepared" for the challenge.

This handicap did not prevent him from setting out on his assignment, however. The turning point in his work for the committee—and, as it turns out—in his life was a visit he made to the town of Bettiah, where he lived for three months, observing the life of the lowest castes at firsthand. He eventually came to the conclusion, he later said, that two core problems of his work were inextricably related: the fate of the lower castes and the sanitation systems available to most Indians. He realized that his challenge was to find ways of "overcom[ing] the violence of caste through non-violent means" by "develop[ing] an effective and affordable toilet system (as an alternative to the expensive Western-style flush toilet and centralized water-borne sewage system) so that manual scavenging could be eliminated and the scavenging dalits freed and rehabilitated in other gainful occupation." With that realization, he set out to educate himself about the technology and economics of simple toilet construction and then to pass on that information to individual Indians for whom open defecation was still the primary means of defecation. In 1970, Pathak founded the Sulabh International Social Service Organization as a means for formalizing the research and activities needed to achieve these goals. Today, more than 50,000 volunteers work for the organization, carrying out research, fund-raising, education, and other activities related to the development and use of simple toilets that can be installed in any home in India.

The best known and most popular system developed by Pathak is called the two-pit pour-flush compost toilet, also known as Sulabh Shauchalaya, or, literally, "easy access to sanitation." This system consists of a toilet pan to which are connected two drains, each leading to a leach pit. At first, one drain is open, and the other closed. Wastes travel out of the toilet pan into the open pit, where liquid wastes leak into the ground and solid wastes are allowed to dry for use as manure. When the first pit is full, the drain pipe to that pit is closed and the other drain pipe opened. After a period of about 18 months, the wastes in the first pit have decayed and are available for use in agriculture or other areas.

The list of Pathak's honors is, according to his Facebook page, "too long to be put in the chapter." They include the Padma Bhushan award from the Government of India, mention in the 2003 Global 500 Roll of Honour, the Energy Globe Award, the Dubai International Award for Best Practices, the Indira Gandhi Priyadarshini Award for Environment, the Stockholm Water Prize for 2009, the 2013 Legend of Planet award from the French senate, and the International Saint Francis Prize for the Environment of the Italian government.

Rajendra Singh (1959–)

Singh is an activist for water conservation in India who was named a winner of the Stockholm Water Prize in 2015 "for his innovative water restoration efforts, improving water security in rural India, and for showing extraordinary courage and determination in his quest to improve the living conditions for those most in need." Singh is sometimes known as the "waterman of India" because of the significant changes he has brought about through education and technological development in many parts of rural India.

Singh is currently chair of the governing board of Tarun Bharat Sangh (India Youth Association), an organization whose purpose it is to "bring dignity and prosperity to the life

of destitute section of the nation through sustainable development measures." The organization was originally founded in
1975 by a group of professors and students at the University of
Rajasthan, although it notes that the organization's "true origin" should probably be traced to a decade later, when four
young men in the organization decided to move to a rural area
and live in the small village of Kisohri in the Alwar district.
There they opened a school for children as a way of beginning
to bring modern education and technology to the region. They
soon became discouraged, however, when villagers seemed to
take little or no interest in the men's projects. Eventually, the
men found greater acceptance in the neighboring village of
Bhikampura, and the first successful outreach for Tarun Bharat
Sangh in rural India was under way.

Rajendra Singh was born on August 6, 1959, in the village of Daula in the state of Uttar Pradesh, India. His father
was a farmer who was responsible for managing a plot of land
60 acres in size. Young Rajendra received his education in the
local village, where he first came into contact with a member of
the Gandhi Peace Foundation, an event that was to change his
life. He readily adopted the principles of Gandhism and decided
to devote his life to helping less fortunate people improve their
lives. One of these first actions in this direction was his participation in a local alcoholism eradication program designed to
help people overcome their addiction to the substance.

After completing his high school education, Singh enrolled
at the Bhartiya Rishikul Ayurvedic Mahavidyalaya College in
Barot, from which he later received his degree in ayurvedic
medicine and surgery. Ayurvedic medicine is a very old system
of healing based on the belief that good health depends on
a balance among mind, body, and spirit. The primary objectives of the practice are to achieve and maintain good health
as a way of preventing disease, although techniques are available for treating specific physical and mental disorders. Singh
decided to put his training to work by starting his own practice
in ayurvedic medicine in his home village. At the time, he also

became increasingly interested in political movements designed to provide aid to the less fortunate, eventually founding the local chapter of a group working for such purposes known as Chhatra Yuva Sangharsh Vahini (Student-Youth Struggle Battalion). Singh then decided to continue his own education, enrolling at a college in Barot affiliated with Allahabad University, where he majored in Hindi literature.

Upon completing his formal education in 1980, Singh took a job with the federal government as a National Service Volunteer. His first assignment was at an adult education program in the Dausa district of Rajasthan. It was during this period of service that he learned about and became a member of Tarun Bharat Sangh and set out to work in the villages. By chance, the region where he ended up living and working was one of the most arid regions in India, where farmers had traditionally practiced water use techniques that continually drained the region's water table without making any provision for recharging that resource. Singh's life was changed at one point when a local farmer pointed out to him that his (Singh's) efforts to educate local children meant far less than helping farmers understand the destructive nature of their water management techniques and find better ways to use their limited water resources in a sustainable manner.

Although Singh had little or no formal training in water conservation technology, he decided to educate himself, largely by studying methods that farmers in the region had once used to capture and store their previous water resources. The key to that technology was the construction of earthen dams (johads) that captured the abundant waters that fell during monsoon season and preserved that water until it was needed during the dry season for irrigating crops. By reminding local farmers of this traditional method of water conservation and beginning to restore abandoned johads in the region, Singh and his neighbors were able to rebuild the traditional system in a matter of only three years, turning the region from a desperately arid landscape into one that could once again sustain crops.

By the time Singh had been awarded the prestigious Ramon Magsaysay Award for community leadership in 2001, his teams had constructed and restored more than 4,500 johads in 850 villages in Rajasthan, and by the time he won the Stockholm Water Prize in 2015, those numbers had increased to 8,600 johads in more than 1,000 villages.

Singh's work has now extended far beyond the restoration and construction of johads. He has organized a number of "water marches" designed to draw people's attention to water issues and to educate them about actions they can take to deal with such issues, has organized five major national conferences on water and other environmental issues, has worked to defeat the proposed Loharinag Pala Hydro Power Project on the Bhagirathi River, an important tributary of the Ganges River, and led a campaign to improve protection of the Aravali wildlife area that resulted in the closing of more than 1,000 polluting mines in Rajasthan. In addition to the Magsaysay and Stockholm awards, Singh has received the Indira Gandhi Environment Award of the government of India, the Joseph C. John Award, and the International River Prize.

Stockholm International Water Institute

The Stockholm International Water Institute (SIWI) was founded in 1991 by the city of Stockholm, Sweden, for the purpose of improving the world's understanding of the importance of water to human survival, the threats that water resources currently face, and the steps that taken be taken to ensure a sustainable access to pure water resources for the world's population. SIWI is funded by the Swedish government and is managed by a board of directors of 10 experts in the field of water technology, economics, management, and related fields, along with a staff of more than 70 individuals who oversee general administrative and programmatic departments. The five major themes around which SIWI activities are organized are water governance; transboundary water management; climate change and water; the water, energy, and food nexus; and water economics. Each of these programmatic areas has associated with a distinct set of knowledge and skills that SIWI is able to bring to bear in dealing with the area. In the field of transboundary water management, for example, the institute develops specific tools and methods to use in dealing with transboundary issues that are based on the best available research and experience on the topic. It also provides mechanisms by which states involved in transboundary issues are able to call upon neutral and trusted third-party observers for assistance in resolving points of dispute. SIWI also offers its services in developing models by which hydroeconomic issues can be studied and resolved. Finally, the institute develops systems that help local water management to extend and improve the resources at their disposal for dealing with a variety of transboundary water management issues.

In addition to the five programmatic areas, SIWI maintains a number of permanent initiatives that focus on specific water management issues: Swedish Water House, The UNDP Water Governance Facility at SIWI, GoAL WaSH (Governance, Advocacy and Leadership in Water, Sanitation and Hygiene), MDG-F Knowledge Management, Shared Waters Partnership, EU Water Initiative Africa Working Group, International Centre for Water Cooperation, and Source to Sea. As an example, the Swedish Water House is a mechanism for bringing together Swedish citizens who are interested in and concerned about specific issues of water management, providing them with an opportunity to get together and exchange new and innovative ideas. The house also provides support for Swedish participants involved with international efforts, groups, meetings, and other exchanges on water-related issues. GoAL WaSH is an initiative that targets countries with special deficiencies in access to clean water and/or adequate sanitation facilities. It assists those countries in assessing those facilities and deriving plans for improving access to pure water and adequate sanitation, provides technological and economic assistance in reaching those goals, and helps governments

to access the progress they have made in this area. WaSH programs are currently in operation in 11 countries around the
world, Bosnia and Herzegovina, Cambodia, El Salvador, Kyrgyzstan, Laos, Liberia, Mongolia, Niger, Paraguay, Tajikistan, and
Togo. Source to Sea is a program that brings together experts in
freshwater, coastal, and marine sciences to discuss and share their
ideas for improving the management and protection of water
systems as a whole, including sources, rivers and streams, estuar-
ies, and oceans.

The Stockholm Institute is especially well known to the general public because of its sponsorship of three major water prizes
awarded annually, the Stockholm Water Prize, the Stockholm
Junior Water Prize, and the Stockholm Industry Water Award,
and of the World Water Week held every year in Stockholm to
address the current status of the world's water problems. The
Water Prize is awarded to the individual or organization "whose
work contributes to the conservation and protection of water
resources, and to the well-being of the planet and its inhabitants." The Junior Prize is awarded to individuals between the
age of 15 and 20 who have completed water-related projects
on environmental, scientific, social, or technological problems
at the local, regional, national, or global level. The Industry
Award goes annually to the business or industry whose work
during the year has made the greatest contribution to improving the world's water situation.

SIWI publishes a monthly magazine (available in English), *Stockholm Water Front*, which provides news updates on
water-related topics as well as in-depth articles on specific subjects, such as hydraulic fracturing, the effects of climate change
on water resources, and the use of water in mining operations.
A number of other publications are also based on or related to
World Water Week and the activities that take place in connection with that event. The institute also produces a number
of reports on water-related subjects, such as water and food
supplies, water in the textile industry, water and energy generation, management of transboundary disputes, and reduction of
water loss in agriculture.

Water and Sanitation Program

The Water and Sanitation Program (WSP) is a division of the World Bank's Water Global Practice. The program was established in 1978 in cooperation with the UNDP with the goal of providing poor people with safe, affordable, and sustainable access to water and sanitation. During its first decade of operation, the program focused on the development of technological devices for achieving this objective for delivery to developing nations. During the 1990s, WSP changed its focus to devising ways in which poor communities could develop their own systems for gaining assured access to safe water and sanitary systems, which remains its primary approach today. WSP currently maintains programs in 25 countries for regions: Africa, East Asia and Pacific, Latin America and Caribbean, and South Asia. These programs are carried out in cooperation with academic institutions, civil society organizations, donors, governments, media, private sector, and other interested groups with the aim of bringing about regulatory and structural changes required for the development of safe and efficient water and sanitation systems.

As a way of achieving these objectives, WSP has identified six core topics as guides for its work in client countries:

Scaling Up Rural Sanitation and Hygiene. One aspect of WSP's work is to find ways of making dependable sanitation systems of proven effectiveness available to small communities that are otherwise less likely to have such systems available to them. In order to do so, WSP programs must also have a strong education component, through which people can learn about the importance of good sanitation and the way to make use of sound sanitation systems.

Creating Sustainable Services through Domestic Private Sector Participation

In addition to seeking support of governmental units, WSP seeks out the cooperation of private domestic companies to scale up the operation of local water and sanitation systems, always making use of the "best practices" available in these areas.

Supporting Poor-Inclusive Water Supply and Sanitation (WSS) Sector Reform. WSP sees as one of its fundamental challenges "fixing the institutions that fix the pipes," which means providing governmental agencies at all levels with information about the best technologies that are available and encouraging those agencies to employ those technologies in support of pro-poor policies.

Targeting the Urban Poor and Improving Services in Small Towns. Although some of the most challenging water and sanitation problems occur in rural areas, towns and cities are not immune from the same problems. WSP also encourages and supports the efforts of governmental units at all levels to improve water and sanitation systems in urban as well as rural areas.

Adapting Water Supply and Sanitation (WSS) Delivery to Climate Change Impacts

Developing countries face a "double whammy" of trying to upgrade existing water and sanitation systems while preparing for a host of new problems expected to arise as a result of climate change. WSP aims to provide current knowledge about such problems, along with the best available suggestions for dealing with those problems of its client states.

Delivering Water Supply and Sanitation (WSS) Services in Fragile States. Not surprisingly, some nations are at greater risk for water and sanitation deficiencies than are others. The most desperate of these countries, the so-called fragile states, require greater interventions like those provided by WSP programs than do other developing nations.

WSP maintains an excellent collection of reports, articles, country profiles, and other publications on its Web site at http://www .wsp.org/library. The Web page provides an interactive browsing feature that allows one to filter by region, country, theme, and copyright year. Some examples of the materials available are :Investing in the Next Generation: Growing Tall and Smart with Toilets," "A Randomized Controlled Study of a Large-Scale Rural Sanitation Behavior Change Program in Madhya Pradesh, India," "A Regional Synthesis of the Service Delivery Assessments for Water Supply and Sanitation in East Asia and the Pacific," "Africa Regional Highlights," "Benin—Innovative Public Private Partnerships for Rural Water Services Sustainability—A Case Study," "Beyond One-Size-Fits-All: Lessons Learned from Eight Water Utility Public-Private Partnerships in the Philippines," "Briefing Note to Support Effective and Sustainable Devolution of Water and Sanitation Services in Kenya," and "Country Profile: Child Feces Disposal in Afghanistan."

One of the most popular of the WSP publications is its annual cartoon calendar. The calendar consists of artwork produced by artists around the world with the goal of presenting fundamental information about WASH issues in a relatively simple, humorous fashion. Past issues of the calendar can be found and orders for upcoming calendars can be placed at http://www.wsp.org/about/Cartoon%20Calendars.

Water for People

Water for People (W4P) was founded in 1991 by three men interested in working on projects that would guarantee a safe and continuous supply of pure water for people in developing countries who currently do not have access to such resources. They were Ken Miller, a former president of the AWWA; John B. Mannion, a former executive director of AWWA; and Wayne Weiss, at the time employed by the engineering, consulting, and construction firm of Black & Veatch. The organization's guiding slogan is Everyone Forever, meaning that it works to develop sustainable water supply systems for every person on the globe, while ensuring that those systems will remain in operation as long as they are needed.

W4P describes its work as representing "a relatively small global footprint" since it is currently in operation in only 30 districts in nine countries around the world, Bolivia, Guatemala,

Honduras, India, Malawi, Nicaragua, Peru, Rwanda, and Uganda in programs that reach an estimated 4 million people. It plans to extend its operations, however, with expectations of providing national coverage in four countries by 2018.

W4P points out that it differs from other organizations interested in water issues in a number of ways, such as

Working toward "full coverage," which means that the organization's ultimate goal is to reach every individual, group, and organization within the area it has chosen to work.

Capacity building, a component of the program that guarantees that not only will water systems be provided for those who need them, but the ability to repair those systems when such repairs are needed will also be supplied.

Cofinance, an important element based on the principle that communities that receive assistance from W4P will be expected to make a financial contribution toward the organization's work in those communities.

Monitoring and evaluation, such that the organization does not walk away from a project once it is completed, but continues to monitor and evaluate the ongoing status of that project.

Market-based approach, based on the organization's commitment to sound business principles in carrying out its goals of providing water systems for communities.

Replication and scale, the principle that systems and programs found to be effective at a local level will then be expanded for use in larger and broader markets.

Focus on sustainability, the expectation that communities that have benefitted from the work of W4P will not expect to survive on foreign interventions forever, but will eventually take over the task of dealing with their own water issues.

Transparency, the organization's commitment to making all of its records available at any time to the general public.

In 2014, W4P invested a total of $16,743,517 in water projects in nine countries, a total that was supplemented by an additional $3,902,052 from governments, local partners, and communities where the new water systems were located. The primary source of revenue for the organization's work is contributions from corporations, nonprofit organizations, and foundations. Individual donations, bequests, and other contributions supplement these sources. Among the most generous of these contributors in 2014 were Charity: Water, Toms Roasting Company, LDS Charities, the Bill and Melinda Gates Foundation, American Water, Kimberly-Clark, the May and Stanley Smith Charitable Trust, the MWA, University of Strathclyde Research & Innovation, and the Skoll Foundation.

W4P depends heavily on individual volunteers in its work, not only for financial donations, but also for support in a variety of other ways. For example, the organization encourages individuals to design and carry out a variety of fund-raising events, assistance for which is provided by the organization on its Web site (see https://www.crowdrise.com/waterforpeople for further information). W4P also offers impact tours, which allows volunteers to spend about a week in a country with which the organization has a working relationship, providing an opportunity to learn firsthand the type of work it does and to interact with staff and local people engaged in the process of developing water systems. Opportunities are also provided for volunteers to work for an extended period of time on one of the organization's in-process projects in one of the cooperating countries.

WaterAid

WaterAid is an international nonprofit organization whose purpose it is to ensure that all people in all parts of the world have access to safe water and proper sanitation and hygiene facilities. The organization was created in Great Britain as a charitable trust in July 1981 in response to the United Nations' declaration of 1981–1991 as the Decade of Drinking Water and Sanitation. Its first two projects were begun almost immediately in Sri Lanka and Zambia, and the severe drought in Africa in 1983 prompted the agency to begin work also in Ethiopia and Tanzania. Two years later, the first water projects were initiated in Ghana, and in 1986, work was extended to Bangladesh, India, and Nepal. As of 2015, WaterAid was operating projects in 26 countries in Central America; Western, Eastern, and Southern Africa; Southeast Asia; and the Pacific Islands. The number of people for whom new water and sanitation facilities were being provided ranged from about 1,000 (sanitation) and 2,000 (water) in Nicaragua to 374,000 (sanitation) and 466,000 (water) in India. Overall, WaterAid's water projects had reached a total of more than 2 million people worldwide by 2015 and its sanitation projects, more than 3 million people. An additional 4 million people had benefitted from new and improved hygiene programs. The vast majority (more than 70%) of these projects were installed in rural settings, with about 20 percent in urban settings, and the remainder in small towns.

WaterAid's main offices are in New York City, but it has regional offices also in the cooperating countries of Australia, Canada (formerly WaterCan), Japan, Sweden, and the United Kingdom. The organization employs more than 900 people in 37 countries and works with 400 distinct local organizations on its projects. Its current annual budget is about $127 million, of which about 82 percent goes directly to its WASH programs and the remainder to administrative, support, and fund-raising activities. Nearly 80 percent of its income comes from foundations and corporations, with another 13 percent coming from governmental agencies, and the balance from individual donations.

WaterAid uses a four-prong approach in its programs to improve WASH services. The first of those prongs begins with an assessment of a community's needs in these three areas and the development of a plan to deal with those needs. The plan involves the use of the best technology available for dealing with WASH needs, as well as the development of an educational program to help people become better aware of the importance of pure water and good sanitation and hygiene practices, as well as the ways in which this knowledge can be put to use. The second prong of WaterAid's approach is empowering individuals in the community to begin taking responsibility for their own WASH systems. The intention is to ensure that the gains made during and as a result of a WaterAid project are not lost when the organization leaves the area, but that local individuals can take over the operation of these systems.

A third element of WaterAid programs involves policy development and advocacy. The organization understands that introducing technological changes in a community and educating local leaders can be only partially successful if governmental agencies at higher levels are not supportive of such changes both from a policy and from a financial standpoint. The organization, therefore, attempts to educate decision- and policy-makers at the state, national, and regional levels to ensure that local communities have the support they need to maintain and improve the WASH systems that WaterAid has helped to develop.

Finally, WaterAid continues to produce a wide variety of publications that can be used to support and encourage the development and implementation of its programs at both the local and national levels. One such publication is the organization's quarterly newsletter, "Oasis," available in print format and online at http://www.wateraid.org/us/google-search?query=oasis. Examples of other publications available from the organization are reports on "The Importance of Water, Sanitation and Hygiene for Lymphatic Filariasis and Leprosy Care and Inclusion"; "Climate Finance and Water Security"; "WASH and Climate Change"; "Financing Sustainable and Resilient Water and Sanitation Infrastructure in African Cities"; and "Compendium of Accessible WASH Technologies." WaterAid has also produced a number of publications on the issue of sustainability, with particular regard to issues of health, hygiene, sanitation, and water. Its series of "framework" documents in this field are suitable for modification by individual communities in various parts of the world with differing resources and needs. (See http://www.wateraid.org/policy-practice-and-advocacy/sustainability.)

Water.org

Water.org was formed in July 2009 through the merger of WaterPartners and H2O Africa. WaterPartners, in turn, had been established in 1990 by civil engineer Gary White, with the goal of empowering people in developing countries to gain access to safe water and sanitation. H2O Africa had been formed in 2006 by actor Matt Damon, director James Moll, the LivePlanet production company, and the Independent Producers Alliance in conjunction with their production of the documentary film *Running the Sahara*. The two groups had broadly similar goals and in 2009 joined forces to form Water.org. Today, White serves as CEO of Water.org and as cofounder along with Damon.

Water.org describes itself as being different from other water organizations in that it sees the vast numbers of people without access to clean water and safe sanitation as having the capacity to take care of themselves and their own needs, providing that they have the education they need to understand how to deal with their problems and the access to resources to take advantage of that education. "They are participants [in solving their own water and sanitation problems]," the organization says, "not recipients." "They know what will work best for them in the long run," Water.org's statement of purpose goes on, and the organization is committed to providing them with the resources to make possible the accomplishment of their goals.

The primary mechanism by which Water.org carries out this initiative is a program called WaterCredit, which makes small loans to individual households for making connections to water systems or the installation of toilets. As the loans are repaid, those funds are then reinvested to other households wishing to make similar upgrades. As of late 2015, the organization had made more than 600,000 such loans, with a repayment rate of more than 99 percent. At that point, $12.9 million in capital investments had produced improvements with a commercial value of $128 million, or a return of about 10 times for the investment made by Water.org in water and sanitation projects. In its most recent annual report, the organization noted that it had funded the installation of 135,682 new toilets and 117,884 new water connections, benefitting more than a million people worldwide who had not previously had access to such resources. During the preceding year (2014), Water.org had added 19 new partner organizations around the world and maintained 55 distinct water and sanitation programs worldwide.

The organization's global headquarters are in Kansas City, with regional offices in Chennai, India; Nairobi, Kenya; Lima, Peru; and Jakarta, Indonesia. It receives about one-fifth of its annual revenue from personal donations, relying on corporations for about an equal income and foundation support for the greatest portion of its budget, about 57 percent of its total income. It spends about three-quarters of its expenses on program activities and the remainder on administrative and support funding. In 2011, Water.org announced the creation of a new program, called the New Ventures Fund, as a way of funding the organization's efforts to design, develop, test, and implement new technologies that can be used in improving the accessibility of individuals and communities to clean water and safe sanitation systems.

Dating back to 2008, Water.org and its predecessor organizations have sought out the assistance of corporations in helping to achieve their objectives. The organization currently has "strategic alliances" with the Pepsico Foundation, Caterpillar Corporation, IKEA Foundation, Cartier Charitable Foundation, Swiss Re Foundation, Stella Artois company, Helmsley Charitable Trust, Bank of America, Conrad N. Hilton Foundation,

Zynga.org, Tarbaca Indigo Foundation, Johnson & Johnson, and Jeep.

World Health Organization

Efforts to establish regional and international health organizations to deal with health and medical problems that transcend national borders extend to the early decades of the 20th century. The first of those organizations was the Office International d'Hygiène Publique (International Office of International Hygiene), created by the League of Nations in 1920. When the United Nations was formed after the end of World War II in 1946, some interest was expressed in creating a similar office in the new organization. Delegates from China and Brazil, in particular, Chinese delegate Dr. Szeming Sze, argued for the immediate formation of such an organization. Delegates unanimously approved Sze's suggestion, and a committee was created to write a constitution for the organization. The organization, the WHO, officially came into being on April 7, 1948, when its constitution was ratified by the 28th member state. As such, WHO became the first specialized agency within the United Nations. (The organization's founding date of April 7 is now celebrated annually as World Health Day.)

WHO is currently a member of the United Nations Development Group (UNDG), a collection of about two dozen separate agencies created in 1997 to bring some order to a disparate variety of organizations developed within the United Nations over the preceding three decades. Other members of UNDG include the Food and Agriculture Organization, United Nations Children's Fund, World Food Programme, United Nations Office on Drugs and Crime, and the United Nations Office of the High Representative for the Least Developed Countries, Landlocked Developing Countries and Small Island Developing States.

Ultimate decision-making authority for WHO resides in the World Health Assembly, whose members are appointed by the 194 member states, which meets annually in May. The assembly debates and decides on general matters of policy and finance and elects 34 members to the organization's Executive Board for terms of three years each. Members of the board are expected to be especially qualified in the field of the health sciences. The primary function of the Executive Board is to carry out the general policy decisions made by the assembly. Day-to-day operation of the organization is carried out under the direction of the director-general who, as of late 2015, was Margaret Chan, formerly director of health in Hong Kong. Chan's term runs until June 2017. More than 8,500 specialists in the health sciences work for WHO in a variety of settings in 147 countries that are organized into six regional offices, Africa, the Americas, Eastern Mediterranean, Europe, Southeast Asia, and Western Pacific.

WHO's work is organized into more than 200 programs focusing on specific health issues, such as aging and life course, buruli ulcer, communicable diseases, drug resistance, food safety, health and human rights, injection safety, oral health, schistosomiasis, substance abuse, yaws, and zoonoses and veterinary public health. Its primary WASH-related programs are household water treatment and safe storage, water sanitation and health (WSH), and the WSPortal, Health through Water. The last of these programs is a collaborative effort of WHO with nine national and regional agencies, such as Health Canada, the New Zealand Ministry of Health, and the U.S. Environmental Protection Agency, designed to outline methods for the development of safe water treatment, storage, and use programs for a variety of local settings. WSH is a broad-ranging program developed to carry out the agency's WASH and NTD Global Strategy for 2015–2020. It deals with a host of WASH-related issues, such as drinking water quality; bathing water issues; water-related diseases; wastewater use; health care waste; water, health, and economics; and household water treatment (for further information, see http://www.who.int/water_sanitation_health/en/).

One of WHO's most important benefits is the very large data bank that it maintains, along with a huge library of reports and other publications. The agency's online data repository, for example, contains a number of user-friendly interactive sites on themes such as Millennium Development Goals (MDGs), mortality and global health estimates, noncommunicable diseases, substance use and mental health, health systems, public health and environment, infectious diseases, injuries and violence, urban health, and general world health statistics. Each of these general categories is further subdivided into more specific topics, such as (for public health and environment) household air pollution; ambient air pollution; joint effects of air pollution; electromagnetic fields; environmental health relating to children; climate change; lead; occupational risk factors; secondhand smoke; ultraviolet radiation; and water, sanitation, and hygiene. The organization's online IRIS (Institutional Repository for Information Sharing) resource also lists nearly 7,000 publications of all kinds on topics ranging from 1-naphthylamine and 1-propanol to zinc and zoonoses, searchable by author, title, subject, community, issue date, and other criteria. More than 2,000 publications are available in the database, for example, on water-related topics, more than 1,500 on topics related to sanitation, and about 60 additional topics on the subject of hygiene. The WHO media center is also a very rich source of news on a host of health-related issues in the form of news reports, events listings and descriptions, fact sheets, multimedia materials, commentaries, feature articles, and other publications and resources.

World Water Council

As far back as the late 1970s, water experts worldwide had been bemoaning the absence of a single international body with responsibility for global water issues. Traditionally, such issues had been the purview of regional, national, state, and local authorities, which seldom dealt with more widespread problems other than those within their boundaries. The 1977 United Nations Conference on Water, held at Mar de Plata, Argentina, was the first attempt to develop an international approach to the world's water problems. But it was still nearly two decades before an actual organization for the governance of water resources worldwide was established. The organization, the WWC, was first proposed at a special session of the International Water Resources Association's Eighth World Water Congress, held in Cairo, in November 1994. Out of that discussion arose the formation of the WWC in March and September 1995. The purpose of the organization is "to promote awareness, build political commitment and trigger action on critical water issues at all levels."

The WWC currently consists of nearly 300 members with diverse functions, except for a common interest in water issues, such as Absheron Water Canal Department (Azerbaijan), Aguas Andinas (Chile), American Society of Civil Engineers—Environmental & Water Resources Institute, Andong City Government (Republic of Korea), Brazilian Business Council for Sustainable Development, China Institute of Water Resources and Hydropower Research, Department of Water Affairs and Forestry—South Africa, Global Institute for Water Environment and Health (Switzerland), Celik Construction Industry and Trade Company, Inc. (Turkey), Scientific Information Center of Interstate Commission for Water Coordination in Central Asia, Water Center for Latin America and the Caribbean (Mexico), Women for Water Partnership International, and World Wildlife Fund—US.

The ultimate authority of the WWC resides in the General Assembly, which includes all members of the organization. The General Assembly meets once every three years and in special session if and when needed. The General Assembly elects and appoints up to 35 members of the Board of Governors, who, in turn, select the council's major officers, including the president, vice president, and treasurer. As of late 2015, the president of WWC is Benedito Braga, secretary for sanitation and water

resources for the state of São Paulo and professor of civil and
environmental engineering at Escola Politecnica of University
of São Paulo, Brazil.

One of the council's major recurring activities is the World
Water Forum, held every three years in a different location.
The most recent session was held from April 12 to 17, 2015, at
the Daegu-Gyeongbuk Free Economic Zone, in South Korea.
The conference drew more than 40,000 participants from 168
nations meeting for more than 400 events and sessions. A total
of 188 memorandums of understanding and 50 bilateral and
multilateral agreements were also signed during the conference. In addition to the World Water Forum, WWC sponsors,
cosponsors, or participates in a number of other international,
regional, and national meetings, such as (in 2015) International Congress & Exhibition of the African Water Association,
Financial Times Water Summit, International River Sympo-
sium, Renewable Energy World Asia, and Catalyst California:
It's a Dry, Dry, Dry, Dry World.

WWC publishes a professional journal, *Water Policy Journal*, six times a year that deals with all aspects of water management, such as ecosystems, engineering, management and
restoration; engineering and design; river basin and watershed
management; multiple uses of water; pollution monitoring
and control; management, use, and sharing of transboundary
waters, treaties, and allocation agreements; flood control and
disaster management; groundwater remediation and conjunc-
tive use of groundwater and surface water; and public participation, consensus building, and confidence building. The
organization provides access to an excellent collection of its
publications on its Web site at http://www.worldwatercouncil
.org/library/official-documents/. These publications include
official documents, activity reports, news of council activities,
annual and special reports, thematic reports (such as water and
green growth), and forum documents produced at each triennial meeting.

5 Data and Documents

Introduction

Useful information about the global water issues in the United States and the rest of the world can often be gleaned from national, state, and local laws; court cases dealing with the topic; and statistics and data about water resources and uses. This chapter provides some of this basic information on the topic of global water issues.

Data

Table 5.1   Quality of Various Water Resources in the United States, 2015

Type of Waterway	Good	Threatened	Impaired
Rivers and streams[1]	490,126	7,657	551,442
Lakes, reservoirs, ponds[2]	5,614,189	145,572	12,188,766
Bays and estuaries[3]	7,566	n/a	26,627
Coastal shoreline[1]	827	n/a	7,159
Ocean near coastal[3]	555	n/a	1,016
Wetlands[2]	574,082	n/a	538,699
Great Lakes shoreline[1]	78	n/a	4,353
Great Lakes open water[3]	62	n/a	53,270

[1] miles
[2] acres
[3] square miles

Source: Assessed Waters of United States. 2015. U.S. Environmental Protection Agency. http://iaspub.epa.gov/waters10/attains_nation_cy.control#total_assessed_waters. Accessed on September 14, 2015.

Many farmers rely on automatic watering systems for the irrigation of their crops. These systems, however, consume enormous quantities of fresh water on an ongoing basis. (OIgor Stevanovic/Dreamstime.com)

Table 5.2 Trends in Water Use in the United States, 1950–2010 (in billions of gallons per day)

Total Withdrawals	1950	1955	1960	1965	1970	1975	1980	1985	1990	1995	2000	2005	2010
Public supply	14	17	21	24	27	29	33	36.4	38.8	40.2	43.2	44.2	42
Rural self-supplied domestic	2.1	2.1	2.0	2.3	2.6	2.8	3.4	3.32	3.39	3.39	3.58	3.83	3.6
Livestock	1.5	1.5	1.6	1.7	1.9	2.1	2.2	2.23	2.25	2.28	2.38	2.14	2.0
Irrigation	89	110	110	120	130	140	150	135	134	130	139	128	115
Thermoelectric power	40	72	100	130	170	200	210	187	194	190	195	201	161
Self-supplied industrial	37	39	38	46	47	45	45.1	25.9	22.6	22.4	19.7	18.2	15.9
Mining	[1]	[1]	[1]	[1]	[1]	[1]	[1]	3.44	4.93	3.72	4.50	4.02	5.32
Commercial	[1]	[1]	[1]	[1]	[1]	[1]	[1]	1.23	2.39	2.89	n/a	n/a	n/a
Aquaculture	[1]	[1]	[1]	[1]	[1]	[1]	[1]	2.24	2.25	3.22	5.77	8.78	9.42

[1] Included in self-supplied industrial

Sources: Trends in Estimated Water Use in the United States, 1950–2005. 2005. U.S. Geological Survey. http://water.usgs.gov/edu/wateruse/pdf/wutrends-2005.pdf. Accessed on September 14, 2015. Summary of Estimated Water Use in the United States in 2010. 2010. U.S. Geological Survey. http://pubs.usgs.gov/fs/2014/3109/pdf/fs2014-3109.pdf. Accessed on September 14, 2015.

Table 5.3 Source of Water Withdrawal, United States, 1950–2010 (billions of gallons per day)

Source	1950	1955	1960	1965	1970	1975	1980	1985	1990	1995	2000	2005	2010
Ground (fresh)	34	47	50	60	68	82	83.1	73.4	79.6	76.4	84.3	79.6	76.0
Ground (saline)	n/a	0.6	0.4	0.5	1.0	1.0	0.93	0.66	1.22	1.11	2.67	3.02	3.29
Surface (fresh)	140	180	190	210	250	260	280	263	255	261	265	270	230
Surface (saline)	10	18	31	43	53	69	71	59.6	68.2	59.7	61.0	58.0	45.0

Sources: Trends in Estimated Water Use in the United States, 1950–2005. 2005. U.S. Geological Survey. http://water.usgs.gov/edu/wateruse/pdf/wutrends-2005.pdf. Accessed on September 14, 2015. Molly A. Maupin, et al. 2014. Estimated Use of Water in the United States 2014. U.S. Geological Survey. http://pubs.usgs.gov/circ/1405/pdf/circ1405.pdf, Table 1, page 9. Accessed on September 14, 2015.

Table 5.4   Quality of Water Resources in the United States for Designated Uses, 2015

Use Group	Good	Threatened	Impaired
Fish, shellfish, and wildlife protection and propagation	58.7	0.6	40.7
Recreation	59.3	1.4	39.3
Agricultural	96.5	0.1	3.4
Aquatic life harvesting	28.8	0.9	70.4
Industrial	97.8	0.0	2.2
Public Water Supply	76.7	0.2	23.1
Other	97.9	0.0	2.1
Aesthetic value	92.7	0.0	7.3
Exceptional recreational or ecological significance	77.7	0.0	22.3

Source: Designated Use Support in Assessed Rivers and Streams. 2015. U.S. Environmental Protection Agency. http://iaspub.epa.gov/waters10/attains_nation_cy.control#total_assessed_waters. Accessed on September 14, 2015.

Table 5.5   Causes of Impairment in Rivers and Streams in the United States, 2015

Cause of Impairment	Miles
Pathogens	173,531
Nutrients	104,910
Mercury	101,837
Sediment	100,466
Organic enrichment/oxygen depletion	84,932
Polychlorinated biphenyls (PCBs)	79,077
Metals (other than mercury)	70,954
Habitat alterations	67,198
Temperature	51,666
Cause unknown	46,048
Turbidity	45,455
Flow alteration(s)	42,546
Cause unknown—impaired biota	42,357
Salinity/total dissolved solids/chlorides/sulfates	34,852
pH/acidity/caustic conditions	27,384

Cause of Impairment	Miles
Pesticides	15,031
Ammonia	11,282
Other cause	11,270
Fish consumption advisory	9,914
Total toxics	7,549
Inorganics	6,802
Algal growth	5,878
Dioxins	5,041
Toxic organics	4,919
Oil and grease	2,992
Nuisance exotic species	1,263
Trash	1,165
Taste, color, and odor	854
Chlorine	754
Radiation	692
Cause unknown—fish kills	678
Noxious aquatic plants	354
Nuisance native species	127
Biotoxins	84

Source: Causes of Impairment in Assessed Rivers and Streams. 2015. U.S. Environmental Protection Agency. http://iaspub.epa.gov/waters10/attains_nation_cy.control#total_assessed_waters

Accessed on September 14, 2015.

Table 5.6   Probable Sources of Impairments in Assessed Rivers and Streams in the United States, 2015

Probable Source	Miles Threatened or Impaired
Agriculture	122,470
Unknown	101,121
Atmospheric Deposition	99,748
Urban-related runoff/storm water	61,250
Municipal discharges/sewage	59,272

(continued)

Table 5.6 (*continued*)

Probable Source	Miles Threatened or Impaired
Natural/wildlife	41,796
Hydromodification	41,179
Unspecified nonpoint source	33,892
Resource extraction	20,086
Habitat alterations (not directly related to hydromodification)	16,266
Industrial	14,788
Land application/waste sites/tanks	8,880
Other	7,878
Legacy/historical pollutants	6,232
Construction	6,060
Silviculture (forestry)	3,751
Spills/dumping	3,013
Recreation and tourism (non-boating)	1,566
Aquaculture	340
Recreational Boating And Marinas	138
Groundwater loadings/withdrawals	62
Commercial harbor and port activities	52
Military bases	20

Source: Probable Sources of Impairments in Assessed Rivers and Streams in the United States, 2015. 2015. U.S. Environmental Protection Agency. http://iaspub .epa.gov/waters10/attains_nation_cy.control#total_assessed_waters

Accessed on September 14, 2015.

Documents

Tyler v. Wilkinson, 24 F. Cas. 472 (C.C.D. R.I. 1827)

The principle of riparian rights is generally said to have its origin in the United States as a result of a case that appeared before Justice Joseph Story of the United States District Court of Rhode Island in 1827. The case arose out of a dispute between two men, Ebenezer Tyler and Abraham Wilkinson, who operated mills on the Pawtucket River as to which man, if either, had rights to use water from the river and, if permitted, to what extent. In the simplest possible terms, Justice Story ruled that each person who owned land on the river had a right to the use of a reasonable amount of water from the river. The key points of Story's decision were later summarized in a compendium of important federal laws from the first century of the nation's history.

Appropriation of water

1. Priority of occupancy of the flowing water of a river creates no right, unless the appropriation be for a period which the law deems a presumption of right.

2. A millowner, as such, has no right to the water of a river beyond what has been legally appropriated to his mill by title, or long uses.

3. The riparian proprietors have a title to all the waters no so appropriated.

4. The exclusive use of flowing water for twenty years is a conclusive presumption of a right.

5. Prima facie, every proprietor upon each bank of a river is entitled to the land covered with water in part of his bank to the middle thread of the river.

6. In virtue of this ownership, he has a right to the use of the water flowing over it in its natural current, without diminution or obstruction. But he has no property in the water itself.

7. Every proprietor may use the water as it flows, according to his pleasure, if the use be not to the prejudice of any other proprietor.

8. There is no difference whether a proprietor be above or below another in the river, for no right is acquired or lost by any such circumstance. No proprietor has a right to throw back water on a proprietor above, or divert it from a proprietor below, to his injury.

Source: Peters, Richard. 1854. *Full and Arranged Digest of the Decisions in Common Law, Equity, and Admiralty of the Courts of the United States from the Organization of the Government in 1789 to 1849*, vol. I. New York: Lewis & Blood. The full decision in this case can be found at John Henry Wigmore. 1912. *Select Cases on the Law of Torts: With Notes, and a Summary of Principles.* Boston: Little, Brown, No. 245, 580–584.

Irwin v. Phillips, 5 Cal. 140 (1855)

The principle of riparian rights in determining control over the use of water has dominated legal thinking in the eastern part of the United States since 1827, when Tyler v. Wilkinson (provided earlier) was decided. Such has not been the case in the western part of the country, however, where doctrines other than those from English Common Law often had a strong influence. One of the earliest cases in which the question of water rights arose was Irwin v. Phillips. This case was based on a situation in which miner Matthew Irwin had settled on a piece of land in 1851, started mining for gold, and built a canal that diverted essentially all of the water from the South Fork of Poor Man's Creek for his mining operations. A few months later, another miner, Robert Phillips, began operations in an adjacent, downstream location from Irwin's mining site, except that no water was available for Phillips's mining operation. Phillips sued Irwin under the riparian doctrine, arguing that anyone living and working along the banks of the river should be guaranteed access to the river's water. The California Supreme Court disagreed with Phillips, thereby establishing the so-called prior appropriation rights document, sometimes described as the "first in time, first in right" doctrine. The court's reasoning was as follows:

Courts are bound to take notice of the political and social condition of the country, which they judicially rule. In this State the larger part of the territory consists of mineral lands, nearly the whole of which are the property of the public. No right or intent of disposition of these lands has been shown either by the

United States or the State governments, and with the exception of certain State regulations, very limited in their character, a system has been permitted to grow up by the voluntary action and assent of the population, whose free and unrestrained occupation of the mineral region has been tacitly assented to by the one government, and heartily encouraged by the expressed legislative policy of the other. If there are, as must be admitted, many things connected with this system, which are crude and undigested, and subject to fluctuation and dispute, there are still some which a universal sense of necessity and propriety have so firmly fixed as that they have come to be looked upon as having the force and effect of *res judicata.* Among these the most important are the rights of miners to be protected in the possession of their selected localities, and the rights of those who, by prior appropriation, have taken the waters from their natural beds, and by costly artificial works have conducted them for miles over mountains and ravines, to supply the necessities of gold diggers, and without which the most important interests of the mineral region would remain without development. So fully recognized have become these rights, that without any specific legislation conferring, or confirming them, they are alluded to and spoken of in various acts of the legislature in the same manner as if they were rights which had been vested by the most distinct expression of the will of the lawmakers. . . .

This simply goes to prove what is the purpose of the argument, that however much the policy of the State, as indicated by her legislation, has conferred the privilege to work the mines, it has equally conferred the right to divert the streams from their natural channels, and as these two rights stand upon an equal footing, when they conflict, they must be decided by the fact of priority upon the maxim of equity, *qui prior est in tempore potior est injure* ("who is first in time is first in law). The miner, who selects a piece of ground to work, must take it as he finds it, subject to prior rights, which have an equal equity, on account of an equal recognition from the sovereign power. If it is upon a stream the waters of which have not been taken from their bed, they cannot be taken to his prejudice; but if they have been already diverted, and for as high, and legitimate a purpose as the one he seeks to accomplish, he has no right to complain, no right to interfere with the prior occupation of his neighbor, and must abide the disadvantages of his own selection.

Source: Wiel, Samuel C. 1911. *Water Rights in the Western States: the Law of Prior Appropriation of Water* . . . San Francisco: Bancroft-Whitney, 8–10.

Colorado River Compact (1922)

In 1917, the states of Arizona, California, Colorado, Nevada, New Mexico, Utah, and Wyoming joined together to form the League of the Southwest, an entity through which the resources of the Colorado River could be developed. Four years later, the states began a discussion of a more formal mechanism by which the water resources of the river could be distributed among the seven states. A year later, the Colorado River Compact, producing this result, was adopted by the seven states and approved by the U.S. government. The major features of that agreement were as follows.

Article I

The major purposes of this compact are to provide for the equitable division and apportionment of the use of the waters of the Colorado River System; to establish the relative importance of different beneficial uses of water, to promote interstate comity; to remove causes of present and future controversies; and to secure the expeditious agricultural and industrial development of the Colorado River Basin, the storage of its waters, and the protection of life and property from floods. To these ends the Colorado River Basin is divided into two Basins, and an apportionment of the use of part of the water of the Colorado River System is made to each of them with the provision that further equitable apportionments may be made.

***

Article III

(a) There is hereby apportioned from the Colorado River System in perpetuity to the Upper Basin and to the Lower Basin, respectively, the exclusive beneficial consumptive use of 7,500,000 acre-feet of water per annum, which shall include all water necessary for the supply of any rights which may now exist.

(b) In addition to the apportionment in paragraph (a), the Lower Basin is hereby given the right to increase its beneficial consumptive use of such waters by one million acre-feet per annum.

(c) If, as a matter of international comity, the United States of America shall hereafter recognize in the United States of Mexico any right to the use of any waters of the Colorado River System, such waters shall be supplied first from the waters which are surplus over and above the aggregate of the quantities specified in paragraphs (a) and (b); and if such surplus shall prove insufficient for this purpose, then, the burden of such deficiency shall be equally borne by the Upper Basin and the Lower Basin, and whenever necessary the States of the Upper Division shall deliver at Lee Ferry water to supply one-half of the deficiency so recognized in addition to that provided in paragraph (d).

(d) The States of the Upper Division will not cause the flow of the river at Lee Ferry to be depleted below an aggregate of 75,000,000 acre-feet for any period of ten consecutive years reckoned in continuing progressive series beginning with the first day of October next succeeding the ratification of this compact.

(e) The States of the Upper Division shall not withhold water, and the States of the Lower Division shall not require the delivery of water, which cannot reasonably be applied to domestic and agricultural uses.

(f) Further equitable apportionment of the beneficial uses of the waters of the Colorado River System unapportioned by paragraphs (a), (b), and (c) may be made in the manner provided in paragraph (g) at any time after October first, 1963, if and when either Basin shall have reached its total beneficial consumptive use as set out in paragraphs (a) and (b).

(g) In the event of a desire for a further apportionment as provided in paragraph (f) any two signatory States, acting through their Governors, may give joint notice of such desire to the Governors of the other signatory States and to The President of the United States of America, and it shall be the duty of the Governors of the signatory States and of The President of the United States of America forthwith to appoint representatives, whose duty it shall be to divide and apportion equitably between the Upper Basin and Lower Basin the beneficial use of the unapportioned water of the Colorado River System as mentioned in paragraph (f), subject to the legislative ratification of the signatory States and the Congress of the United States of America.

Source: Colorado River Compact, 1922. U.S. Bureau of Reclamation. https://www.usbr.gov/lc/region/pao/pdfiles/crcompct .pdf. Accessed on September 11, 2015.

Article 10, California State Constitution (1928)

In 1926, the California Supreme Court heard a case, Heminghaus v. Southern California Edison, *in which the owner of a large private ranch (Heminghaus) complained about plans by a large electric utility (Southern California Edison) to withdraw large quantities of water upstream of her ranch, essentially depriving her of the water needed to irrigate her fields. The court ruled in favor of Southern California Edison because the Heminghaus family held riparian rights to the river water, while the electric company held only appropriated rights. The fact that the Heminghaus use of essentially all of the river's water to irrigate its lands seemed to be an unreasonable use of the river water, while the electric company's use seemed to be very reasonable was thought by the court to be irrelevant to its final decision in the case. The court's decision produced a sense of outrage among many California businesses, who saw a desperate need for more reasonable use of the state's water resources. They formed a coalition that fought for an amendment to the state constitution requiring just such a plan when requests for use of state water resources were made. In 1928, that amendment was adopted and is now Article 10 of the state constitution. Its most important sections read as follows:*

SECTION 1. The right of eminent domain is hereby declared to exist in the State to all frontages on the navigable waters of this State.

SEC. 2. It is hereby declared that because of the conditions prevailing in this State the general welfare requires that the water resources of the State be put to beneficial use to the fullest extent of which they are capable, and that the waste or unreasonable use or unreasonable method of use of water be prevented, and that the conservation of such waters is to be exercised with a view to the reasonable and beneficial use thereof in the interest of the people and for the public welfare. The right to water or to the use or flow of water in or from any natural stream or water course in this State is and shall be limited to such water as shall be reasonably required for the beneficial use to be served, and such right does not and shall not extend to the waste or unreasonable use or unreasonable method of use or unreasonable method of diversion of water. Riparian rights in a stream or water course attach to, but to no more than so much of the flow thereof as may be required or used consistently with this section, for the purposes for which such lands are, or may be made adaptable, in view of such reasonable and beneficial uses; provided, however, that nothing herein contained shall be construed as depriving any riparian owner of the reasonable use of water of the stream to which the owner's land is riparian under reasonable methods of diversion and use, or as depriving any appropriator of water to which the appropriator is lawfully entitled.

Source: California State Constitution. Article 10. http://www
.leginfo.ca.gov/.const/.article_10. Accessed on September 10, 2015.
For further information on *Heminghaus v. Southern California Edison*, see M. Catherine Miller. 1989. "Water Rights and the Bankruptcy of Judicial Action: The Case of Herminghaus v. Southern
California Edison." *Pacific Historical Review.* 58(1): 83–107.

Clean Water Act of 1972

*The Clean Water Act of 1972 is, technically, a set of amendments
to an earlier "clean water act," the Federal Water Pollution Control Act of 1948. The purpose of the 1972 amendments was to
restore and maintain the quality of the nation's water resources by
controlling the release of pollutants into rivers, streams, lakes, and
other water sources. A major provision of the amendments was the
creation of a permitting system, the National Pollutant Discharge
Elimination System (NPDES), designed to control the release of
pollutants from municipalities, industrial operations, and some
agricultural facilities. A few of the relevant sections from the long
and complex act are cited here.*

National Pollutant Discharge Elimination System

Declaration of Goals and Policy

"SEC. 101. (a) The objective of this Act is to restore and maintain the chemical, physical, and biological integrity of the
Nation's waters. In order to achieve this objective it is hereby
declared that, consistent with the provisions of this Act—

"(1) it is the national goal that the discharge of pollutants into
the navigable waters be eliminated by 1985;

"(2) it is the national goal that wherever attainable, an interim
goal of water quality which provides for the protection
and propagation of fish, shellfish, and wildlife and provides for recreation in and on the water be achieved by
July 1,1983;

"(3) it is the national policy that the discharge of toxic pollutants in toxic amounts be prohibited;

"(4) it is the national policy that Federal financial assistance be provided to construct publicly owned waste treatment works;

"(5) it is the national policy that area wide waste treatment management planning processes be developed and implemented to assure adequate control of sources of pollutants in each State;

and

"(6) it is the national policy that a major research and demonstration effort be made to develop technology necessary to eliminate the discharge of pollutants into the navigable waters, waters of the contiguous zone, and the oceans.

. . .

"SEC. 402. (a)(1) Except as provided in sections 318 and 404 of this Act, the Administrator may, after opportunity for public hearing, issue a permit for the discharge of any pollutant, or combination of pollutants, notwithstanding section 301(a), upon condition that such discharge will meet either all applicable requirements under sections 301, 302, 306, 307, 308, and 403 of this Act, or prior to the taking of necessary implementing actions relating to all such requirements, such conditions as the Administrator determines are necessary to carry out the provisions of this Act.

"(2) The Administrator shall prescribe conditions for such permits to assure compliance with the requirements of paragraph (1) of this subsection, including conditions on data and information collection, reporting, and such other requirements as he deems appropriate.

"(3) The permit program of the Administrator under paragraph (1) of this subsection, and permits issued thereunder, shall be subject to the same terms, conditions, and requirements as apply to a State permit program and permits issued thereunder under subsection (b) of this section.

"(4) All permits for discharges into the navigable waters issued pursuant to section 13 of the Act of March 3,1899, shall be deemed to be permits issued under this title, . . .

Source: Public Law 92–500. 1972. U.S. Statutes. http://www .gpo.gov/fdsys/pkg/STATUTE-86/pdf/STATUTE-86-Pg816 .pdf. Accessed on September 12, 2015.

Safe Drinking Water Act of 1974

The Safe Drinking Water Act of 1974 was passed for the purpose of protecting the nation's freshwater supply. The act was amended twice, in 1986 and 1996, and, today, constitutes the general guidelines for ensuring the safety of the nation's drinking water supplies. The initial 1974 act focused primarily on the treatment of water to ensure its purity and safety, while the 1986 and 1996 amendments concentrated primarily on monitoring and protecting the sources of freshwater. Relevant portions of the original act and later amendments are cited here.

"National Drinking Water Regulations

"Sec. 1412 (a)(1) The Administrator shall publish proposed national interim primary drinking water regulations within 90 days after the date of enactment of this title. Within 180 days after such date of enactment, he shall promulgate such regulations with such modifications as he deems appropriate. Regulations under this paragraph may be amended from time to time.

"(2) National interim primary drinking water regulations promulgated under paragraph (1) shall protect health to the extent feasible, using technology, treatment techniques, and other means, which the Administrator determines are generally available (taking costs into consideration) on the date of enactment of this title.

[Much of this section is devoted to an explanation of the way rules and regulations for water safety are to be determined. The key provision in the section is as follows:]

"(B) Within 90 days after the date the Administrator makes the publication required by subparagraph (A), he shall by rule establish recommended maximum contaminant levels for each contaminant which, in his judgment based on the report on the study conducted pursuant to subsection (e), may have any adverse effect on the health of persons. Each such recommended maximum contaminant level shall be set at a level at which, in the Administrator's judgment based on such report, no known or anticipated adverse effects on the health of persons occur and which allows an adequate margin of safety. In addition, he shall, on the basis of the report on the study conducted pursuant to subsection (e), list in the rules under this subparagraph any contaminant the level of which cannot be accurately enough measured in drinking water to establish a recommended maximum contaminant level and which may have any adverse effect on the health of persons. Based on information available to him, the Administrator may by rule change recommended levels established under this subparagraph or change such list.

. . .

"State Primary Enforcement Responsibility

"SEC. 1413. (a) For purposes of this title, a State has primary enforcement responsibility for public water systems during any period for which the Administrator determines (pursuant to regulations prescribed under subsection (b)) that such State—

"(1) has adopted drinking water regulations which (A) in the case of the period beginning on the date the national interim primary drinking water regulations are promulgated under section 1412 and ending on the date such regulations take effect are no less stringent than such regulations, and (B) in the case of the period after such effective date are no less stringent than the interim and revised national primary drinking water regulations in effect under such section;

"(2) has adopted and is implementing adequate procedures for the enforcement of such State regulations, including conducting such monitoring and making such inspections as the Administrator may require by regulation;

"(3) will keep such records and make such reports with respect to its activities under paragraphs (1) and (2) as the Administrator may require by regulation;

"(4) if it permits variances or exemptions, or both, from the requirements of its drinking water regulations which meet the requirements of paragraph (1), permits such variances and exemptions under conditions and in a manner which is not less stringent than the conditions under, and the manner in, which variances and exemptions may be granted under sections 1415 and 1416; and

"(5) has adopted and can implement an adequate plan for the provision of safe drinking water under emergency circumstances.

Source: Public Law 93-523. 1974. U.S. Statutes. http://www.gpo.gov/fdsys/pkg/STATUTE-88/pdf/STATUTE-88-Pg1660-2.pdf. Accessed on September 12, 2015.

Amendments of 1996

[Among the many provisions of the 1996 amendments was a new focus on protecting the sources of drinking water, rather than treating water after it had left the source. The primary section dealing with this new emphasis was the following.]

"Source Water Quality Assessment

"SEC. 1453. (a) SOURCE WATER ASSESSMENT.—

"(1) GUIDANCE.—Within 12 months after the date of enactment of the Safe Drinking Water Act Amendments of 1996, after notice and comment, the Administrator shall publish guidance for States exercising primary enforcement responsibility for public water systems to carry out directly or through delegation (for the protection and benefit of public water systems and for the support of monitoring flexibility) a source water assessment program within the State's boundaries. Each State adopting modifications to monitoring requirements pursuant to section 1418(b) shall, prior to adopting such modifications, have an approved source water assessment program under this section and shall carry out the program either directly or through delegation.

"(2) PROGRAM REQUIREMENTS.—A source water assessment program under this subsection shall—

"(A) delineate the boundaries of the assessment areas in such State from which one or more public water systems in the State receive supplies of drinking water, using all reasonably available hydrogeologic information on the sources of the supply of drinking water in the State and the water flow, recharge, and discharge and any other reliable information as the State deems necessary to adequately determine such areas; and

"(B) identify for contaminants regulated under this title for which monitoring is required under this title (or any unregulated contaminants selected by the State, in its discretion, which the State, for the purposes of this subsection, has determined may present a threat to public health), to the extent practical, the origins within each delineated area of such contaminants to determine the susceptibility of the public water systems in the delineated area to such contaminants.

Source: Public Law 104–182. 1996. U.S. Statutes. http://www .gpo.gov/fdsys/pkg/PLAW-104publ182/pdf/PLAW-104publ182.pdf. Accessed on September 12, 2015.

(For a complete review of amendments to the Safe Drinking Water Act of 1974, see Mary Tiemann. 2014. "Safe Drinking Water Act (SCWA): A Summary of the Act and Its Major Requirements." Congressional Research Service. https://www. fas.org/sgp/crs/misc/RL31243.pdf. Accessed on September 12, 2015.

National Audubon Society v. the Superior Court of Alpine County, 33 Cal. 3d 419; 189 Cal. Rptr. 346 (1983)

One of the confounding points about many water issues is that two or more legal, regulatory, or other factors may apply at the same time to a controversy. Such was the case with this dispute between an environmental organization on the one hand and the city of Los Angeles on the other. The city had obtained permits from the state as early as 1940 to draw water from five streams that feed Mono Lake in the northern part of the state, a lake of considerable natural beauty that was popular with visitors. By the time the city had actually constructed all of the diversion canals needed to withdraw water from the streams, the level of the lake had begun to drop significantly. At that point, the Audubon Society brought legal action to invalidate the city's petition arguing that the so-called doctrine of public trust outweighed the legal right of appropriation under which the state had awarded the permits to the city. The public trust doctrine is a very ancient theory that says that certain resources are so valuable that they cannot be sold, rented, or otherwise awarded to private parties. The waters of Lake Mono, the Audubon Society argued, were protected by such a doctrine. In a long and somewhat complex decision, the California Supreme Court found for the Audubon Society, agreeing that the state had an obligation to protect the natural beauty of the Lake Mono waters. In its summary in the case, the court said that:

This has been a long and involved answer to the two questions posed by the federal district court. In summarizing our opinion, we will essay a shorter version of our response.

The federal court inquired first of the interrelationship between the public trust doctrine and the California water rights system, asking whether the "public trust doctrine in this context [is] subsumed in the California water rights system, or . . . [functions] independently of that system?" Our answer is "neither." The public trust doctrine and the appropriative water rights system are parts of an integrated system of water law. The public trust doctrine serves the function in that integrated system of preserving the continuing sovereign power of the state to protect public trust uses, a power which precludes anyone from acquiring a vested right to harm the public trust, and imposes a continuing duty on the state to take such uses into account in allocating water resources.

Restating its question, the federal court asked: "[Can] the plaintiffs challenge the Department's permits and licenses by arguing that those permits and licenses are limited by the public trust doctrine, or must the plaintiffs . . . [argue] that the water diversions and uses authorized thereunder are not 'reasonable or beneficial' as required under the California water rights system?" We reply that plaintiffs can rely on the public trust doctrine in seeking reconsideration of the allocation of the waters of the Mono Basin.

The federal court's second question asked whether plaintiffs must exhaust an administrative remedy before filing suit. Our response is "no." The courts and the Water Board have concurrent jurisdiction in cases of this kind. If the nature or complexity of the issues indicate that an initial determination by the board is appropriate, the courts may refer the matter to the board.

This opinion is but one step in the eventual resolution of the Mono Lake controversy. We do not dictate any particular allocation of water. Our objective is to resolve a legal conundrum in which two competing systems of thought—the public trust doctrine and the appropriative water rights system—existed independently of each other, espousing principles which seemingly suggested opposite results. We hope by integrating these two doctrines to clear away the legal barriers which have so far prevented either the Water Board or the courts from taking a new and objective look at the water resources of the Mono Basin. The human and environmental uses of Mono Lake—uses protected by the public trust doctrine—deserve to be taken into account. Such uses should not be destroyed because the state mistakenly thought itself powerless to protect them.

Source: *National Audubon Society v. the Superior Court of Alpine County*, 33 Cal. 3d 419; 189 Cal. Rptr. 346 *[etc.]*. 1983. California Courts. The Official Case Law of the State of California. http://www.lexisnexis.com/clients/CACourts/. Accessed on September 13, 2015.

Convention on the Protection and Use of Transboundary Watercourses and International Lakes (1992)

One of the fundamental documents on water policy adopted by the United Nations was the Convention on the Protection and Use of Transboundary Watercourses and International Lakes, which was adopted in 1992 and entered into force in 1996. The document attempts to provide guidelines that countries can use in resolving disputes over water resources that are in contact with two or more discrete governmental entities. Some key provisions of the convention are the following.

Article 2

General Provisions

1. The Parties shall take all appropriate measures to prevent, control and reduce any transboundary impact.

2. The Parties shall, in particular, take all appropriate measures:

   (a) to prevent, control and reduce pollution of waters causing or likely to cause transboundary impact;

   (b) to ensure that transboundary waters are used with the aim of ecologically sound and rational water management, conservation of water resources and environmental protection;

   (c) to ensure that transboundary waters are used in a reasonable and equitable way, taking into particular account their transboundary character, in the case of activities which cause or are likely to cause transboundary impact;

   (d) to ensure conservation and, where necessary, restoration of ecosystems.

3. Measures for the prevention, control and reduction of water pollution shall be taken, where possible, at source.

4. These measures shall not directly or indirectly result in a transfer of pollution to other parts of the environment.

5. In taking the measures referred to in paragraphs 1 and 2 of this Article, the Parties shall be guided by the following principles:

   (a) the precautionary principle, by virtue of which action to avoid the potential transboundary impact of the release of hazardous substances shall not be postponed on the ground that scientific research has not fully proved a causal link between those substances, on the one hand, and the potential transboundary impact, on the other hand;

(b) the polluter-pays principle, by virtue of which costs of pollution prevention, control and reduction measures shall be borne by the polluter;

(c) water resources shall be managed so that the needs of the present generation are met without compromising the ability of future generations to meet their own needs.

. . .

Article 3

Prevention, Control and Reduction

1. To prevent, control and reduce transboundary impact, the Parties shall develop, adopt, implement and, as far as possible, render compatible relevant legal, administrative, economic, financial and technical measures, in order to ensure, inter alia, that:

(a) the emission of pollutants is prevented, controlled and reduced at source through the application of, inter alia, low and non-waste technology.

(b) transboundary waters are protected against pollution from point sources through the prior licensing of waste water discharges by the competent national authorities, and that the authorized discharges are monitored and controlled;

(c) limits for waste water discharges stated in permits are based on the best available technology for discharges of hazardous substances;

(d) stricter requirements, even leading to prohibition in individual cases, are imposed when the quality of the receiving water or the ecosystem so requires;

(e) At least biological treatment or equivalent processes are applied to municipal waste water, where necessary in a step-by-step approach;

(f) appropriate measures are taken, such as the application of the best available technology, in order to reduce nutrient inputs from industrial and municipal sources;

(g) appropriate measures and best environmental practices are developed and implemented for the reduction of inputs of nutrients and hazardous substances from diffuse sources, especially where the main sources are from agriculture (guidelines for developing best environmental practices are given in Annex II to this Convention);

(h) environmental impact assessment and other means of assessment are applied;

(i) sustainable water-resources management, including the application of the ecosystems approach, is promoted:

(j) contingency planning is developed;

(k) additional specific measures are taken to prevent the pollution of groundwaters;

(l) the risk of accidental pollution is minimized.

Source: Convention on the Protection and Use of Transboundary Watercourses and International Lakes, Helsinki, 17 March 1992. United Nations, *Treaty Series*, vol. 1936, p. 269. Reprinted by permission of the United Nations.

Standards for the Growing, Harvesting, Packing and Holding of Produce for Human Consumption (2014)

One of the responsibilities of the U.S. Food and Drug Administration (FDA) is to establish standards that will minimize the risk of serious adverse health consequences as a result of eating contaminated food products. As a step in that direction, the FDA proposes a long and detailed list of rules for ensuring food safety in 2013. Among those rules were a number that dealt with the safety and purity of agricultural water. The provisions of a key section of those rules are summarized here.

A. General Requirement

Proposed § 112.41 would establish the requirement that all agricultural water must be safe and of adequate sanitary quality for its intended use. The principle of "safe and of adequate sanitary quality for its intended use" contains elements related both to the quality of the source water used and the activity, practice, or use of the water. Uses vary significantly, including: Crop irrigation (using various direct water application methods); crop protection sprays; produce cooling water; dump tank water; water used to clean packing materials, equipment, tools and buildings; and hand washing water. The way in which water is used for different commodities and agricultural practices can determine how effectively pathogens that may be present are transmitted to produce.

. . .

B. Measures Regarding Agricultural Water Sources and Distribution Systems

Proposed § 112.42(a) would establish that at the beginning of a growing season, you must inspect the entire agricultural water system under your control (including water source, water distribution system, facilities, and equipment), to identify conditions that are reasonably likely to introduce known or reasonably foreseeable hazards into or onto covered produce or food-contact surfaces in light of your covered produce, practices, and conditions, including consideration of the following:

(1) The nature of each agricultural water source (for example, ground water or surface water);

(2) The extent of your control over each agricultural water source;

(3) The degree of protection of each agricultural water source;

(4) Use of adjacent or nearby land; and

(5) The likelihood of introduction of known or reasonably foreseeable hazards to agricultural water by another user of agricultural water before the water reaches your covered farm.

*[The proposed rules then give detailed information about each
of these five conditions.]*

. . .

C. Requirements for Treating Agricultural Water

Water treatment is an effective means of decreasing the number
of waterborne outbreaks in sources of drinking water (Ref. 146).
However, treatments that are inadequate or improperly applied,
interrupted, or intermittent have been associated with waterborne
disease outbreaks (Ref. 146). Failures in treatment systems are
largely attributed to suboptimal particle removal and treatment
malfunction (Ref. 147). For this reason, when treating water,
it is important to monitor the treatment parameters to ensure
the treatment is delivered in an efficacious manner. Monitoring
treatment can be performed in lieu of microbial water quality
monitoring, if under the intended conditions of the treatment,
the water is rendered safe and of adequate sanitary quality for
its intended use. Many operations choose to perform microbial
water quality testing in addition to monitoring the water treatment as a further assurance of treatment effectiveness (Ref. 148).

Proposed § 112.43 would establish requirements related
to treatment of agricultural water. *[Details about the process of
treating agricultural water then follow.]*

. . .

D. Testing and Frequency of Testing of Agricultural Water

Proposed § 112.44 would establish requirements related to testing of agricultural water and subsequent actions based on the
test results. Specifically, proposed § 112.44(a) would require that
you test the quality of agricultural water according to the requirements in § 112.45 using a quantitative, or presence-absence

method of analysis provided in subpart N to ensure there is no detectable generic E. coli in 100 ml agricultural water when it is:

(1) Used as sprout irrigation water;

(2) Applied in any manner that directly contacts covered produce during or after harvest activities (for example, water that is applied to covered produce for washing or cooling activities, and water that is applied to harvested crops to prevent dehydration before cooling), including when used to make ice that directly contacts covered produce during or after harvest activities;

(3) Used to make a treated agricultural tea;

(4) Used to contact food-contact surfaces, or to make ice that will contact food-contact surfaces; or

(5) Used for washing hands during and after harvest activities.

. . .

E. Requirements for Water Used in Harvesting, Packing, and Holding Activities

Proposed § 112.46 would establish the measures you must take for water that you use during harvest, packing, and holding activities for covered produce. Specifically, proposed § 112.46(a) would require that you manage the water as necessary, including by establishing and following water-change schedules for re-circulated water, to maintain adequate sanitary quality and minimize the potential for contamination of covered produce and food-contact surfaces with known or reasonably foreseeable hazards (for example, hazards that may be introduced into the water from soil adhering to the covered produce)

. . .

[Section F deals with requirements for record-keeping related to all of the above rules.]

Source: Standards for Growing, Harvesting, Packing, and Holding of Produce for Human Consumption. 2013. Regulations.gov. http://www.regulations.gov/#!documentDetail;D= FDA-2011-N-0921-0001. Accessed on September 23, 2015.

Communication from the Commission on the European Citizens' Initiative "Water and Sanitation Are a Human Right! Water Is a Public Good, Not a Commodity!" (2014)

One provision of the Lisbon Treaty of 2009 is that initiatives for action by the European Commission (EC) may be submitted by groups who collect at least a million signatures from at least seven member states on some topic in which they are interested. The first such petition was presented to the EC on February 17, 2014, on the subject of water and sanitation. The key element in that petition was the wish by petitioners to clarify that water is a human right, not a commodity, a dispute that has gone on in the international community for a number of years. That is, petitioners argue that access to water and adequate sanitation should not be a function of market forces, but a guaranteed right to all people of the world. Portions of the commission's response to that petition are provided here. (Footnotes are omitted in the excerpt.)

Access to safe drinking water and sanitation is inextricably linked to the right to life and human dignity and to the need for an adequate standard of living.

Over the last decade, international law has acknowledged a right to safe drinking water and sanitation, most prominently at the United Nations (UN) level. The UN General Assembly Resolution 64/292 recognises *"the right to safe and clean drinking water and sanitation as a human right that is essential for the full enjoyment of life and all human rights"*. Moreover, in the final outcome document of the 2012 UN Conference on Sustainable Development (Rio+20), heads of State and Government and high level representatives reaffirmed their *"commitments regarding the human right to safe drinking water and sanitation, to be progressively realized for [their] populations with full respect for national sovereignty".*

At the European level, the Parliamentary Assembly of the Council of Europe declared *"that access to water must be recognised as a fundamental human right because it is essential to life on earth and is a resource that must be shared by humankind".* The EU has also reaffirmed that "all States bear human rights obligations regarding access to safe drinking water, which must be available, physically accessible, affordable and acceptable".

These principles have also inspired EU action. The EU Water Framework Directive recognises that *"water is not a commercial product like any other but, rather, a heritage which must be protected, defended and treated as such".*

. . .

In response to the citizens' call for action, the Commission is committed to take concrete steps and work on a number of new actions in areas that are of direct relevance to the initiative and its goals. In particular, the Commission:

- will reinforce implementation of its water quality legislation, building on the commitments presented in the 7th EAP and the Water Blueprint;
- will launch an EU-wide public consultation on the Drinking Water Directive, notably in view of improving access to quality water in the EU;
- will improve transparency for urban wastewater and drinking water data management and explore the idea of benchmarking water quality;
- will bring about a more structured dialogue between stakeholders on transparency in the water sector;
- will cooperate with existing initiatives to provide a wider set of benchmarks for water services;
- will stimulate innovative approaches for development assistance (e.g. support to partnerships between water operators

and to public-public partnerships); promote sharing of best practices between Member States (e.g. on solidarity instruments) and identify new opportunities for cooperation.

- will advocate universal access to safe drinking water and sanitation as a priority area for future Sustainable Development Goals.

Source: Communication from the Commission. 2014. European Commission. http://ec.europa.eu/transparency/regdoc/rep/1/2014/EN/1–2014–177-EN-F1–1.Pdf. Accessed on September 12, 2015.

Climate Change Impacts in the United States (2014)

One of the provisions of the Global Change Research Act of 1990 was that the National Science and Technology Council provide the U.S. Congress with regular reports on the status of climate change worldwide and its anticipated effects on the United States. The section of the most recent of those reports dealing with water begins with a listing of 11 "key messages" about the effects of climate change on water resources in the United States. Those key messages are as follows:

1. Annual precipitation and river-flow increases are observed now in the Midwest and the Northeast regions. Very heavy precipitation events have increased nationally and are projected to increase in all regions. The length of dry spells is projected to increase in most areas, especially the southern and northwestern portions of the contiguous United States.

2. Short-term (seasonal or shorter) droughts are expected to intensify in most U.S. regions. Longer-term droughts are expected to intensify in large areas of the Southwest, southern Great Plains, and Southeast.

3. Flooding may intensify in many U.S. regions, even in areas where total precipitation is projected to decline.

4. Climate change is expected to affect water demand, groundwater withdrawals, and aquifer recharge, reducing groundwater availability in some areas.

5. Sea level rise, storms and storm surges, and changes in surface and groundwater use patterns are expected to compromise the sustainability of coastal freshwater aquifers and wetlands.

6. Increasing air and water temperatures, more intense precipitation and runoff, and intensifying droughts can decrease river and lake water quality in many ways, including increases in sediment, nitrogen, and other pollutant loads.

7. Climate change affects water demand and the ways water is used within and across regions and economic sectors. The Southwest, Great Plains, and Southeast are particularly vulnerable to changes in water supply and demand.

8. Changes in precipitation and runoff, combined with changes in consumption and withdrawal, have reduced surface and groundwater supplies in many areas. These trends are expected to continue, increasing the likelihood of water shortages for many uses.

9. Increasing flooding risk affects human safety and health, property, infrastructure, economies, and ecology in many basins across the United States.

10. In most U.S. regions, water resources managers and planners will encounter new risks, vulnerabilities, and opportunities that may not be properly managed within existing practices.

11. Increasing resilience and enhancing adaptive capacity provide opportunities to strengthen water resources management and plan for climate change impacts. Many institutional, scientific, economic, and political barriers present challenges to implementing adaptive strategies.

Source: Melillo, Jerry M., Terese (T.C.) Richmond, and Gary W. Yohe, eds., 2014. "Climate Change Impacts in the United States: The Third National Climate Assessment. U.S. Global Change Research Program."

Executive Order B-29-15 (California) 2015

In response to the continuing drought in the state of California, Governor Jerry Brown released the following Executive Order, designed to take aggressive action to deal with this ongoing crisis in the state. The order contains 31 sections, only some of which are summarized here.

2. The State Water Resources Control Board (Water Board) shall impose restrictions to achieve a statewide 25% reduction in potable urban water usage through February 28, 2016.

3. The Department of Water Resources (the Department) shall lead a statewide initiative, in partnership with local agencies, to collectively replace 50 million square feet of lawns and ornamental turf with drought tolerant landscapes.

5. The Water Board shall impose restrictions to require that commercial, industrial, and institutional properties, such as campuses, golf courses, and cemeteries, immediately implement water efficiency measures. . . .

6. The Water Board shall prohibit irrigation with potable water of ornamental turf on public street medians.

7. The Water Board shall prohibit irrigation with potable water outside of newly constructed homes and buildings that is not delivered by drip or microspray systems.

8. The Water Board shall direct urban water suppliers to develop rate structures and other pricing mechanisms, including but not limited to surcharges, fees, and penalties, to maximize water conservation consistent with statewide water restrictions.

10. The Water Board shall require frequent reporting of water diversion and use by water right holders, conduct inspections to determine whether illegal diversions or wasteful and unreasonable use of water are occurring, and bring enforcement actions against illegal diverters and those engaging in the wasteful and unreasonable use of water.

12. Agricultural water suppliers that supply water to more than 25,000 acres shall include in their required 2015 Agricultural Water Management Plans a detailed drought management plan that describes the actions and measures the supplier will take to manage water demand during drought.

25. The Energy Commission shall expedite the processing of all applications or petitions for amendments to power plant certifications issued by the Energy Commission for the purpose of securing alternate water supply necessary for continued power plant operation.

Source: Executive Order B-29-15. 2015. State of California. https://www.gov.ca.gov/docs/4.1.15_Executive_Order.pdf. Accessed on September 11, 2015.

WaterSense (2015)

WaterSense is a program introduced by the U.S. Environmental Protection Agency (EPA) in 2006 to promote the wise use of water in a host of consumer products and services. The program is a partnership between EPA and more than a thousand companies in a wide variety of fields including builders, governmental agencies, product manufacturers, retailers, certifying agencies, trade associations, and utilities. The program provides a label that indicates that a product or service meets certain standards for the wise use of water. The criteria on which the label issuance is based are as follows:

- WaterSense labels products that are 20 percent more water-efficient and perform as well as or better than standard models.

- WaterSense labeled faucets—or aerators that can be installed on existing bathroom faucets—are about 30 percent more efficient than standard faucets while still providing sufficient flow.

- WaterSense labeled toilets use 20 percent less water per flush but perform as well as or better than today's standard toilets and older toilets that use much more water.

- The WaterSense label is now found on more than 1,600 models of showerheads, 1,900 models of tank-type toilets, 6,800 models of faucet or faucet accessory models, and 150 models of weather-based irrigation controllers that are independently certified to meet EPA's criteria for both water efficiency and performance.

- To design, service, or audit your in-ground landscape irrigation system, look for an irrigation professional certified by a WaterSense labeled program.

Some basic data and statistics on which the WaterSense program is based are as follows:

- Approximately 5 to 10 percent of American homes have water leaks that drip away 90 gallons a day or more! Many of these leaks reside in old fixtures, such as leaky toilets and faucets. In fact, water lost by these leaky residences could be reduced by more than 30,000 gallons if new, efficient fixtures were installed. If the 5 percent of American homes that leak the most corrected those leaks—it could save more than 177 billion gallons of water annually!

- Using WaterSense labeled faucets or faucet accessories could reduce a household's faucet water use by more than 500 gallons annually—that's enough water to do 14 loads of laundry.

- WaterSense labeled faucets and faucet accessories can reduce excessive flow volumes by more than 30 percent without sacrificing performance.

- If one in every 10 homes in the United States were to install WaterSense labeled faucets or faucet accessories in their bathrooms, it could save 6 billion gallons of water, and more than $50 million in the energy costs to supply, heat, and treat that water.

• If all inefficient toilets in U.S. homes were converted to WaterSense labeled models, we could save more than 640 billion gallons of water per year—the equivalent to 15 days of flow over Niagara Falls.

• If homeowners with irrigation systems use a certified irrigation professional to perform regular maintenance, they can reduce irrigation water use by 15 percent or nearly 8,800 gallons of water annually. That's the equal to the amount of water used to take 500 showers.

Source: WaterSense. 2015. United States Environmental Protection Agency. http://www.epa.gov/watersense/about_us/facts .html#watersense. Accessed on September 25, 2015.

LET'S TURN · NOT BURN

IT'S TIME TO BUILD A
RENEWABLE ENERGY ECONOMY
IN NEW YORK.

SIERRA
CLUB
FOUNDED 1872

RENEWA... ...PAIGN

...d Pr... ...the Earth

...woRow... 2013

SIERRAC...

FRACK

NYAgainstFra...

KEEP THE
FRACK
OUT OF MY
WATER

SIERRACLUB.ORG/FRACKING

SIERRA
CLUB
FOUNDED 1872

KE...
FR...
OUT...
WA...

6 Annotated Bibliography

Introduction

Water is perhaps the single most important chemical compound on Earth. It is essential for human life in some fundamental ways, such as drinking, and critical for other uses, such as sanitation and power production. People have been thinking about and writing about the importance of water in human civilization for many centuries. No bibliography of the length available here can even begin to touch on the great variety of books, articles, reports, and Internet commentaries on water in general and on the present world crisis in water availability and use. This bibliography can be seen, therefore, as primarily an introduction to some of the most recent publications available on the topic.

Some resources are available in more than one format, usually as articles and as Internet reproductions of those articles. In such cases, information about both formats is provided. The reader is reminded that this list of resources is not meant to be exhaustive, but is provided as a source of references with which one might continue his or her research on the topic. The reader is also encouraged to review the references for Chapters 1 and 2, which contain a number of other valuable resources, most of which are not duplicated in this bibliography.

Books

Antonelli, Marta, and Francesca Greco, eds. 2015. *The Water We Eat: Combining Virtual Water and Water Footprints.* Cham, Switzerland: Springer.

Water used in the fracking of a single well ranges in the millions of gallons per well, much too high for a world that is increasingly running out of water, according to some observers. (David Grossman/Alamy Stock Photo)

The essays that comprise this book focus on so-called green water, water that is contained in plants. It considers issues of sustainability and food security that depend on a ready supply of green water. Some chapter titles are "Water in Food," "Virtual Water in Diet, Shopping and Food Waste," "Aware Eaters of Water: An Idea for Water Labeling," and "The Virtual Water in a Bottle of Wine."

Baba, A., et al., eds. 2011. *Climate Change and Its Effects on Water Resources*. Dordrecht, South Holland: Springer.
This book is part of the NATO Science for Peace and Security Series. Its chapters deal with a variety of climate- and water-related topics such as impacts of climate change on recharge rates of groundwater resources; management of karst reservoirs during climate change; potential effects of climate change on specific water resources, such as those in Turkey, Azerbaijan, and Armenia; and the threat of nanoparticles to groundwater resources.

Bell, Alexander. 2013. *Peak Water: How We Built Civilisation on Water and Drained the World Dry*. New York: Luath Press.
This book takes a strongly historical view of the world's current water situation, arguing that human civilization was originally based to a large extent on the ability of humans to capture and put water to use for a host of different activities. The author then shows how various societies have increasingly ignored their key link to water resources, producing the global water crisis that exists today. He shows how many different aspects of society will suffer if efforts are not made to make better use of the water resources available to humans.

Berlatsky, Noah. 2012. *Water*. Detroit: Greenhaven Press.
This book is part of the publisher's Global Viewpoints series for young adults, which outlines important contemporary issues and presents a variety of viewpoints about various aspects of those issues.

Booth, Colin, and Susanne Charlesworth, eds. 2014. *Water Resources for the Built Environment: Management Issues and Solutions*. Chichester: Wiley Blackwell.

This book includes a number of essays dealing with a variety of issues related to the use of water resources in urban settings and other so-called built environments. Individual sections deal with topics related to deficiency and excess of water resources, water policy and legislation, water privatization, urban water economics, the impact of dams and reservoirs, hydropower, water quality and treatment, desalination, delivering potable water to buildings, water conservation, rainwater harvesting, and gray water harvesting.

Buckley, Michael. 2014. *Meltdown in Tibet: China's Reckless Destruction of Ecosystems from the Highlands of Tibet to the Deltas of Asia*. New York: Palgrave Macmillan.

This book focuses on the changes in water resources that have been taking place in Tibet and neighboring countries largely as a result of development projects initiated by the Chinese government. Individual chapters deal with topics such as "what are Chinese engineers up to?," "what is the fate of the mighty rivers of Tibet?," "why is China snuffing out Tibetan nomad culture?," and "what does a rain of black soot have to do with this?."

Callow, Roger, Eva Ludi, and Josephine Tucker, eds. 2013. *Achieving Water Security: Lessons from Research in Water Supply, Sanitation and Hygiene in Ethiopia*. Rugby, UK: Practical Action Publishing.

The authors report on a five-year study on the effects of investing in water and WASH programs on water security in Ethiopia. They argue that such investments produce significant returns, not only for Ethiopia, but also for other nations in sub-Saharan Africa and beyond.

Chávarro, Jimena Murillo. 2015. *The Human Right to Water: A Legal Comparative Perspective at the International, Regional and Domestic Level.* Cambridge, UK: Intersentia.

The author reviews the history of the doctrine of water as a human right and then explores the way in which that doctrine has been interpreted and put into practice at the domestic, national, and international levels.

Chellaney, Brahma. 2013. *Water, Peace, and War: Confronting the Global Water Crisis.* Lanham, MD: Rowman & Littlefield.

This book provides an excellent general introduction to the current global water crisis, based on the author's presumption that water issues lie at the basis of many, if not all, major international conflicts in the world today. For a good review of the book, see http://www.globalpolicyjournal.com/blog/19/02/2014/book-review-water-peace-and-war-confronting-global-water-crisis-brahma-chellaney.

De Villiers, Marq. 2015. *Back to the Well: Rethinking the Future of Water.* Fredericton, NB: Goose Lane Editions.

This book is a follow-up on the author's 2003 overview of the world water crisis (see later), with extended discussions of some basic issues, such as who actually owns the world's water supplies, is access to water a basic human right, whose responsibility is it to ensure that adequate supplies of clean water are available, and what relative claims to individuals and society as a whole have on water resources?

De Villiers, Marq. 2003. *Water: The Fate of Our Most Precious Resource*, 2nd ed. Toronto, ON: M&S.

The author takes a grand overview of the world's water status in the early 21st century, starting with a broad general introduction to the topic that includes data and history of water use by humans, followed by a discussion of factors that have brought about significant changes in the quality of water, the amount of water available, and the uses to which it is put. He next discusses specific water issues in places such as the Middle East, northern Africa, China, and the United States, before concluding with a section on "What Is to Be Done?"

Dong, Bo. 2014. *Climate Change and the Water Cycle Hydrological Impacts of Climate Change in the Continental United States.* Saarbrücken, Germany: LAP LAMBERT Academic Publishing.
One may think of the water cycle as a relatively fixed phenomenon in which water is recycled through Earth's atmosphere, lithosphere, and hydrosphere. Yet, that cycle is subject to change by a variety of factors, one of which is climate. This book explores measurable changes that have occurred in Earth's water cycle, with particular reference patterns to the United States, along with a consideration of the practical effects these changes may have on weather patterns, food production, and other elements of the nation's economy.

Filho, Walter Leal, and Vakur Sümer, eds. 2015. *Sustainable Water Use and Management: Examples of New Approaches and Perspectives.* Cham, Switzerland: Springer.
Problems relating to ways in which water scarcity and insecurity can be dealt with are of growing interest to a variety of groups and individuals around the world. The chapters in this book present ideas for water management from individual projects in countries in all parts of the world including Canada, the United States, Lithuania, Australia, Kenya, Afghanistan, Turkey, Finland, and India.

Free Flow: Reaching Water Security through Cooperation. 2013. Paris: UNESCO Publishing; London: Tudor Rose.
This excellent book contains dozens of essays on various aspects of water issues by experts from around the world. The essays are arranged into eight major sections on water diplomacy; transboundary water management;

water education and institutional development; financing; legal framework at national and international levels; water cooperation, sustainability, and poverty eradication; economic development and water; and international cooperation on water sciences and research.

Gleick, Peter H. 2014. *The World's Water. Volume 8: The Biennial Report on Freshwater Resources.* Washington, DC: Island Press.
This book is the latest volume in a biennial report on the state of the world's water resources. It includes chapters on topics such as sustainable water management, desalination, hydraulic fracturing, water governance, transboundary disputes over water ownership and use, water funding, access to water and sanitation in various countries, and water resources globally and by country.

Gulbenkian Think Tank on Water and the Future of Humanity. 2013. *Water and the Future of Humanity: Revisiting Water Security.* Dordrecht, South Holland: Springer.
This anthology consists of a number of papers on various aspects of the world's current water resources situation. Some topics include drivers of water demand, lessons from the past, climate change and water management, recent changes in water availability, human impact on the environment, changing approaches to water management, urban centers and urban water systems, smarter management of food and water systems, water and energy, and strategies for moving to a positive future.

Jagerskog, Anders, Ashok Swain, and Joakim Ojendal. 2015. *Water Security*, 4 vols. Los Angeles: SAGE.
As issues of water scarcity become more widespread and more common among nations of the world, questions have arisen as to how governments can guarantee water security within their own borders, ensuring that citizens will continue to have access to the amounts and quality of water that they expect and require. The four volumes

in this series consider all aspects of that issue, including origin and foundations, international conflict and cooperation, water security and development, and current dilemmas and future challenges.

Kallen, Stuart A. 2015. *Running Dry: The Global Water Crisis.* Minneapolis: Twenty-First Century Books.
This book is intended as an introduction to water issues in today's world for readers at the secondary school level. It provides a good general introduction to the topic.

Kluge, Thomas. 2015. "Water Gap: The Overuse of Fresh Water." In Susanne Hartard and Wolfgang Liebert, eds. *Competition and Conflicts on Resource Use.* Cham, Switzerland: Springer, Ch. 14, 213–229.
The author presents a general overview of the problem of freshwater shortages worldwide, explains how the problem can lead to conflict between nations and regions, and also explains the steps that can be taken to deal with those conflicts.

Lassiter, Allison, ed. 2015. *Sustainable Water: Challenges and Solutions from California.* Oakland, CA: University of California Press.
Most of the major issues surrounding water scarcity and related problems arising around the world have their counterparts in California. This volume brings together essays from experts in a wide variety of fields, including policymakers, lawyers, economists, hydrologists, ecologists, engineers, and planners, each of whom discusses water problems confronted by the state of California and solutions that have been devised to deal with those problems.

Meija, Abel. 2014. "Water Scarcity in Latin America and the Caribbean: Myths and Reality." In Mardechai Shechter, ed. *Water for the Americas: Challenges and Opportunities.* Abingdon; New York: Routledge, Taylor and Francis, Ch. 3.

This book provides a particularly interesting analysis of the factors that combine to make water shortages (in Latin America, but in other parts of the world also) largely a result of political, social, and economic decisions rather than a matter of shortages in physical supplies of water.

Nakayama, Mikiyasu, and Ryo Fujikura. 2014. *Restoring Communities Resettled after Dam Construction in Asia*. Abingdon, UK; New York: Routledge.

Research on the short-term consequences of dam construction on local communities is relatively abundant. Similar research 5, 10, or more years later is rare. This book attempts to fill that gap by reporting on the long-term changes that have occurred in five countries—Indonesia, Japan, Laos, Sri Lanka, and Turkey—as a result of dam construction.

Peppard, Christiana Z. 2014. *Just Water: Theology, Ethics, and the Global Water Crisis*. Maryknoll, NY: Orbis Books.

The author notes that the world's current water problems have fundamental and important moral and ethical cognates. She analyzes those problems within that context.

Piper, Karen Lynnea. 2014. *The Price of Thirst: Global Water Inequality and the Coming Chaos*. Minneapolis: University of Minnesota Press.

Piper takes her cue for this book from a 2006 headline in *The New York Times*, "There's money in thirst," raising questions about the economic aspects of the current global water crisis. She begins with historical stories of the economic aspects of water shortages in California and Chile, before moving on to more recent conflicts over water in South Africa and India. She concludes her story with a retelling of wars that have been fought over water rights in Egypt and Iraq.

Postel, Sandra. 2014. *The Last Oasis: Facing Water Scarcity*. Hoboken, NJ: Taylor and Francis.

This book provides a general overview of the water problems facing the world today, the way in which these problems have developed, and some of the solutions that have been devised for dealing with these problems.

Richter, Brian D. 2014. *Chasing Water: A Guide for Moving from Scarcity to Sustainability.* Washington, DC: Island Press.
The author reviews the history of the development of the current global water crisis and points out some solutions that have been developed by governmental agencies at the national and international levels. He then argues that water issues often require the attention of individual communities, who can only devise solutions that are appropriate to their own unique settings.

Shrestha, Sangam, ed. 2015. *Managing Water Resources under Climate Uncertainty: Examples from Asia, Europe, Latin America, and Australia.* Cham, Switzerland; New York: Springer.
As the evidence for climate change continues to become available, questions about ways of dealing with potential water shortages become of greater significance. This book brings together a number of articles dealing with specific ways in which authorities from a variety of countries have begun to explore ways of solving this problem of the future. Examples come from Vietnam, Indonesia, Laos, India, Cambodia, Bhutan, Australia, and Europe.

Tang, Qiuhong, ed. 2015. *The Terrestrial Water Cycle: Natural and Human-induced Changes.* Washington, DC: American Geophysical Union.
The essays in this book focus on the changes that have been made, intentionally and unintentionally, in the Earth's water cycle.

Tannahill, Kim, Peter Mills, and Colin A. Booth. 2014. "Impacts and Issues of Dams and Reservoirs." In Colin Booth and Susanne Charlesworth, eds. *Water Resources for the Built Environment:*

Management Issues and Solutions. Chichester: Wiley Blackwell, Ch. 5.

> The authors provide a general overview of the status of dams worldwide as of 2014 and then discuss the environmental and socioeconomic impacts of those dams.

Tanzi, Attial, et al., eds. *The UNECE Convention on the Protection and Use of Transboundary Watercourses and International Lakes: Its Contribution to International Water Cooperation.* Leiden, South Holland; Boston: Brill Nijhoff.

> The chapters in this book review the history of the water convention and the influence it has had on countries having to deal with transborder and related water issues over the past decade or more.

Thielbörger, Pierre. 2014. *The Right(s) to Water: The Multi-Level Governance of a Unique Human Right.* Heidelberg, Baden-Württemberg; New York; Dordrecht, South Holland; London: Springer.

> The three main sections of this book deal with (1) the current legal status of water rights in Europe and other parts of the world, (2) philosophical approaches to determining the right to water, and (3) implementation of principles governing decisions as to how water rights ought to be distributed internationally.

Tilt, Bryan. 2015. *Dams and Development in China: The Moral Economy of Water and Power.* New York: Columbia University Press.

> This excellent book reviews one very specific aspect of global water issues, the interaction between moral and economic issues that occur as a result of the accelerated construction of dams on many of China's largest and most important rivers.

Tortajada, Cecilia, Asit K. Biswas, and Avinash Tyagi, eds. 2015. *Water Management and Climate Change: Dealing with Uncertainties.* Milton Park, UK: Routledge.

The chapters in this book deal with some of the problems involving water management caused by significant climate and other types of changes in coming years. The chapters focus on such issues in a variety of nations, such as Australia, Mexico, Spain, Greece, Italy, and the United States.

Vajpeyi, Dhirendra K., ed. 2014. *Water Resource Conflicts and International Security: A Global Perspective.* Lanham, MD: Lexington Books.

The editor notes that modern technology has created the possibility of increasing numbers and intensities of disputes between and among countries for the use of water from shared resources, such as rivers and lakes that lie between those countries. The essays in this book focus on some specific issues of this kind that have arisen with regard to the Tigris and Euphrates Rivers, the Nile and Jordan River basins, water resources in South Africa, and debates over the Aral Sea Basin.

Weber, Karl. 2012. *Last Call at the Oasis: The Global Water Crisis and Where We Go from Here.* New York: Public Affairs.

This book is a companion publication written to accompany the motion picture *Last Call at the Oasis*, which discusses the current global water crisis. The book can be read alone for the information and stories it provides about the present situation, but is probably used more effectively along with a viewing of the film.

Articles

Aiken, S. Robert, and Colin H. Leigh. 2015. "Dams and Indigenous Peoples in Malaysia: Development, Displacement and Resettlement." *Geografiska Annaler: Series B, Human Geography.* 97(1): 69–93.

This article provides a comprehensive and very interesting review of the effects of dam construction and operation on a very specific population in rural Malaysia.

Akpabio, Emmanuel M., and Kaoru Takara. 2014. "Understanding and Confronting Cultural Complexities Characterizing Water, Sanitation and Hygiene in Sub-Saharan Africa." *Water International.* 39(7): 921–932.

The authors argue that a number of nonscientific factors are involved in the acceptance or lack of acceptance of WASH programs in the communities of sub-Saharan Africa. They review some of the cultural and religious factors that may be involved in limiting the acceptance and effectiveness of such programs.

Akter, T., and Ali A. Mehrab. 2014. "Factors Influencing Knowledge and Practice of Hygiene in Water, Sanitation and Hygiene (WASH) Programme Areas of Bangladesh Rural Advancement Committee." *Rural and Remote Health.* 14(3): 2628. Epub.

This article focuses on some of the factors that affect the implementation or non-implementation of WASH programs in a number of the subdistricts of the Bangladesh Rural Advancement Committee.

Bain, Robert, et al. 2014. "Global Assessment of Exposure to Faecal Contamination through Drinking Water Based on a Systematic Review." *Tropical Medicine & International Health.* 19(8): 917–927.

The authors use data from published studies to attempt to estimate the number of individuals worldwide who are at risk for diseases from water contaminated with fecal matter. They conclude that about 1.8 billion people worldwide are exposed to drinking water that contains at least some level of fecal contamination and that about 60 percent of that number face at least a "moderate" risk from such contamination.

Campbell, Suzy J., et al. 2014. "Water, Sanitation, and Hygiene (WASH): A Critical Component for Sustainable Soil-Transmitted Helminth and Schistosomiasis Control." *PLoS Neglected Tropical Diseases.* 8(4): e2651.

The authors discuss the reasons that WASH and nutritional programs can be critical in the fight against two major tropical diseases, helminth infestation and schistosomiasis. They also review some of the factors related to the implementation of such programs as well as factors that may inhibit their broader use.

Chartres, Colin J., and Andrew Noble. 2015. "Sustainable Intensification: Overcoming Land and Water Constraints on Food Production." *Food Security: The Science, Sociology and Economics of Food Production and Access to Food.* 7(2): 235–245.

The authors review the water demands that will be created by a growing agricultural enterprise that will be needed to provide food for the world's population in coming demands and make a number of recommendations as to how these demands can be met.

Chaturvedi, Vaibhav, et al. 2015. "Climate Mitigation Policy Implications for Global Irrigation Water Demand." *Mitigation and Adaptation Strategies for Global Change: An International Journal Devoted to Scientific, Engineering, Socio-Economic and Policy Responses to Environmental Change.* 20(3): 389–407.

The authors ask two questions about the effects of climate change on water resources for irrigation: (1) how large will the demand for irrigation water be over the next century, and (2) what will be the effects of efforts to deal with climate change have on these demands? They argue that "increasing population and economic growth could more than double the demand for water for agricultural systems in the absence of climate policy, and policies to mitigate climate change further increase agricultural demands for water."

Famiglietti, J. S. 2014. "The Global Groundwater Crisis." *Nature Climate Change.* 4: 945–948.

The author argues that the world's groundwater crisis is "a far greater threat to global water security than is currently acknowledged." He reviews the nature of that crisis and the kinds of actions that are necessary to deal with the crisis.

Freeman, Matthew C., et al. 2014. "Systematic Review: Hygiene and Health: Systematic Review of Handwashing Practices Worldwide and Update of Health Effects." *Tropical Medicine & International Health.* 19(8): 906–916.
The authors attempt to estimate the effects worldwide of appropriate handwashing practices as a preventative for contagious diseases and conclude that handwashing after contact with excreta is "poorly practiced globally, despite the likely positive health benefits."

Gorijan, Shiva, and Barat Ghobadian. 2015. "Solar Desalination: A Sustainable Solution to Water Crisis in Iran." *Renewable and Sustainable Energy Reviews.* 48: 571–584.
The authors describe the water crisis that currently exists in Iran, where more than 70 percent of the land area is arid. They explain how and why desalination is a reasonable and perhaps best available approach to solving the nation's water shortage.

Groll, M., et al. 2015. "Water Quality, Potential Conflicts and Solutions—An Upstream-Downstream Analysis of the Transnational Zarafshan River (Tajikistan, Uzbekistan)." *Environmental Earth Sciences.* 73(2): 743–763.
This article provides a superb analysis of the water issues related to the flow of a river that passes through two countries and the way that water resource is affected by global climate change, growing demands for fresh water by humans living in the area, the needs of agriculture in the two nations, and a host of political factors determining appropriate distribution of water rights.

Ireson, A.M., et al. 2015. "The Changing Water Cycle: the Boreal Plains Ecozone of Western Canada." *Water.* 2(5): 505–521.

Virtually all experts in the field acknowledge that climate change will make significant changes in the fundamental features of water distribution and use on Earth. This article describes in some detail a careful study of the nature of those changes to be expected in one very specific region, the boreal plains of Western Canada. A must read for anyone concerned with potential changes in the water cycle as a result of climate change.

Islam, Shafiqul, and Amanda C. Repella. 2015. "Water Diplomacy: A Negotiated Approach to Manage Complex Water Problems." *Journal of Contemporary Water Research & Education*. 155(1): 1–10.
The authors point out that, at one time, water issues tended to be relatively simple disputes that could be solved fairly easily as long as disputants were willing to put forward the effort. Now, they say, such disputes tend to be far more complicated, requiring a more sophisticated approach to reaching solutions. They review some of the elements that might be involved in such efforts.

Jaeger, W. K. 2013. "Toward a Formal Definition of Water Scarcity in Natural-Human Systems." *Water Resources Research*. 49(7): 4506–4517.
The term *water scarcity* is widely used in articles about the global water crisis, but is not always carefully defined. This article attempts to provide a precise technical definition for the term and a detailed analysis of the factors involved in discussions of the phenomenon.

Jones, Peter, David Hillier, and Daphne Comfort. 2015. "Water Stewardship and Corporate Sustainability: A Case Study of Reputation Management in the Food and Drinks Industry." *Journal of Public Affairs*. 15(1): 116–126. http://onlinelibrary.wiley.com/doi/10.1002/pa.1534/epdf. Accessed on June 15, 2015.
A number of corporations have begun to acknowledge their role in dealing with national and global problems

of water use. These authors attempt to learn more about the motivations for such concerns and the types of actions being taken by companies to deal with sustainable use of water in their businesses.

Le Roux, C. E., Michael Van der Laan, and Mark Gush. 2015. "Agricultural Water Management." *Water Wheel.* 14(2): 22–26.
This article provides an interesting and very readable explanation of the important role that water plays in a traditional agricultural enterprise, some of the problems associated with water use, and some methods that have been developed for dealing with those problems.

Liechti, T. Cohen, et al. 2015. "Influence of Hydropower Development on Flow Regime in the Zambezi River Basin for Different Scenarios of Environmental Flows." *Water Resources Management.* 29(3): 731–747.
This technical article explores the question of how and to what extent a balance can be achieved in building a hydropower dam that is needed to increase energy supplies in a country while reducing the dam's environmental effects to their lowest possible level.

Liu, Yongbo, Xubin Pan, and Junsheng Li. 2015. "Current Agricultural Practices Threaten Future Global Food Production." *Journal of Agricultural and Environmental Ethics.* 28(2): 203–216.
The authors review global agricultural data for the past 50 years and find that the amount and quality of land available for agriculture have declined during the time period. But demands for food from a growing population are almost certain to increase the need for productive agricultural practices. They outline the challenges that are likely to arise because of this conflict.

Liuzzo, Lorena, et al. 2015. "Modifications in Water Resources Availability under Climate Changes: A Case Study in a Sicilian Basin." *Water Resources Management.* 29(4): 1117–1135.

The authors make use of a climate modeling system to predict the effects of climate change on water resources in a southern region of Italy, with some interesting predictions as to what such changes are likely to produce.

Martínez-Ibarra, Emilio. 2015. "Climate, Water and Tourism: Causes and Effects of Droughts Associated with Urban Development and Tourism in Benidorm (Spain)." *International Journal of Biometeorology*. 59(5): 487–501.
This article explores an interesting sub-issue about global water problems, the interaction of water shortages in regions that depend heavily on tourism for their economic survival. The author reviews the ways in which the Benidorm region has dealt (essentially successfully) with water shortages in the past, the deleterious effects of such shortages on the local economy, and prospects for the region's continued success in maintaining an adequate water supply.

Molden, David, Charlotte De Fraiture, and Frank Rijsberman. 2007. "Water Scarcity: The Food Factor." *Issues in Science and Technology*. 23(4): 39–48.
The authors discuss the role of water resources in food production and point out that the "water crisis" is actually, to a large extent, "the role of water in food production" crisis. They remind readers that there are abundant supplies of water and that the main problem is finding ways to get water to people who need it to grow food.

Ngure, Francis M., et al. 2014. "Water, Sanitation, and Hygiene (WASH), Environmental Enteropathy, Nutrition, and Early Child Development: Making the Links." *Annals of the New York Academy of Sciences*. 1308: 118–128.
The authors discuss the possible role of WASH and nutritional programs in health programs for very young children for which, they say, little clinical evidence is available. They recommend that greater attention be paid to the

inclusion of such programs in early childhood health programs, largely as a way of dealing with endemic enterological problems among young children.

Panjabi, Ranee Khooshie Lal. 2014. "Not a Drop to Spare: The Global Water Crisis of the Twenty-First Century." *Georgia Journal of International and Comparative Law.* 42(2): 277–424.

The author, professor at Memorial University in Newfoundland, Canada, provides a long and detailed analysis of the elements of the world's current water crisis with special focus on some political and legal aspects of that issue.

Prüss-Ustün, Annette, et al. 2014. "Burden of Disease from Inadequate Water, Sanitation and Hygiene in Low- and Middle-Income Settings: A Retrospective Analysis of Data from 145 Countries." *Tropical Medicine & International Health.* 19(8): 894–905.

The authors examined available data to estimate the number of deaths and cases of disease resulting from inadequate water and sanitation systems worldwide. They concluded that, in 2012, 502,000 deaths from diarrhea could be attributed to inadequate drinking water systems and 280,000 deaths from inadequate sanitation systems. An additional 297,000 deaths were attributable to inadequate handwashing systems.

Richey, Alexandra S., et al. 2015. "Quantifying Renewable Groundwater Stress with GRACE." *Water Resources Research.* 51(7): 5217–5238.

This article describes a process developed and used by the National Aeronautics and Space Administration (NASA) to measure changes in the world's 37 largest aquifers. The data collected suggest that 21 of those aquifers are currently losing water faster than it is being replenished.

Schmidt, Wolf-Peter. 2014. "The Elusive Effect of Water and Sanitation on the Global Burden of Disease." *Tropical Medicine & International Health.* 19(5): 522–527.

Schmidt briefly discusses the history of WASH programs in developing countries and then raises the issue as to how researchers can adequately access the importance of such programs in the health of communities in those nations. He reviews the problems associated with carrying out research on this topic and obtaining good evidence for the success or failure of WASH programs. He concludes that "[i]t is not esoteric to believe that water and sanitation are upstream interventions, likely to have a broad impact on well-being and health."

Swatuk, Larry., et al. "Seeing "Invisible Water": Challenging Conceptions of Water for Agriculture, Food and Human Security." *Canadian Journal of Development Studies/Revue Canadienne D'études du Développement.* 36(1): 24–37.

The authors argue that broad concerns about the availability of adequate amounts of freshwater in the present and the future are incorrect in that they do not take into account the vast amounts of "green water" available on the planet. When that source of freshwater is taken into account, they say, "there is enough water and land for food security for all."

Teague, Jordan, E. Anna Johnston, and Jay P. Graham. 2014. "Water, Sanitation, Hygiene, and Nutrition: Successes, Challenges, and Implications for Integration." *International Journal of Public Health.* 59(6): 913–921.

Through interviews with 16 stakeholders in the WASH and nutrition sectors, the authors of this article attempt to discover the factors that contribute to and tend to discourage the integration of good WASH and nutrition practices in child health programs.

Vogel, Richard M., et al. 2015. "Hydrology: The Interdisciplinary Science of Water." *Water Resources Research.* 51(6): 4409–4430.

This article focuses on the nature of hydrology in the 21st century. They point out that rather being considered as a relatively straightforward scientific topic—the study of the properties, distribution, and circulation of water on and below Earth's surface—the field has now become a much more interdisciplinary subject that takes into account social, political, economic, and other considerations in its study of water.

Zarfl, Christiane, et al. 2015. "A Global Boom in Hydropower Dam Construction." *Aquatic Sciences: Research across Boundaries.* 77(1): 161–170.

The authors of this article comment on the very large number of dams currently under construction or being planned worldwide (about 3,700 major dams) and express their concerns about the social, economic, and ecological ramifications of this dam construction boom.

Zhang, Y., et al. 2015. "Ethiopia's Grand Renaissance Dam: Implications for Downstream Riparian Countries." *Journal of Water Resources Planning and Management.* 141(9): 5001–5002.

The authors discuss the potential environmental impacts of the construction of a new dam, which will be the largest dam in Africa. They suggest that little or nothing is known about the multitude of ways in which the mammoth dam will affect countries downstream of it once it begins to fill.

Zhou, Dingyan, Zhuoying Zhang, and Minjun Shi. 2015. "Where Is the Future for a Growing Metropolis in North China under Water Resource Constraints?" *Sustainability Science.* 10(1): 113–122.

The Beijing-Tianjin metropolis in northern China presents a classic case of water shortages for a region that is growing rapidly in population, increasing in industrial complexity, and largely lacking in the water resources needed to meet these changes. The authors review the recent history of this problem and suggest some possible solutions for dealing with water issues in the region in the future.

Reports

Bigas, Harriet, Tim Morris, Bob Sandford, and Zafar Adeel, eds. 2012. "The Global Water Crisis: Addressing an Urgent Security Issue. Papers for the InterAction Council." Hamilton, ON: UNU-INWEH.

This report consists of a selection of papers by experts in the field with regard to water issues facing the world in the 21st century. They cover topics such as when and where the next war over water will be fought; water resources and climate change; water and political security; water, sanitation, and hygiene; women's role in water issues; the right to water; and legal and ethical issues related to water use.

Callow, Roger, et al. 2011. "Climate Change, Water Resources and WASH: A Scoping Study." Overseas Development Institute. http://www.odi.org/sites/odi.org.uk/files/odi-assets/publications-opinion-files/7322.pdf. Accessed on September 21, 2015.

This report investigates the interrelationships among climate change, water resources, and water, hygiene, and sanitation problems and practices in sub-Saharan Africa and southern Asia. The report summarizes the current status of programs in these areas and suggests steps to prepare the two regions more fully for changes that are likely to occur as a result of climate change.

"Climate Change: Evaluating Your Local and Regional Water Resources." 2015. U.S. Geological Survey. Reston, VA: U.S. Department of the Interior, U.S. Geological Survey.

This booklet is designed specifically for watershed management experts, but it provides an interesting insight into the types of problems and potential solutions for watersheds posed by climate change.

"Collaboration: Preserving Water through Partnering That Works." 2015. PWC. http://www.pwc.com/us/en/corporate-sustainability-climate-change/publications/assets/pwc-access-to-water-for-businesses.pdf. Accessed on September 21, 2015.

This report is intended for businesses and other stakeholders who are interested in and concerned about water use in their industry. It discusses ways in which a business can partner with other businesses and other entities to make the wisest and best use of water in their activities.

Douglas, Colin, ed. 2009. "Charting Our Water Future: Economic Frameworks to Inform Decision-making." The 2030 Water Resources Group. [n.p.]. http://www.mckinsey.com/cli ent_service/sustainability/latest_thinking/charting_our_water_ future. Accessed on September 19, 2015.

The 2030 Water Resources Group consists of representatives from a number of major corporations, including the Coca-Cola Company, the International Finance Corporation, Nestlé SA, and Syngenta. This report summarizes some of the impacts that water scarcity worldwide is likely to have on the economic community. It also recommends some specific actions that business can take to ameliorate the effects of water shortages on their operations.

Economic Commission for Europe and the International Network of Basin Organizations. 2015. "Water and Climate Change Adaptation in Transboundary Basins: Lessons Learned and Good Practices." Geneva: United Nations.

Climate change is causing a greater number of countries to begin thinking about transboundary water issues and to look for ways of identifying and solving those issues. This document brings together a number of lessons that have been learned about dealing with transboundary issues in the past, with suggestions as to how those lessons can be applied to new problems arising out of climate change.

Faeth, Paul, et al. 2014. "A Clash of Competing Necessities: Water Adequacy and Electric Reliability in China, India, France, and Texas." CNA Analysis and Solutions. http://www.indiaenviron mentportal.org.in/files/file/Water%20Adequacy%20and%20 Electric%20Reliability.pdf. Accessed on September 20, 2015.

This report was prepared by researchers at CNA Corporation, Aarhus University in Denmark, and the University of Vermont Law School. It concludes that the competition between electricity generation and domestic uses of water will become increasingly severe, leading to a 40 percent gap between water demands and resources by the year 2030.

Food and Agriculture Organization of the United Nations. 2012. "Coping with Water Scarcity: An Action Framework for Agriculture and Food Security." Rome: Food and Agriculture Organization.

This report offers a detailed analysis of the existing water shortages present and developing in nations around the world, with a review of the causes for such shortages and future potential water scarcity patterns. The focus of the report is on how these shortages will affect food production and how shortages of food production are likely to affect the world's communities and economies. The report ends with a number of suggestions for ways of dealing with future water shortages and their potential effects on food production.

Freyman, Monica. 2014. "Hydraulic Fracturing & Water Stress: Water Demand by the Numbers." Ceres. http://www.ceres.org /resources/reports/hydraulic-fracturing-water-stress-water-demand-by-the-numbers/view. Accessed on September 21, 2015.

One of the major causes of stress on water resources in some regions of the world is the recently developed fossil fuel recovery technology of hydraulic fracturing, or "fracking." This report provides detailed information on the use of water resources by that technology.

Gassert, Francis, et al. 2013. "Aqueduct Country and River Basin Rankings: A Weighted Aggregation of Spatially Distinct Hydrological Indicators." Working paper. Washington, DC: World Resources Institute. wri.org/publication/aqueduct-country-river-basin-rankings. Accessed on September 21, 2015.

This report provides a comprehensive and technical overview of the world's nations with regard to their levels of water stress. An excellent general introduction to the topic of water stress.

Melillo, Jerry M., Terese (T.C.) Richmond, and Gary W. Yohe, eds. 2014. "Climate Change Impacts in the United States: The Third National Climate Assessment. U.S. Global Change Research Program." Washington, DC: U.S. Global Change Research Program.

This report was prepared in response to the Global Change Research Act, which requires the Global Change Research Program to prepare a review for Congress every four years of the assessment of global climate change effects in the United States. This report is organized around 13 sectors, such as water, energy, transportation, agriculture, and forests; 10 geographic regions in the United States; and 5 different response strategies, such as mitigation, adaptation, and continuing assessment. The primary parts of the report dealing with water are to be found on pages 69–112 and 257–281.

Molden, David, ed. 2007. "Water for Food. Water for Life. A Comprehensive Assessment of Water Management in Agriculture." London: Earthscan.

This very important report considers the water needs for agriculture in coming years, expressing the view that enough water will be available provided that different approaches be adopted for the way water is used in agriculture. The report makes eight recommendations for policy actions that will help to bring about this situation.

Pegram, Guy. 2010. "Global Water Scarcity: Risks and Challenges for Business." Lloyd's 360° Risk Insight. London: Lloyd's.

This report makes and discusses four major points about water scarcity: "Global Water Resources Are under Threat and Businesses Are Affected"; "Different Types of

Business Face Different Threat Levels"; "Water Is Different to Other Natural Resources—It Needs to Be Managed on a Local, Basin or National Scale"; and "Tools and Approaches for Managing Business Risk from Water Scarcity Are Already Being Developed."

Ringersma, Jacquelijn, Niels Batjes, and David Dent. 2003. "Green Water: Definitions and Data for Assessment." Wageningen, The Netherlands.

This report explores a number of basic questions about so-called green water, including what the term means, the physical principles of water storage in the soil, the availability of data about green water on the planet, ways of optimizing green water use, models available for estimating the efficiency of green water use, and applications of remote sensing for determining the availability of green water worldwide.

World Health Organization. 2015a. "Water, Sanitation, and Hygiene in Health Care Facilities: Status in Low- and Middle-income Countries and Way Forward." Geneva: World Health Organization. http://apps.who.int/iris/bitstream/10665/154588/1/978924150 8476_eng.pdf?ua=1. Accessed on September 19, 2015.

This report claims to be "the first comprehensive, multi-country analysis on water, sanitation and hygiene services in health-care facilities." It summarizes extensive research on the use of WASH in such facilities, some important issues revealed by this research, and steps that can be taken to improve the use of WASH in health care facilities in the future.

World Health Organization. 2015b. "Water, Sanitation and Hygiene for Accelerating and Sustaining Progress on Neglected Tropical Diseases." Geneva: World Health Organization. http://apps.who.int/iris/bitstream/10665/182735/1/WHO_FWC_WSH_15.12_eng.pdf?ua=1. Accessed on September 19, 2015.

This report lays out a new global plan for using WASH programs to target and attack 17 neglected tropical diseases. The plan involves increasing public awareness of the problem of NTDs and putting into practice new and tested methods for introducing and promoting the use of reliable WASH techniques to address these diseases.

"World Water Development Report." Annual. Geneva: UN Water. Detailed information at http://www.unwater.org/publications/world-water-development-report/en/. Accessed on September 16, 2015.

This report was first issued in 2003 in conjunction with the World Water Forum. It was originally conceived of as a triennial publication and was produced again in 2006, 2009, and 2012. In 2014, it was reconfigured as an annual publication and appeared again in 2015. The report focuses in each edition on a specific aspect of global water issues, such as "water for people, water for life" (2003), "water in a changing world" (2009), "managing water under uncertainty and risk" (2012), and "water and energy" (2014). All reports are available at no cost on the Internet.

WWAP (United Nations World Water Assessment Programme). 2015. "The United Nations World Water Development Report 2015: Water for a Sustainable World." Paris: UNESCO.

This report takes a look at the current and probable future characteristics of the world's water supplies. It comes to some pessimistic conclusions, including the prediction that the world will have access to only 60 percent of the water it needs by the year 2030. The report suggests a number of policies and actions that nations can take to deal with future water issues.

Internet

"Agricultural Water." 2015. National Sustainable Agriculture Coalition. http://sustainableagriculture.net/fsma/learn-about-the-issues/agricultural-water/. Accessed on September 19, 2015.

Farmers, cattlemen, dairy operators, and others in the field of agriculture use very large amounts of water for a variety of purposes. A number of provisions of the Clean Water Act and other federal legislation prescribe practices designed to help such individuals and businesses to conserve the water they use and make sure that it is as clean as possible before, during, and after use. This Web page provides an excellent overview of those regulations as of 2015.

"Aqueduct: Measuring and Mapping Water Risk." 2015. World Resources Institute. http://www.wri.org/our-work/project/aque duct. Accessed on September 21, 2015.

Water risk is a term used to describe the damage that might be caused by some water-related event, such as water scarcity or water stress. This Web site contains interactive maps that show places and severity where water risk is a problem today and in the future.

Bliss, Laura. 2015. "Contaminated and Unregulated: A Worrying New 'Water Atlas' of L.A. County." Citylab. http://www.citylab .com/tech/2015/05/contaminated-and-unregulated-a-worrying- new-water-atlas-of-la-county/393332/. Accessed on September 20, 2015.

This article provides interesting insights into the water problems faced by a single community in the United States, albeit the second largest city in the nation. The problems described by the new "atlas" are not, however, unique to Los Angeles.

Bosman, Dawid. 2015. "Alternative Water Supply." The Water Wheel. http://www.wrc.org.za/Lists/Knowledge%20Hub%20 Items/Attachments/11184/WW_May2015_desalination.pdf. Accessed on June 14, 2015.

This article reviews the history of Australia's attempts to deal with serious long-term droughts with the construction and use of desalination plants, and how this history can and should affect future policy decisions about desalination.

Brown, Lester. 2013. "The Real Threat to Our Future Is Peak Water." http://www.theguardian.com/global-development/2013/jul/06/water-supplies-shrinking-threat-to-food. Accessed on September 19, 2015.

This long-time writer on environmental issues adopts the principle of "peak oil" and "peak coal" to argue that the most serious problem about water scarcity is that some nations have reached or are approaching a point at which they simply no longer have adequate freshwater supplies to meet their needs. He then considers the consequences of such a situation in any particular country.

Choy, Janny, and Geoff McGhee. 2014. Groundwater: Ignore It, and It Might Go Away." Water in the West. http://waterinthewest.stanford.edu/groundwater/overview/index.html. Accessed on September 16, 2015.

This article takes a close look at the role that groundwater plays in meeting the state of California's water needs and the troublesome changes that have occurred in aquifers because of the underregulated use of groundwater over past history. Also see other articles by Water in the West associated with this topic and linked to this article.

"Climate Change and Water News." Regular publication. U.S. Environmental Protection Agency. http://www2.epa.gov/climate-change-water-sector/climate-change-and-water-news. Accessed on September 21, 2015.

The EPA publishes a regular electronic newsletter carrying information and news on the relationship between climate change and water resources. A recent issue of the newsletter, for example, had articles on managing water quality in the face of uncertainty, "early warning systems on algal blooms," a regional storm water conference, and the national Resilient Cities Challenge.

Damayanti, Okty. 2014. "Connecting Indonesian Communities to Clean Water." *Cornerstone* magazine. http://cornerstonemag.net/tag/water-energy-nexus/. Accessed on September 23, 2015.

Cornerstone magazine is the official journal of the world coal industry. The article cited here is one of a number at the Cornerstone Web site that discusses ways in which the coal industry is attempting to ameliorate the negative environmental effects of its mining operations around the world. In this case, Damayanti outlines ways in which the PT Adaro Indonesia company attempts to recycle a portion of its waste waters in such a way as to provide neighbors of the mine with a reliable source of freshwater, which they currently do not have.

Dimick, Dennis. 2014. "If You Think the Water Crisis Can't Get Worse, Wait until the Aquifers Are Drained." *National Geographic.* http://news.nationalgeographic.com/news/2014/08/140819-groundwater-california-drought-aquifers-hidden-crisis/. Accessed on September 16, 2015.

This article provides an excellent overview of the risks posed by increasing withdrawal of water from the nation's aquifers. It contains a number of links to other very good related print and electronic articles on the topic.

"Drought Basics." 2015. National Drought Mitigation Center. http://drought.unl.edu/DroughtBasics.aspx. Accessed on September 21, 2015.

The National Drought Mitigation Center is an agency whose purpose it is to help people prepare for droughts and to deal with the effects of droughts. This Web site has many useful sections, one of which is a general introduction to the characteristics of drought, called "Drought Basics."

"El Salvador Mining Ban Could Establish a Vital Water Security Precedent." 2013. *The Guardian.* http://www.theguardian.com/global-development/poverty-matters/2013/jun/10/el-salvador-mining-ban-water-security. Accessed on September 23, 2015.

This article reports on the attempt by the government of El Salvador to prevent a Canadian mining company from operating an open-pit gold mine near one of the country's major rivers, the San Jose River, because of the potential pollution mine wastes would cause in the river and surrounding countryside.

"Facts about Pollution from Livestock Farms." 2013. Natural Resources Defense Council. http://www.nrdc.org/water/pollution/ffarms.asp. Accessed on September 23, 2015.

One of the threats to the world's freshwater resources is wastes from large livestock operations. This Web site summarizes some of the most important of those effects.

"Freshwater Crisis." 2015. National Geographic. http://environment.nationalgeographic.com/environment/freshwater/freshwater-crisis/. Accessed on September 19, 2015.

This Web site provides a good general overview on the topic of water scarcity, but is especially strong in the visual presentations that accompany the text, along with many links to Web pages with related information.

"Great Pacific Garbage Patch." 2015. National Geographic. http://education.nationalgeographic.com/encyclopedia/great-pacific-garbage-patch/. Accessed on September 23, 2015.

This article provides a good general overview of the topic of ocean "garbage patches" in general and of the Great Pacific Garbage Patch in particular. A number of links to other references on the same topic are provided.

"Groundwater in the News." 2015. University of California. Division of Agriculture and Natural Resources. http://groundwater.ucdavis.edu/Groundwater_in_the_News/. Accessed on September 20, 2015.

This Web site may well provide the most complete list of articles on the subject of groundwater to be found anywhere on the Internet. It is an invaluable resource for anyone interested in the status of groundwater issues in the United States and around the world.

Hertsgaard, Mark. 2015. "If You Only Read One Book about the Water Crisis: 'Cadillac Desert.'" *The Daily Beast*. http://www

.thedailybeast.com/articles/2015/07/11/if-you-only-read-one-book-about-the-water-crisis-cadillac-desert.html. Accessed on September 19, 2015.

This long and thoughtful article is a review of two books on the role that dams play in today's water crisis in the American West and, by analogy, in other parts of the world.

Holland, Lynn. 2015. "The Open Pit and the Great Green Macaw in Costa Rica." Council on Hemispheric Affairs. http://www.coha.org/the-open-pit-and-the-great-green-macaw-in-costa-rica/. Accessed on September 23, 2015.

Holland, Lynn. 2015. "For the Love of Water: The Ban on Mining in El Salvador." Council on Hemispheric Affairs. http://www.coha.org/for-the-love-of-water-the-ban-on-mining-in-el-salvador/. Accessed on September 23, 2015.

The waste produced during mining operations is often responsible for a host of environmental problems, water pollution being one of them. The problem exists in all types of mining operations in many parts of the world. This series of three articles deals with specific cases of water pollution and other environmental damage caused by actual or proposed mining operations in Central America. (The third article in the series is "to be published soon.")

"Infiltration—The Water Cycle." 2015. USGS Water Science School. http://water.usgs.gov/edu/watercycleinfiltration.html. Accessed on September 20, 2015.

This Web site provides a good general introduction to the subject of infiltration and the role it plays in the water cycle.

"Introduction to Global Water Scarcity." 2015. eSchoolToday. http://www.eschooltoday.com/global-water-scarcity/global-water-shortage-for-kids.html. Accessed on September 16, 2015.

This Web site provides a comprehensive and easily understood general introduction to the subject of water scarcity, with sections on the water cycle, drinking water treatment, threats to the water supply, and effects of water shortages.

"Irrigation and Water Use." 2015. Economic Research Service. U.S. Department of Agriculture. http://www.ers.usda.gov/topics/ farm-practices-management/irrigation-water-use.aspx. Accessed on September 19, 2015.

This Web site provides a good general introduction to the ways in which water is used in irrigation systems in the United States, along with some of the problems involved with agricultural water.

Kershner, Isabel. 2015. "Aided by the Sea, Israel Defeats Old Foe: Drought." *The New York Times.* http://www.nytimes.com/ 2015/05/30/world/middleeast/water-revolution-in-israel- overcomes-any-threat-of-drought.html?_r=0. Accessed on September 21, 2015.

This article explains how the state of Israel has apparently overcome a long-standing national problem, drought, by putting into practices a number of practices and technologies, including water conservation, reuse of waste water, and desalination such that for Israelis "the fear [of water scarcity] is now gone."

"Mission 2012: Water." 2015. Massachusetts Institute of Technology. http://web.mit.edu/12.000/www/m2012/finalwebsite/ index.shtml. Accessed on September 19, 2012.

This Web site was developed by a group of freshmen at the Massachusetts Institute of Technology who were challenged "to develop a comprehensive solution to a complex problem facing the world." The problem chosen by this class was to design a program that would ensure the availability of clean freshwater in western North America for the next 100 years. The Web site does a very thorough job of defining the nature of this problem and of laying out a number of solutions for the region's future water problems.

Morain, Dan. 2015. "Swimming Upstream to Save a Victim of State's Water Crisis." Sacramento Bee. http://www.sacbee.com/opinion/opn-columns-blogs/dan-morain/article17351492.html. Accessed on September 20, 2015.

    The three-inch-long Delta smelt is threatened by extinction in California because so much of its natural water resource is being diverted to deal with the state's ongoing water shortage. Morain reviews the status of that situation and asks what steps can and should be taken to help the smelt survive this crisis.

Paulson, Linda Dailey. 2015. "What Is Water Scarcity?" RWL Water. http://www.rwlwater.com/what-is-water-scarcity/. Accessed on September 21, 2015.

    This essay defines water scarcity, explains the difference between physical and economic water scarcity, and outlines some methods for dealing with water scarcity.

Pearce, Fred. 2012. "Beyond Big Dams: Turning to Grassroots Solutions on Water." Environment 360. http://e360.yale.edu/feature/beyond_big_dams_turning_to_grass_roots_solutions_on_water/2571/. Accessed on September 19, 2015.

    The author begins this article with the view that "[m]ega-dams and massive government-run irrigation projects are not the key to meeting world's water needs." He then goes on to review a host of much simpler technologies for water diversion, storage, and use that can be developed and/or implemented by water users in both developing and developed countries.

Pottinger, Lori. 2009. "The Wrong Climate for Big Dams." International Rivers. http://www.internationalrivers.org/resources/the-wrong-climate-for-big-dams-1730. Accessed on September 19, 2015.

    African countries have gone on a dam-building "spree" in recent decades as a way of producing the hydropower they need for development. This author explains why this line of development is not good for the continent's environment and discusses alternative sources of energy for African nations. Also see related links at the end of the article for additional essays on this topic.

Powers, Madison. 2015. "Water Scarcity." http://www.fewre sources.org/water-scarcity-issues-were-running-out-of-water .html. Accessed on September 16, 2015.
This Web site provides a comprehensive and well-presented introduction to the subject of water scarcity in today's world along with many useful links to Web sites on related topics.

"Problems with Big Dams." 2015. International Rivers. http://www.internationalrivers.org/problems-with-big-dams. Accessed on September 19, 2015.
This Web site is devoted to a discussion of the environmental and other effects of dams. The home page provides some useful general information, which can be supplemented by a large number of individual articles on discrete aspects of the issue.

Ramachandran, Sudha. 2015. "Water Wars: China, India and the Great Dam Rush." *The Diplomat.* http://thediplomat .com/2015/04/water-wars-china-india-and-the-great-dam-rush/. Accessed on September 19, 2015.
The construction of dams is frequently the basis for transboundary disputes over the use of water. This article focuses on some of the specific problems created between China and India as a result of dam building in one or the other of the two countries.

Ruby, Emily. 2015. "How Urbanization Affects the Water Cycle." California Water and Land Use Partnership. http://www.coastal .ca.gov/nps/watercyclefacts.pdf. Accessed on September 21, 2015.
This concise and well-written pamphlet outlines the major ways in which urbanization affects water issues in a region or community.

Schulte, Peter. 2014. "Defining Water Scarcity, Water Stress, and Water Risk: It's Not Just Semantics." Pacific Institute. http://pacinst.org/water-definitions/. Accessed on September 21, 2015.

Three terms commonly used to describe shortage of water are water scarcity, water stress, and water risk. This article explains the difference among the three terms and explains why that difference is important.

"Selected USGS Groundwater Publications." 2015. U.S. Geological Survey. http://water.usgs.gov/ogw/pubs.html. Accessed on September 16, 2015.

This Web site is an excellent resource on a wide variety of government publications on the topic of groundwater, including subjects such as estimated use in the United States, depletion by wells, basic groundwater hydrology, aquifer basics, maps of the principle aquifers in the United States, and a glossary of water resource terms.

Stallard, Brian. 2015. "Groundwater Crisis Is Driving World Conflict." Nature World News. http://www.natureworldnews.com/articles/10153/20141108/global-groundwater-crisis-driving-conflict.htm. Accessed on September 20, 2015.

Stallard writes about recent reports and opinion pieces that suggest that groundwater shortages may be responsible for disputes among nations that have or may lead to armed conflict. These conflicts appear to be most common in India and the Middle East, but may begin to develop also in China and the United States.

"U.S. Drought Monitor." 2015. Center for Climate and Energy Solutions. http://www.c2es.org/science-impacts/extreme-weather/drought. Accessed on September 21, 2015.

This Web page provides a brief introduction to drought issues, but has a number of useful links to other sources of information and background data.

"Water." 2015. The World Bank. http://www.worldbank.org/en/topic/water. Accessed on September 16, 2015

The World Bank is very active in funding a number of general and specific water programs around the world. This Web page describes these activities, which include programs in transboundary cooperation, solar-powered irrigation pumps in Bangladesh, innovative methods for finding water and sanitation projects, collaborative management of water resources in the Zambezi River, and water-powered energy projects in central Asia.

"Water Properties and Measurement." 2015. The USGS Water Science School. http://water.usgs.gov/edu/waterproperties.html. Accessed on September 16, 2015.

This Web page provides an excellent overview of the major properties of water, such as its chemical and physical properties, the water cycle, and water in the environment.

"Water Resources." 2015. GreenFacts. http://www.greenfacts .org/en/water-resources/. Accessed on September 16, 2015.

This Web page provides a comprehensive overview of the major factors essential to an understanding of the current global water crisis, including information on where and how much water is found on Earth, what the current pressures on water resources are, how human activities affect water resources, and how water resources can be sustainably developed and used.

"Water Resources of the United States." 2015. U.S. Geological Survey. http://www.usgs.gov/water/. Accessed on September 16, 2015.

This Web site provides basic information on all of the major topics dealing with water resources in the United States, such as water data; streams, lakes, and reservoirs; groundwater, aquifers, and wells; quality of water resources; and water use.

"Water Rights Law: Prior Appropriation." 2015. FindLaw. http://corporate.findlaw.com/business-operations/water-rights-law-prior-appropriation.html. Accessed on September 16, 2015.

This Web page provides a good general introduction to the legal principles involved in the doctrine of prior appropriation of water rights.

"Water Scarcity." 2015. Bat Conservation International. http://www.batcon.org/our-work/regions/usa-canada/address-serious-threats/water-scarcity. Accessed on September 20, 2015.
This Web page provides an excellent overview of the importance of water to the survival of one order of animals and explains how water shortages in many parts of the world are contributing to the decline of that order.

"Water Scarcity." 2015. World Wildlife Fund. http://www.world wildlife.org/threats/water-scarcity. Accessed on September 19, 2015.
This excellent Web site provides a general introduction to the problem of water scarcity worldwide, with special emphasis on its effects on threatened and endangered plant and animal life. The Web site also provides information on the activities being undertaken by the organization to deal with problems of water scarcity.

"Water Stewardship." 2013. World Wildlife Fund. http://awsas sets.panda.org/downloads/ws_briefing_booklet_lr_spreads.pdf. Accessed on September 20, 2015.
As part of its effort to protect threatened and endangered species worldwide from water shortage issues, the World Wildlife Fund has prepared this booklet outlining some of the steps that businesses can take to make sure that they are conserving water and protecting water quality to the maximum extent possible. The booklet represents an interesting and promising effort to combine the best interests of enlightened corporations with wildlife conservationists.

"Water Use in Agriculture." 2015. OECD (The Organisation for Economic Co-Operation and Development). http://www.oecd.org/tad/sustainable-agriculture/wateruseinagriculture.htm. Accessed on September 19, 2015.

Agricultural water is a topic of major interest to the OECD. This Web page provides an excellent introduction to the topic with basic statistics and information about problems related to the use of water in agriculture. Of special interest is a wide variety of reports, papers, datasets, and other sources of information about the topic.

"World Water Crisis." 2015. *BBC News.* http://news.bbc.co.uk/hi/english/static/in_depth/world/2000/world_water_crisis/default.stm. Accessed on September 20, 2015.

This Web site provides a good general overview of the world's global water crisis, along with an interactive map for a dozen specific places around the world, each with its own unique water issues.

Yacoub, Sameer. 2015. "ISIS Reduces Water Supply to Areas in Iraq's Anbar." *The World Post.* http://www.huffingtonpost.com/2015/06/04/isis-iraq-anbar-water_n_7510174.html. Accessed on September 21, 2015.

This article describes a contemporary example of the way that disruption of water supply can be used as a weapon of war.

7 Chronology

Introduction

Water is a critical substance in the survival of individual humans and of human civilization. It should hardly be surprising, then, that human history is studded with a variety of important events, from the origins of civilization to the present day. The chronology presented here mentions only a few of the most important of those events over the preceding thousands of years.

ca. 6000 BCE   The first irrigation systems are constructed in the area known as the Fertile Crescent as a way of collecting and making use of water from the Tigris and Euphrates Rivers.

ca. 5500 BCE   This date is often mentioned as the earliest period during which the first human settlements were established in the Fertile Crescent formed by the confluence of the Tigris and Euphrates Rivers in ancient Mesopotamia.

5469–5098 BCE   The first water wells in human history are dug in eastern Germany.

ca. 3000 BCE   The world's first human-made dam (a gravity dam) is constructed on the wadi (river) Rajil near the town of Jawa in modern-day Lebanon.

The dust bowl that swept the American Plains region in the 1920s was one of the most dramatic and most severe droughts in modern history. This dust storm struck Elkhart, Kansas, in May 1937. (New York Public Library/ Getty)

ca. 2700 BCE The world's first embankment dam is built at Sadd Al-Kafara in Egypt.

ca. 2550 BCE A long-running battle between the Lagash and Umma states of ancient Mesopotamia is thought to have been brought to an end by an agreement now known as the Treaty of Mesilim.

ca. 2200 BCE This date marks the beginning of the period during which the first human communities were established in the Indus Valley of modern-day India.

ca. 1790 The Code of Hammurabi, instituted by the Babylonian king of that name, contains the first laws establishing water rights within the kingdom.

ca. 1700 BCE This date is mentioned by many authorities as marking the origin of human civilization in China, usually in the Yellow River basin.

ca. 1700 BCE Egyptian inventors create the shaduf (or shadoof), a device for raising water from a lower level, such as an underground source, to an irrigation system.

ca. 550 BCE The qanat, a system for collecting underground water for use in irrigation, is invented in Mesopotamia.

ca. 500 BCE The sakia, or Persian water wheel, is invented. It consists of a set of pots attached to a rope, which, when turned on a wheel, collects water from one source and moves it to a second location.

Third-century BCE Greek inventor Archimedes is credited with inventing the first mechanical device for lifting water from one level to another level, a device known as Archimedes' screw. The invention may date a few centuries earlier, however, to a device used in Assyria for that purpose.

312 BCE The first Roman aqueduct is begun as part of a program to ensure an adequate supply of freshwater for the city's residents.

First-century BCE Archaeological research suggests that the town of Qaryat al-Faw was created around an oasis at about this period. It was probably the first major city to be established in pre-Islamic Arabia.

First-century BCE   The world's first arch dam is built in the Vallon de Baume in France.

528 CE   The Roman emperor Justinian attempts to codify all civil laws developed over the preceding 13 centuries, some of which deal with water rights, the world's first attempt to bring together all such laws in a single document. Among the doctrines codified in the Justinian Code was the principle of riparian rights.

537 CE   In the last days of the Roman Empire, the Goths besiege the city of Rome and cut off nearly its water supply by blocking all but one of the aqueducts leading into the city.

ca. 750–900 CE   Sustained droughts in Mesoamerica are thought to be responsible for or contributed to the downfall of the Mayan civilization.

1627   English polymath Sir Francis Bacon describes a method for obtaining pure water from saltwater by the process of desalination.

1672   In one of a number of similar events, the Dutch protect their country from the attacking armies of the French Army under Louis XIV by opening the dikes that hold back the North Sea, flooding the land and repelling the invaders.

1747   The world's first buttress dam (according to many authorities) is built at Almendralejo (or Al-Mendralejo or Albuera de Feria or Feria) in Spain.

1804   The world's first water treatment plant is opened in Paisley, Scotland.

1826   In the case of *Tyler v. Wilkinson*, the rule of riparian rights is established as a guiding principle for the use of waterways in the United States.

1828   The city of London begins to purify its drinking water by passing it through thick layers of sand.

1854   English physician John Snow proves that water from an impure source is responsible for an outbreak of cholera in

London, thus establishing the modern theory of disease contagion by waterborne contaminants.

1855 In the case of *Irwin v. Phillips*, the California Supreme Court establishes the policy of prior appropriation as a legitimate (and alternative to riparian rights) basis for determining water rights in the state (and later, for much of the West).

1860–1865 Both sides in the Civil War make use of water resources in their battles against the enemy, such as cutting new canals or building dams that divert important rivers and streams and contaminating freshwater sources by dumping sand, dead animal and human bodies, and other materials into wells and other sources of freshwater.

1881 The beginning of the so-called fence-cutting wars in the American West between farmers and cattle raisers over access to the limited supplies of freshwater available in the region. The wars continued until the end of the decade.

1882 The world's first commercial hydroelectric power plant begins operation on the Fox River in Wisconsin.

1890s Geologist N. H. Darton first describes and names (in 1898) the Ogallala aquifer.

1899 The U.S. Congress passes the Rivers and Harbors Act in an attempt to guarantee that contaminants would not interfere with the navigation of ships on the nation's waterways. The act is sometimes described as the nation's first environmental legislation.

1900 The world's first water treatment plant using chlorine as a disinfectant is established in Ostend, Belgium. The plant operates only two years. (Also see **1902**.)

1902 The world's second, and more efficient, chlorine-based water treatment plant opens in Middelkerke, Belgium.

1908 In the case of *Winters v. United States*, the U.S. Supreme Court takes up the question as to what water rights accrue to Native Americans from sources shared with non-Indian lands. The decision essentially sets the underlying principles of Native American water rights for future history.

1917   The states of Arizona, California, Colorado, Nevada, New Mexico, Utah, and Wyoming join together to form the League of the Southwest in order to adopt plans for the development of the Colorado River, its tributaries, and adjoining basins. The league is later instrumental in the adoption of the Colorado River Compact of 1922 (q.v.).

1921–1922   An extended drought in the Soviet Union is blamed for the death of at least 5 million people.

1922   The Colorado River Compact is signed, allotting proportional water rights from the river to the states of Arizona, California, Colorado, Nevada, New Mexico, Utah, and Wyoming.

1924   Residents of Owens Valley, California, dynamite a portion of the Los Angeles Viaduct that carries water from the valley to the city. The action is among the most violent objections raised by Owens Valley's residents to the "theft" of their water by the city that had begun with the construction of the viaduct in 1907.

1928   The world's first commercial desalination plant begins operation on the island of Curacao.

1931   The first in a series of cases known as *Arizona v. California* is decided by the U.S. Supreme Court. The cases all deal with the amount of water that can be taken from the Colorado River by the two states and, in some later decisions, by other states in the West. The court revised its 1931 decision on a number of occasions, including 1934, 1936, 1963, 1964, 1968, 1979, 1983, 1984, and 2000.

1934   The first wave of the American dust bowl drought hits the Midwest.

1936   The second wave of the American dust bowl drought hits the Midwest.

1939–1940   The dust bowl drought in the American Midwest returns.

1948   The U.S. Congress passes the Federal Water Pollution Control Act (also known as the Clean Water Act), which, in its many amended forms, has become the basis for the nation's regulation of water quality.

1955 Signing of the Unified (Johnston) Water Plan by Israel and the Arab League for determining the development and use of the waters of the Jordan River. Although the plan was never formally ratified by individual Arab states, many of its provisions were carried out de facto as a way of resolving differences over the use of that water resource by the nations of the Middle East.

1960 The International Bank for Reconstruction and Development (now the World Bank) brokers an agreement between India and Pakistan over the use of water resources in the Indus River basin. A dispute between the two nations over the river's water resources had begun in 1947 with partition of the two countries from the formerly British India. Since signing of the treaty, the two nations have been largely successful in resolving new issues over Indus River water.

1964 The Cuban government cuts off the only supply of freshwater to the small U.S. enclave at Guantanamo Bay in retaliation for the arrest and fining of four Cuban fishermen off the coast of Florida. The United States solves the problem by disassembling a desalination plant at Point Loma, California, shipping it to Guantanamo Bay, and reassembling it there.

1967–1972 The U.S. military forces attempt to use artificial rainmaking over North Vietnam as a way of increasing precipitation and making the land so muddy that the movement of troops is difficult or impossible. The operation, known as Operation Popeye, is only a partial success.

1972 The U.S. Congress adopts the Clean Water Act as an amendment to the Federal Water Pollution Control Act of 1948. The Clean Water Act is the strongest and most effective of the many amendments to the 1948 act and serves as the guide for current U.S. policy on water quality and pollution issues.

1974   The U.S. Congress passes the Safe Drinking Water Act (SDWA), which establishes standards for drinking water quality obtained from rivers, lakes, springs, underground sources, reservoirs, and almost all other sources, with the exception of wells serving fewer than 25 individuals. The law was amended in 1986 and again in 1996.

1976   In a rerun of the 1924 bombing of the Los Angeles Viaduct, two teenage residents of Owens Valley, Mark Berry and Robert Howe, dynamite a set of gates holding back water in the viaduct, causing the backflow of some 100 million gallons back into the valley.

1990   The U.S. Supreme Court reaches a decision in the case of *Georgia v. South Carolina*, a dispute as to the precise location of the boundary between the two states. That boundary lies along the Savannah River, but since the river changes course and creates new islands from time to time, questions arise as to where the border actually lies and who owns the new islands that have been created.

1991   Iraq ruler Saddam Hussein orders the draining of the Mesopotamian Marshes southeast of Bagdad in retaliation for their use by enemies of his regime as hiding places. The marshes are restored with limited success beginning in late 2003.

1991   The U.S. government institutes a policy of destroying water and sanitation systems in Iraq as part of an effort to bring the country to its needs. U.S. plans also call for an embargo on materials that could be used to rebuild and operate the water and sanitation systems.

1992   A dispute that continues today among Uzbekistan, Kyrgyzstan, and Kazakhstan over shared water resources begins. At its peak, the dispute has resulted in the ordering of more than 100,000 troops by one country or another to disputed regions, threats of diverting all or most of the river water, and other actions designed to increase the flow of water into one nation or another.

1992 The United Nations General Assembly adopts a resolution, A/RES/47/193, declaring March 22, 1993, and every subsequent March 22 as World Water Day for the purpose of conducting "concrete activities such as the promotion of public awareness through the publication and diffusion of documentaries and the organization of conferences, round tables, seminars and expositions related to the conservation and development of water resources and the implementation of the recommendations of Agenda 21." (Agenda 21 is a comprehensive plan of action adopted by the United Nations Conference on Environment and Development [UNCED] held in Rio de Janeiro in June 1992.)

1992 The Stockholm International Water Institute announces the first World Water Week, a weeklong conference focusing on issues of water use, development, and sustainability. The event is held annually in September or October of each year and in 2001 was officially renamed the World Water Week in Stockholm. During the event, a number of prestigious prizes are awarded, including the Stockholm Water Prize, the Stockholm Junior Water Prize, and the Stockholm Industry Water Award.

1992 The United Nations Economic Commission adopts the Convention on the Protection and Use of Transboundary Watercourses and International Lakes (also known as the Water Convention), providing guidance for ways in which nations that share water resources can work for sustainable management of those resources and find ways of sharing them in a reasonable and equitable way.

1997 The United Nations General Assembly adopts by a vote of 103 to 3 the Convention on the Law of the Non-Navigational Uses of International Watercourses, which establishes a set of general principles for the resolution of disputes over transboundary water issues. The treaty finally goes into force in 2014.

1997 Yachtsman Charles J. Moore and his companions discover a region of the Pacific Ocean that is heavily contaminated with waste products from human activities, a region that is to become known as part of the Great Pacific Garbage Patch (GPGP).

1999 The United Nations Economic Commission for Europe's (UNECE) Protocol on Water and Health is signed in London. The purpose of the protocol is to protect human health by developing and implementing better systems of water management to risk the dangers of waterborne diseases.

2000 The United Nations Millennium Summit establishes eight Millennium Development Goals (MDGs), targets for improving the human condition worldwide in areas such as poverty and hunger, primary education, gender equality, and child mortality. MDG Target Goal #7.C called for halving, by 2015, the proportion of the world population without sustainable access to safe drinking water and basic sanitation.

2002 Botswana president Festus Mogae sends troops to force ethnic Khoisan (Bushmen) out of their ancestral homes in the Kalahari Desert. His stated objective is to begin integrating the Khoisan into Botswana society, although most observers believe that the real reason was the discovery of diamonds in the area some years earlier, creating the possibility of extended mining operations there. Officials seal off all wells used by the Khoisan and forbid their digging of new wells, the only source of freshwater in the desert region. In 2011, the Botswana Supreme Court decrees that the Khoisan may return to their native homes and may once again use their former wells and dig new ones.

2002 Title IV of the Public Health Security and Bioterrorism Preparedness and Response Act of 2002 (Bioterrorism Act) creates a number of new requirements for water districts and water systems designed to ensure the safety of such systems in the case of various types of bioterrorism attacks.

2003 Four water districts in California sign the Quantification Settlement Agreement (QSA), which allocates waters from the Colorado River sent to California annually. The agreement settles a long-term dispute among the water districts as to how much water each district is allowed to take each year from the state's total allocation.

2006 A drought called the worst in modern history is responsible for the death of more than 8 million people and an equal number of cattle.

2008 The United Nations General Assembly declares 2008 to be the International Year of Sanitation, with the purpose of improving public understanding of worldwide issues of sanitation and cutting the number of people globally who do not have access to safe sanitation systems in half by the year 2015.

2009 The UNECE publishes "Guidance on Water and Adaptation to Climate Change," a document designed to consider the effects of climate change on (primarily) transboundary water resources in the European continent with suggestions for ways of dealing with potential political, social, economic, technical, and other problems that may arise because of these changes.

2011 The United Nations General Assembly adopts resolution A/RES/63/124, on the Law of Transboundary Aquifers, which encourages nations "to make appropriate bilateral or regional arrangements for the proper management of their transboundary aquifers, taking into account the provisions of these draft articles."

2011 Berber peoples living near the foot of the Atlas Mountains in Morocco attack the water supply used by the nation's largest silver mining company. The Berbers claim that the company takes more than its share of water in its mining operations and returns impure water to the rivers from which it comes.

2012 The Food and Agriculture Organization (FAO) releases a report, "Coping with Water Scarcity: An Action Framework for Agriculture and Food Security," attempting to predict the status of water resources in coming decades and the effects of these estimates on food production worldwide.

2013 The United Nations declares 2013 to be the International Year of Water Cooperation. The year is celebrated with a number of regional and international conferences on water issues, as well as other special events focusing on the special problems associated with water use worldwide.

Glossary

Introduction

A study of global water issues often requires the use of specialized terminology. This glossary defines some of the most common terms used in such discussions.

Acre-foot A measurement of water volume equal to the amount of water required to cover one acre of land to the depth of one foot. One acre-foot is equivalent to 325,851 gallons, or 43,560 cubic feet.

Aquifer A bed of porous rock or sand that holds water and from which water can be extracted.

Arch dam A dam that is usually made of concrete and with a curved shape that is facing upstream.

Best available technology (BAT) A method of water treatment that has been determined to be the most effective such technology for that application.

Blue water A term used to describe groundwater and surface water.

Buttress dam A dam that consists of a sloping concrete wall that faces upstream and that is supported by vertical columns attached to the wall.

Chlorination The application of chlorine to water usually for the purpose of disinfecting that water.

Coliform bacteria A group of bacteria found in soils, in water, and in the intestines of warm-blooded animals. Although usually harmless themselves, they are used as an indicator of the potential presence of disease-causing organisms in water.

Desalination   The process of removing dissolved salts from a solution, usually seawater, so that it can be used for human consumption, industrial operations, agriculture, or other purposes.

Drought   A period of time with less than normal precipitation that lasts for an extended period of time, such that plants are unable to grow successfully, and widespread death of animals results.

Dysentery   A disease especially common among children, often caused by waterborne organisms, characterized by severe diarrhea with passage of mucus and blood.

Economic water scarcity   A situation in which natural sources of freshwater may be available to a region, but insufficient efforts have been expended to make those resources available to human inhabitants of the region.

Embankment dam   A dam made of unconsolidated materials, such as rock, sand, clay, and/or soil.

Finished water   Water that has been treated and is ready to be delivered for use by humans.

Fossil water   Water that has been trapped underground in an aquifer for very long periods of times, usually tens or hundreds of thousands or millions of years.

Freshwater   Water that contains no or very low amounts of dissolved salts.

Gravity dam   A dam made of a dense material, such as concrete, that holds back water largely because of its weight.

Gray water   Water required to carry away the waste products of some industrial, municipal, agricultural, or other human activities, that is, polluted water.

Green water   Rainwater that falls on the land and soaks into the ground, where it is available for growing plants.

Groundwater   Water that occurs beneath the surface of the ground.

Highly saline   Saline water that contains 10,000 to 35,000 parts per million of dissolved salts.

Hydrology   The science dealing with Earth's waters, their occurrences, distribution, and circulation through the water cycle.

Infiltration   The process by which rainwater falls on the ground, soaks into the earth, and then remains there or slowly travels through the earth.

Maximum contaminant level (MCL)   A term used to describe the highest concentration of a substance considered to be safe in drinking water.

Moderately saline   Saline water that contains 3,000 to 10,000 parts per million of dissolved salts.

Open defecation   The discharge of feces from the body in fields, forests, bodies of water, or other open spaces.

Physical water scarcity   The lack of access to potable water because of insufficient natural resources, such as lakes, rivers, and underground reservoirs.

Potable water   Water that is safe to drink. More specifically, water that is pure enough to meet certain government standards such as the U.S. Public Health Service Drinking Water Standards (available at http://water.epa.gov/drink/contaminants/upload/mcl-2.pdf).

Primary drinking water standards   A group of legally enforceable standards designed to protect the general public by limiting the amount of various contaminants found in drinking water.

Prior appropriation   Priority in the use of a water resource is determined by the priority of beneficial use or, is sometimes commonly noted, "first in time, first in use."

Qanat   A system consisting of a long sloping underground tunnel that can be used to collect water from underground and deliver it to a holding tank on the surface of the land.

Raw water   Water that is taken untreated from a natural source, such as a river or lake.

Reverse osmosis A method that is commonly used in the desalination of water in which water is forced through a semi-permeable membrane from a region of low concentration to one of high concentration.

Riparian rights A legal doctrine that allows any person whose property borders on a water resource to have access for any beneficial use to that water.

Saline A water solution containing dissolved salts. *Also see* slightly saline; moderately saline; highly saline.

Secondary drinking water standards A set of standards designed to protect the public health that are provided as guidelines for water purification technology, but that are not legally enforceable.

Shaduf (or shadoof) A simple kind of water-transferring machine that consists of a long horizontal pole that pivots on a vertical post. A bucket hangs from one end of the horizontal pole and a weight (e.g., a rock) at the opposite end.

Slightly saline Saline water that contains 1,000 to 3,000 parts per million of dissolved salts.

Waterborne disease A type of illness caused by a pathogen (e.g., a virus, bacterium, parasite, chemical, or other potentially harmful material) that occurs in drinking water or water used for recreation (e.g., swimming).

Water risk A measure of the probability and severity of the damage caused by some water-related event to a community, a business, or some other entity.

Water scarcity The lack of a sufficient supply of freshwater or of access to such a supply. Technically, the term is used to describe regions where there are fewer than 1,000 cubic meters of freshwater available per person per year.

Water-stressed A term describing an area with a severe lack of freshwater supplies, usually one with between 1,000 and 1,667 cubic meters per person per year.

Water table An underground region in which the ground is permanently saturated.

Index

323

About the Author

David E. Newton holds an associate's degree in science from Grand Rapids (Michigan) Junior College, a BA in chemistry (with high distinction), an MA in education from the University of Michigan, and an EdD in science education from Harvard University. He is the author of more than 400 textbooks, encyclopedias, resource books, research manuals, laboratory manuals, trade books, and other educational materials. He taught mathematics, chemistry, and physical science in Grand Rapids, Michigan, for 13 years; was professor of chemistry and physics at Salem State College in Massachusetts for 15 years; and was adjunct professor in the College of Professional Studies at the University of San Francisco for 10 years.

The author's previous books for ABC-CLIO include *Global Warming* (1993), *Gay and Lesbian Rights—A Resource Handbook* (1994, 2009), *The Ozone Dilemma* (1995), *Violence and the Mass Media* (1996), *Environmental Justice* (1996, 2009), *Encyclopedia of Cryptology* (1997), *Social Issues in Science and Technology: An Encyclopedia* (1999), *DNA Technology* (2009), *Sexual Health* (2010), *The Animal Experimentation Debate* (2013), *Marijuana* (2013), *World Energy Crisis* (2013), *Steroids and Doping in Sports* (2014), *GMO Food* (2014), *Science and Political Controversy* (2014), *Wind Energy* (2015), and *Fracking* (2015). His other recent books include *Physics: Oryx Frontiers of Science Series* (2000); *Sick!* (4 volumes; 2000); *Science, Technology, and Society: The Impact of Science in the 19th Century* (2 volumes; 2001); *Encyclopedia of Fire* (2002); *Molecular Nanotechnology: Oryx Frontiers of Science Series* (2002); *Encyclopedia of Water* (2003); *Encyclopedia of Air* (2004); *The New Chemistry* (6 volumes; 2007); *Nuclear Power* (2005); *Stem Cell Research* (2006); *Latinos in the Sciences, Math, and Professions* (2007); and *DNA Evidence and Forensic Science* (2008). He has also been an updating and consulting editor on a number of books and reference works, including *Chemical Compounds* (2005), *Chemical Elements* (2006), *Encyclopedia of Endangered Species* (2006), *World of Mathematics* (2006), *World of Chemistry* (2006), *World of Health* (2006), *UXL Encyclopedia of Science* (2007), *Alternative Medicine* (2008), *Grzimek's Animal Life Encyclopedia* (2009), *Community Health* (2009), *Genetic Medicine* (2009), *The Gale Encyclopedia of Medicine* (2010–2011), *The Gale Encyclopedia of Alternative Medicine* (2013), *Discoveries in Modern Science: Exploration, Invention, and Technology* (2013–2014), and *Science in Context* (2013–2014).